D0374642

QUESTIONS OF TASTE:
THE PHILOSOPHY OF WINE

QUESTIONS OF TASTE:
THE PHILOSOPHY OF WINE

Edited by
Barry C. Smith

With a foreword by Jancis Robinson

Oxford University Press

Oxford University Press, Inc., publishes works that further
Oxford University's objective of excellence in research, scholarship, and
education.

Oxford New York
Auckland   Cape Town   Dar es Salaam   Hong Kong   Karachi
Kuala Lumpur   Madrid   Melbourne   Mexico City   Nairobi
New Delhi   Shanghai   Taipei   Toronto

With offices in
Argentina   Austria   Brazil   Chile   Czech Republic   France   Greece
Guatemala   Hungary   Italy   Japan   Poland   Portugal   Singapore
South Korea   Switzerland   Thailand   Turkey   Ukraine   Vietnam

Published in by Oxford University Press, Inc.
198 Madison Avenue, New York, New York 10016
www.oup.com

by arrangement with Signal Books Ltd,
36 Minster Road, Oxford IX4 1LY, UK

Oxford is a registered trademark of Oxford University Press

US Cataloguing-in-Publication Data Available

ISBN-13: 978-0-19-533146-2
ISBN-10: 0-19-533146-X

CONTENTS

Contributors

KENT BACH is a philosopher of mind and language from San Francisco State University who has written extensively on mind and language. He is the author of *Thought and Reference* (OUP 1994), and *Linguistic Communication and Speech Acts* (1979) with Michael Harnish.

STEVE CHARTERS is a Master of Wine who lectures in Wine Studies at Edith Cowan University in Australia. He is the author of *Wine and Society: The Social and Cultural Context of a Drink* (2006) and the entry on 'Wine quality' in *The Oxford Companion to Wine* (2006). From 2007 he will be Professor of Champagne Management at Reims Management School.

TIM CRANE is a philosopher of mind and metaphysics at University College, London and Director of the University of London's Institute of Philosophy. He has written extensively on the philosophy of mind and consciousness. He is author of *The Mechanical Mind* (Penguin 1997) and *Elements of Mind* (OUP 2004). He has written on excess in *The World of Fine Wine*.

OPHELIA DEROY has the *agrégation* in philosophy. She is a member of the Institut Jean Nicod in Paris, and has written articles on metaphysics. She lectures in philosophy of science at the University of Paris XII.

PAUL DRAPER is a graduate in philosophy from Stanford University and chief wine-maker at Ridge Wines, California. He was *Decanter* Man of the Year in 2001. In 2006 his 1970 Montebello was ranked first in the anniversary tasting of the Judgment of Paris comparison between Bordeaux and Californian wines.

JAMIE GOODE is a trained biochemist and an accomplished wine writer who runs the highly informative website, wineanorak.com. He is the author of *Wine Science* (2006) for which he won a Glenfiddich Food and Drink Award.

ANDREW JEFFORD is a distinguished wine writer and critic. He has won five Glenfiddich Food and Drink awards, and is the author of the highly acclaimed *The New France*, and *Peat, Smoke and Spirit* on Islay whisky.

ADRIENNE LEHRER is a Professor Emerita in the Linguistics Department of Arizona and author of *Wine and Conversation* (Indiana University Press 1983) in which she analyses the language people use to talk about wine.

GLORIA ORIGGI is a philosopher who specialises in social epistemology. She is a member of the CNRS and the Institut Jean Nicod in Paris. She was a visiting fellow at the Italian Institute at Columbia University, and has published widely on the philosophy of mind, language, and the social transmission of knowledge.

ROGER SCRUTON is a distinguished philosopher and writer, and also wine correspondent for the *New Statesman*. He has written books on music, art, architecture, Kant and Hegel and is the author of *A Guide to Modern Philosophy*.

BARRY C. SMITH is a philosopher at the School of Philosophy at Birkbeck College and Deputy Director of the University of London's Institute of Philosophy. He has held visiting positions at the University of California, Berkeley and the École Normale Supérieure in Paris. He edited *The Oxford Handbook of Philosophy of Language* (OUP 2006 with E. Lepore) and has written on 'Wine and Philosophy' for *The Oxford Companion to Wine* (2006).

Foreword

Could this book represent the most fun you can have with wine without drinking a single drop?

Admittedly as a wine writer and one of Oxford's first graduates in maths and philosophy, I might be expected to find a book on philosophy and wine of particular interest, but I must admit that I have not read any philosophy for thirty years so I approached this manuscript with my mind in shamefully untutored state. Yet I found these articles perfectly comprehensible, even quite gripping. I believe that any intelligent wine drinker—and even some teetotal philosophers—will find an enormous amount to savour in the pages that follow.

Of course no-one will agree with every word. That is hardly the point of philosophy. But this book is hugely enjoyable and admirably clearly written. I can imagine a legion of wine lovers lapping up its bracing engagement with so many of the topics that concern us all every time we sip a wine or read a tasting note. There is no shortage of good taste, cogent argument, intriguing allusion and above all rich stimulation here. It deserves a wide non-academic readership and should give every bit as much pleasure as a favourite lecturer or particularly treasured wine.

Jancis Robinson
London, October 2006

Acknowledgements

The current collection of essays develops ideas originally pursued at an international conference entitled *Philosophy and Wine: from Science to Subjectivity*, run by the Institute of Philosophy (then The Philosophy Programme) at the University of London's School of Advanced Study in December 2004. It was the first ever conference on the philosophy of wine, and it brought together scholars, wine writers and wine-makers to discuss philosophy and wine. The success of the conference and subsequent press attention demonstrated the wide interest in the topic. This volume is based on the proceedings of that conference together with additional commissioned essays.

The plans for the conference were conceived at a dinner party held by Jean Hewitson, and it is with deep affection that I would like to thank her for her warmth, generosity and encouragement for this project. At that planning dinner were Jancis Robinson, Nick Lander and Tim Crane, and I would like to thank them for excellent advice and ready enthusiasm. On that occasion we drank Ridge Montebello 1992 and 1993 and Jancis Robinson suggested that we invite Paul Draper to speak at the conference. I am grateful to Paul for participating in the conference and for very generously providing the wines at the dinner that followed. The conference included a tutored tasting of Olivier Leflaive's white burgundies, led by Adam Brett Smith of Corney and Barrow, and I would like to thank him for such an informative and engaging talk, and also thank his assistant Laura Taylor for organizing the wines. The red tasting of Ridge wines was led by Paul Draper, and I would like to thank Jasper Morris of Berry Bros. and Rudd for organizing the wines and for his contributions at the conference. Andrew Jefford played an invaluable role at the tastings, stepping in as resident critic and offering his precise and rapier like responses to each wine. I am very grateful to him for treating all who were there to such a display of skill. The complex arrangements for the conference, before and on the day, were conducted in the usual exemplary way under the excellent stewardship of Dr. Shahrar Ali and I would like to offer personal thanks and gratitude to him for all his help. My greatest thanks goes to Michael Dwyer, an exemplary editor whose good sense, sound editorial advice, patience and commitment made this project possible.

The final work on volume was completed in Burgundy and I would like to thank Laurent Glaise, Yann Lioux, Nicolas Potel, Xavier Meney, Vincent Dauvissat, Jean-Claude Rateau, Peter Piouze, Jean-Pierre Cropsal and Ophelia Deroy for generously sharing with me their knowledge, passion and wines.

Introduction

Philosophy and wine have many connections and some similarities, yet there has been to date no sustained study of the relationship between the two. The time has come to examine these themes and continue where philosophers of the past left off.

Wine was part of philosophy's early origins in ancient Greece where wine was drunk at the symposium to ease the tongue and encourage discussion, but it was not itself the subject of discussion. When philosophers attended to wine they often departed from philosophy as we see in Plato's apology for wine at the beginning of *The Laws*, or in the British Empiricist philosopher John Locke's study of wine and agricultural practices in France. Wine was often appreciated by philosophers and they saw fit to tell us which wines they favoured. The Scottish philosopher David Hume liked claret and the Rhennish wines, while the German transcendental idealist, Immanuel Kant, declares that he likes the wine of the Canary Islands. Both philosophers valued wine and company. Hume recommended drinking and making merry with friends whenever philosophy seemed to lead us to frustration or despair. Kant believed that wine, drunk in moderation, could soften men's characters and lead them to show the very best of their natures. In this way, wine was seen as means to something else, and for Kant it was not worth considering in itself. For Hume, however, wine provides the best example when contemplating the issue of whether there is a standard of taste. We shall return to Hume's concerns below. But first let us reflect on the way we consider wine. We do not take it simply as a means to an end. We pay a good deal of attention to it, as an object of care, value and specific pleasure. We buy bottles and keep them, knowing when to open them, choosing which dishes best accompany them. We try to discover more about wines and about the labels on precious bottles. We seem to take wine as an end and not a means: a worthy object for contemplation; and it is here, in our attempt to get closer to the thing itself that philosophy begins.

For these reasons, drinking fine wine provides an occasion for pleasure, and an opportunity for thought. Voltaire put it well when he said, "Taste invites reflection". And there is much to reflect upon. We know, for example, that the pleasure we take in a fine wine is best shared with another. And yet we may begin to wonder why this is the case if taste is subjective, as we are always told it is. Can we really share the experience of the wine we are drinking? If taste were subjective, the answer would have to be, "no". But this runs counter to attitudes and practices with wine. When friends gather to drink wine, they talk happily about what they are tasting; they share impressions, agree or disagree about the aromas or flavours they perceive the wine to have; they rate its quality. Each taster attempts to come closer to a true description of the wine's qualities or faults. We are persuaded by another's identification of prune notes, we appreciate yet another's skill at pinpointing an elusive aroma. We treat wines as objects for talk and reflection, and we take ourselves to be reflecting on the same thing. What properties of the wine are we reflecting on? What are the features, qualities and character of the wines we talk about? How accurate or objective is the language we use for describing them? How much trust should we place in wine connoisseurs or experts? Can they impart knowledge to the beginner? Does knowledge of wine bring us closer to the true character of a wine? Does greater dis-crimination mean more knowledge of tastes and flavours or of the chemical analysis of the wine? Will the increase in scientific knowledge of wine lead to better tasting experiences?

Further questions emerge beyond this point. Can knowledge affect the pleasure we take in a wine? Is the intoxicating property of wine an essential part of its nature, and what importance does it have for us? Can there be a standard to judge or evaluate a wine's quality in anything other than subjective terms? All these questions are the concern of the philoso-pher, and the answers that can be given provide the basis for larger questions about the significance of wine and the value it has for us in our lives. These questions are all addressed in detail by the philosophers and wine practitioners writing in this volume. Let us look at some of them a little more closely.

THE ISSUE OF OBJECTIVITY

To know the chemical composition of a wine and its method of vinifi-cation is not yet to know how it tastes, so how then does what we taste relate to the liquid in front of us? This is a question explored by Ophelia Deroy in her chapter. To know how a wine tastes one must, of course, experience the wine for ourselves. But in tasting a wine are we discovering properties the wine has or just noting our subjective responses to it? I raise this issue in chapter 3, and go on to ask whether every response is as good as any other. Here we have a key philosophical question: how subjective are tastes and tasting, or to put it in ontological terms: what are we tasting? On one view, the only objective knowledge we can have of wine is that provided by scientific analysis: the chemist describes the way the wine is, the wine critic describes the way it tastes. The former is objective, the latter is merely subjective. But are the two clearly connected? Wine-makers rely on scientific analysis to achieve the taste they are aiming for and to correct faults. Experienced wine tasters like Paul Draper rely on taste to identify and describe compounds of flavours or aromas that arise from fermentation. For this to be so, wine tasters must draw objective conclusions about a wine from their subjective responses to it, and wine-makers must create conditions they hope will produce a certain taste for us. (See Draper and Jefford's chapter for a discussion about the natural versus the scientific aspect of wine making.)

A revised view would be that while tasting is a subjective experience of individual tasters, *what* we taste, the tannins, or acidity in a wine, are objective properties or characteristics of the wine itself. Nevertheless, many of the qualities we value in wine such as finesse, balance and length can only be confirmed by tasting. And some philosophers would argue that these more complex properties depend on us and should be conceived as some kind of relation between the wines and our responses to them. The problem for this view is whether to treat all such responses as equally correct. If we differ in opinion about whether a wine is round or balanced, does this mean there is no fact of the matter about who is right? Is it balanced for me but not for you? On the subjectivist view, matters of taste are neither right nor wrong: the conclusion is *de gustibus non est disputandum*. Another option is to adopt relativism about tastes. The facts about whether the wine is acidic are relative to individuals or populations of tasters. But are such tasters representative?

As well as the science of wine, we must ask what we know about the science of tasters. What facts from psychology and neuroscience about the perceptions of taste and the processing of multimodal judgments about the colour, feel, taste and smell of wine can help with the questions of objectivity and shared experience? These are among the issues raised by Jamie Goode in his chapter on wine and the brain.

TASTES AND TASTING

Philosophers who reject the conclusion that taste is subjective argue that taste properties, such as a wine's length or balance, *are* among its objective features and that under the right conditions, and with the right experience and training as tasters, they are revealed to us by means of perception. Tasting a wine involves the taster's subjectivity but verdicts based on those subjective experiences are not mere matters of opinion: so not subjective in that sense. Certain experiences will be more accurate than others, some people will be better tasters then others, and judgments of a wine may be right or wrong. On this objectivist view, defended in my chapter, *tastes* are in the wine, not in us, and by improving the skills of *tasting* we can come to know them more accurately.

WHAT IS MEANT BY "FINE WINE"?

A large and related issue concerns the evaluation of wines and whether there is a clear separation between describing a wine and assessing its quality. In their different ways, both Gloria Origgi and Steve Charters address this topic. Part of the problem is how we should characterize fine wine. From the absence of a definition we should not infer there is no category of fine wine any more than our inability to define "chair" satisfactorily should lead us to conclude that there are no chairs. We can give criteria for fine wine that stop short of providing a definition, as when we can say that a fine wine is one whose complex, individual character rewards the interest and attention paid to it, and affords the degree of discrimination we exercise in assessing its qualities and characteristics. We trust experts to help us sort and select fine wines, and perhaps great wines, on occasion. But is a fine wine a wine that must be appreciated? Or can experienced wine tasters assess the qualities of a wine without enjoying it? The alternative view is that recognizing a wine's merits depends on the enjoyment, pleasure or preferences of the individual taster. The dispute here concerns the ultimate nature of wine tasting and wine appreciation. Charters raises this issue explicitly in his chapter, while, in his, Tim Crane makes out a case for an aesthetics of fine wine.

Do we directly perceive the quality of a wine, or do we assess its quality on the basis of what we first perceive? Tasting seems to involve both perception and judgment. But does the perceptual experience of tasting—which relies on the sensations of touch, taste and smell—already involve a judgment of quality? Is such judgment a matter of understanding and assessment, and does assessment require wine knowledge in order to arrive at a correct verdict?

Some philosophers would claim that one cannot assess a wine's quality on the basis of perceptual experience alone and that evaluation goes beyond what one finds in a description of its objective characteristics. According to these thinkers something else is required to arrive at an assessment of a wine's merits. This may be the pleasure the taster derives from the wine, the valuing of certain characteristics, or the individual preferences of the taster. Is there room among such views for non-subjective judgments of wine quality?

To say that assessments of quality rest on interpretation is to say that one cannot recognize a wine's quality on the basis of perceptual experience alone. And yet according to Kent Bach, a novice taster can recognize the merits of wine by taste without the expert knowledge of the wine critic. In my chapter I disagree. Expert knowledge may enable one to recognize a wine as an excellent example of its type, but if that style of wine offers the taster no pleasure, could one, as a wine critic, still judge or admire it as a great wine? Many philosophers would think not, but then on what basis does one judge something to be a great wine, and what would separate the experienced and the novice taster in evaluating wines? Is each taster's opinion equally good?

A further and pressing topic is how we use wine vocabulary and which properties of wine it tracks, and which perceptions of the taster it shapes. These issues are discussed in detail by Adrienne Lehrer in her chapter on the use of language in wine appreciation. Differences are drawn that highlight other factors in our descriptions beyond those that correlate objectively with the wine.

A Standard of Taste

The philosopher, David Hume, asked whether there could be a standard of taste. Hume's solution was to rely on the excellence of judges or critics who showed delicacy of judgment; were free from prejudice; could draw on a wide range of experience for comparisons; paid due attention; and were unclouded by mood. These may be prerequisites for accurate tasting but on what basis does such an excellent critic appreciate a truly great wine? Origgi asks whether trust in expertise reflects the accuracy or merely the authority in the wine market. Another answer to this question can be found in Kant's account of aesthetic judgment (which he did not himself extend to wine). To claim that a wine is great is not just to judge for oneself alone, but to judge for all. The judgment is made on the basis of pleasure but this is not a claim about what one finds personally pleasant or agreeable. It is a judgment about the pleasure the wine affords anyone suitably equipped to taste it. There is no such thing as a wine that is great *for me*. In claiming to recognize a great wine I am claiming something about *the wine itself*, about how it will (and should) strike others. It is thus a universal claim about the delight all can take in it, and others would be mistaken were they not so to judge it.

Kant's solution fails to solve all problems of the objectivity of taste, however. Disagreements about a wine's qualities are still disagreements among ourselves, and not disagreements settled solely by the properties of the wine itself.

A further problem is created when two (or more) experienced, unprejudiced wine critics differ in their opinions regarding the excellence of a wine. (Robert Parker and Jancis Robinson famously disagreed about the merits of 2003 Château Pavie.) Perhaps they agree in their descriptions of the wine's objective characteristics but diverge in evaluating its merits. If they merely point to divergent qualities one can argue for pluralism about the qualities and tastes of a wine. However if they genuinely conflict in judgment, neither has overlooked any aspect of the wine's identifiable properties, and both agree in the terms they use to describe and classify wines, we may be tempted to conclude neither is right and neither is wrong. Subjectivism about standards of taste can be resisted in this case by embracing relativism about matters of taste. According to relativist doctrines both critics are right: both make true judgments about the wine in question. It is simply that the truth of each judgment is *relative* to a standard of assessment, or set of preferences, not shared by the other. Cultural differences could account for these divergences and there would still be a right answer according to one set of standards, or the other. In effect, this is to claim there can be more than one standard of taste, and each critic is right relative to his or her own standard of assessment.

Finally, philosophers have stressed the meaning and value wine has in our lives as a celebration of our relationship with our natural surroundings. The place, culture and history of a people that fall under the concept *terroir* are celebrated and acknowledged in drinking a wine that reflects that *terroir* and the wine-makers' efforts to uphold and maintain the traditions with which they transformed soil and vine into grape, and grape into wine. The final transformation, according to Roger Scruton, occurs when we take wine into ourselves and through its intoxicating effects it transforms us and opens us up to one another.

The reflections of philosophers can do only so much to illuminate the wines we appreciate and value, but to understand more about how such wines are produced, and about which decisions the wine-maker or grower takes in guiding him to the critically sought outcome, we turn finally to the chapter by the philosophy-trained wine grower of Ridge wines, Paul Draper, and the distinguished wine critic Andrew Jefford.

Barry C. Smith
Beaune, August 2006

chapter one

THE PHILOSOPHY OF WINE

Roger Scruton

Philosophers have probably drunk more than their fair share of wine; but they have not had a fair share in the words written about it. In particular, they have largely avoided discussing the most important philosophical issue with which wine acquaints us, which is that of intoxication. This is the issue that I shall be considering, and I shall be exploring the epistemological, moral and metaphysical meaning of intoxication and its place in the life of a rational being. I shall also make a few remarks about taste, and about the particular perspective on the problem of taste that is opened by wine.

Questions immediately arise. What exactly is intoxication? Is there a single phenomenon that is denoted by this word? Is the intoxication induced by wine an instance of the same general condition as the intoxication induced by whisky say, or that induced by cannabis? And is "induced" the right word in any or all of the familiar cases?

There is a deft philosophical move which can put some order into those questions, which is to ask whether intoxication is, to put it in technical terms, a *natural kind*—in other words, a condition whose nature is to be determined by science, rather than philosophy. The question "what is water?" is not a philosophical question, since philosophy cannot, by reflecting on the sense of the term "water", tell us anything about the stuff to which that term refers, except that it is *this* kind of stuff, pointing to some example. Now we can point to a case of intoxication—a drunken man say—and explain intoxication as *this* kind of state, thereupon leaving the rest to science. Science would explore the temporary abnormalities of the case, and their normal or typical causes. And no doubt the science could be linked to a general theory, which would connect the behavioural and mental abnormalities of the drunk with those of the spaced-out cannabis user, and those of the high-flying junkie. That theory would be a general one of intoxication as a natural kind. And it would leave the philosopher with nothing to say about its subject-matter.

However, we can quickly see that the question that concerns us cannot be so easily ducked. The drunk is intoxicated, in that his nervous system has been systematically disrupted by an intoxicant (i.e. an agent with just this effect). This intoxication causes predictable effects on his visual, intellectual, and motor-sensory pathways. When the heart and soul light up with the first sip from a bowl of old Falernian, however, the experience *itself* is intoxicating, and it is as though we taste the intoxication as a quality of the wine. We may compare this quality with the intoxicating quality of a landscape or a line of poetry. It is fairly obvious from the comparison and from the grammar of the description that we are not referring to anything like drunkenness. There are natural kinds to which the experience of drinking wine and that of hearing a line of poetry both belong: for one thing they are both experiences. But the impulse to classify the experiences together is not to be understood as the first step in a scientific theory. It is the record of a perceived similarity— one that lies on the surface, and which may correspond to no underlying neuro-physiological resemblance. When we ask what we understand this intoxication to be, therefore, we are asking a philosophical rather than a scientific question.

Furthermore there is a real question about the relation between the intoxication that we experience through wine, and the state of drunkenness. The first is a state of consciousness, whereas the second is a state of unconsciousness—or which tends towards unconsciousness. Although the one leads in time to the other, the connection between them is no more transparent than the connection between the first kiss and the final divorce. Just as the erotic kiss is neither a tame version nor a premonition of the bitter parting to which it finally leads, so is the intoxicating taste of the wine neither a tame version nor a premonition of drunkenness: they are simply not the "same kind of thing", even if at some level of scientific theory they are discovered to have the same kind of cause.

It is also questionable to speak of the intoxication that we experience through wine as "induced by" the wine. For this implies a separation between the object tasted and the intoxication felt, of the kind that exists between drowsiness and the sleeping pill that causes it. When we speak of an intoxicating line of poetry, we are not referring to an effect in the person who reads or remembers it, comparable to the effect of an energy pill. We are referring to a quality in the line itself. The poetic intoxication of Mallarmé's line *aboli bibelot d'inanité sonore* lies there on the page, not here in my nervous system. Are the two cases of intoxicatingness—wine and poetry—sufficiently alike to enable us to use the one to cast light on the other? Yes and no.

Non-rational animals sniff for information, and are therefore interested in smells. They also discriminate between the edible and the inedible on grounds of taste. But they relish neither the smell nor the taste of the things that they consume. For relishing is a reflective state of mind, in which an experience is held up for critical inspection. Only rational beings can relish tastes and smells, since only they can take an interest in *the experience itself*, rather than in the information conveyed by it. The temptation is therefore to assimilate relishing to the interest we have in colour and pattern, in the sound of music and in works of literary and visual art. Like aesthetic interest relishing is tied to sensory experience, and like aesthetic experience it involves holding our normal practical and information-gathering interests in abeyance. Why not say, therefore, that wine appeals to us in something like the way that poetry, painting or music appeal to us, by presenting an object of experience that is meaningful in itself? Why not say that the intoxicating quality is in the wine, in just the way that the intoxicating quality lies in the line of poetry? Our question about wine will then reduce to a special case of the general question, concerning the nature of aesthetic qualities.[1]

Philosophers have tended to regard gustatory pleasures as purely sensory, without the intellectual intimations that are the hallmark of aesthetic interest. Sensory pleasure is available whatever the state of your education; aesthetic pleasure depends upon knowledge, comparison and culture. The senses of taste and smell, it is argued, provide purely sensory pleasure, since they are intellectually inert. Unlike the senses of sight and hearing, they do not represent a world independent of themselves, and therefore provide nothing, other then themselves, to contemplate. This point was argued by Plato, and emphasised by Plotinus. It was important for Aquinas, who distinguished the cognitive senses of sight and hearing from the non-cognitive senses of taste and smell, arguing that only the first could provide the perception of beauty.[2] Hegel too, in the introduction to his *Lectures on Aesthetics*, emphasises the distinction between the pleasures of the palate and aesthetic experience, which is "the sensuous embodiment of the Idea".

In an unjustly neglected article, Frank Sibley suggests that this philosophical tradition is founded on nothing more than prejudice, and that the relishing of tastes and smells is as much an aesthetic experience as the relishing of sights and sounds.[3] All those features commonly thought to characterise aesthetic experience attach also to our experience of tastes and smells. A smell or taste can be enjoyed "for its own sake"; it can possess aesthetic qualities, such as finesse, beauty, harmony, delicacy; it can bear an emotional significance or tell a story, like the taste of the *madeleine* in Proust; it can be moving, exciting, depressing, intoxicating and so on. And there is good and bad taste in smells and tastes just as there is good and bad taste in music, art and poetry. All attempts to drive a wedge between merely sensory and truly aesthetic pleasures end up, Sibley thinks, by begging the question. We should not be surprised, therefore, if there are art forms based on smell and taste, just as there are art forms based on sight and sound: the Japanese incense game, for example, or the somewhat extravagant but by no means impossible keyboard of olfactory harmonies envisaged by Huysmans in *À rebours*. Perhaps *haute cuisine* is such an art form: and maybe wine too is an aesthetic artefact, comparable to those products like carpentry that bridge the old and no longer very helpful division between the "fine" and the "useful" arts.

Sibley's argument is challenging, but not, it seems to me, successful. Consider smells: the object of the sense of smell is not the thing that smells but the smell emitted by it. We speak of smelling a cushion, but the smell is not a quality of the cushion. It is a thing emitted by the cushion that could exist without the cushion, and indeed does exist in a space where the cushion is not—the space around the cushion. The visual appearance of the cushion is not a thing emitted by the cushion, nor does it exist elsewhere than the cushion. Moreover, to identify the visual appearance we must refer to visual properties of the cushion. The object of my visual perception when I see the cushion is the cushion— not some other thing, a "sight" or image, which the cushion is not. To put it another way: visual experience reaches through the "look" of a thing to the thing that looks. I don't "sniff through" the smell to the thing that smells, for the thing is not represented in its smell in the way that it is represented in its visual appearance. Crucial features of visual appearances are therefore not replicated in the world of smells. For example, we can see an ambiguous figure now as a duck, now as a rabbit; we can see one thing in another, as when we see a face in a picture. There seems to be no clear parallel case of "smelling as" or "smelling in", as opposed to the construction of rival hypotheses as to the cause of a smell.

One conclusion to draw from that is that smells are ontologically like sounds—not qualities of the objects that emit them but independent objects. I call them "secondary objects", on the analogy with secondary qualities, in order to draw attention to their ontological dependence on the way the world is experienced.[4] Smells exist *for* us, just as sounds do, and must be identified through the experiences of those who observe them. Now it is undeniable that sounds are objects of aesthetic interest, and this in three ways—first as sounds, as when we listen to the sound of a fountain in a garden, second as tones, when we listen to sound organised as music, and third as poetry or prose, when we listen to sound organised semantically. Only the first of those experiences is replicated by smells. For smells cannot be organised as sounds are organised: put them together and they mingle, losing their character. Nor can they be arranged along a dimension, as sounds are arranged by pitch, so as to exemplify the order of between-ness. They remain free-floating and unrelated, unable to generate expectation, tension, harmony, suspension or release. You could concede the point made by Sibley, that smells might nevertheless be objects of aesthetic interest, but only by putting them on the margin of the aesthetic—the margin occupied by the sound of fountains, where beauty is a matter of association rather than expression, and of context rather than content. But it would be more illuminating to insist on the radical distinction that exists, between these objects of sensory enjoyment which acquire meaning only by the association of ideas, and the objects of sight and hearing, which can bear within themselves all the meaning that human beings are able to communicate.

If asked to choose therefore I would say, for philosophical reasons, that the intoxication that we experience in wine is a sensory but not an aesthetic experience, whereas the intoxication of poetry is aesthetic through and through. Still, there is no doubt that the intoxicating quality that we taste in wine is a quality that we taste in *it*, and not in ourselves. True, we are raised by it to a higher state of exhilaration, and this is a widely observed and very important fact. But this exhilaration is an effect, not a quality bound into the very taste of the stuff, as the intoxication seems to be. At the same time, there is a connection between the taste and the effect—which is why we call the taste intoxicating—just as there is a connection between the exciting quality of a spectacle and the excitement that is produced by it. But—just as with the spectacle—if you wish to describe the effect you must do so in terms of its cause.

Here is a first clue to understanding the intoxicating quality of wine. My excitement at a football match is not a physiological condition that could have been produced by a drug. It is directed towards the game: it is excitement *at* the spectacle and not just excitement *caused by* the spectacle; it is an effect directed at its cause. And that is true too of the wine. The intoxication that I feel is not just caused by the wine: it is, to some extent at least, *directed at* the wine, and is not just a cause of my relishing the wine, but in some sense a form of it. The intoxicating quality and the relishing are internally related, in that the one cannot be properly described without reference to the other. The wine lives in my intoxication, as the game lives in the excitement of the fan: I have not swallowed the wine as I would a tasteless drug; I have taken it into myself, so that its flavour and my mood are inextricably bound together.

The first clue to understanding the question of intoxication is, then, this: that the intoxication induced by the wine is also directed at the wine, in something like the way the excitement produced by a football game is directed at the game. The cases are not entirely alike, however. It is without strain that we say that we were excited at the game, as well as by it; only with a certain strain can we say that we were intoxicated at the wine, rather than by it. We should bear this difference in mind, even though it is unclear at present what weight to place upon it.

It is also important to keep hold of the difference that Aquinas points to, in distinguishing cognitive from non-cognitive senses. Visual experience has a content that must be described in conceptual terms. When I see a table I also see it as a table (in the normal case). In describing my experience I am describing a visual world, in terms of concepts that are in some sense *applied in* the experience and not deduced from it. Another way of putting this is to say, as I said earlier, that visual experience is a *rep-*

resentation of reality. Now taste and smell are not like that, as I noted above. I might say of the ice-cream in my hand that it tastes *of* chocolate or that it tastes *like* chocolate, but not that I taste it *as* chocolate, as though taste were in itself a form of judgment. The distinction here is reflected in the difference between the cogent accounts of paintings given by critics, and the far-fetched and whimsical descriptions of wines given by the likes of Robert Parker. Winespeak is in some way ungrounded, for it is not describing the way the wine is, but merely the way it tastes. And tastes are not representations of the objects that possess them.

Before returning to that difficult point, I want to say a little more about the phenomenology of wine and its relation to other forms of intoxicant. Our experience of wine is bound up with its nature as a drink—a liquid that slides smoothly into the body, lighting the flesh as it journeys past. This endows wine with a peculiar inwardness, an intimacy with the body of a kind that is never achieved by solid food, since food must be chewed and therefore denatured before it enters the gullet. Nor is it achieved by any smell, since smell makes no contact with the body at all, but merely enchants without touching, like the beautiful girl at the other end of the party.

The features of vinous intoxication that I have been describing have important consequences in the world of symbolism. An intoxicating drink, which both slides down easily and warms as it goes, is a symbol of—and also a means to achieve—an inward transformation, in which a person *takes something in* to himself. Hence you find wine, from the earliest recorded history, allotted a sacred function. It is a means whereby a god or demon enters the soul of the one who drinks it, and often the drinking occurs at a religious ceremony, with the wine explicitly identified with the divinity who is being worshipped. I do not refer only to the very obvious cult of Dionysus, but also to the Eleusian mysteries, the Athenian festivals such as the *thesmophoria,* the mystery cults of Diana and the Egyptian child Horus. For the anthropologist the Christian Eucharist, in which the blood of the sacrificed lamb is drunk in the form of communion wine, is downstream from the mystery cults of antiquity, which are in turn downstream from those ceremonies that accompanied the vinification of the grape among the great heroes who first discovered how to do it and believed, with commendable piety, that it was the work of a god.

This symbolic use of wine in religious cults is reflected too in art and literature, in which magic drinks are conceived as mind-changing and even identity-changing potions, which slide down the gullet taking their spiritual burden into the very source of life. Wagner makes potent use of this symbolism, both in the drink of forgetting which represents the corruption of Siegfried's soul in the world of human ambition, and in the celebrated *Sühnetrank*, or drink of atonement, which dedicates Tristan to Isolde and Isolde to Tristan forever. We find this symbolism easy to understand, since it draws on the way in which intoxicating drinks, and wine pre-eminently, are "taken into oneself", in a way that tempts one almost to a literal interpretation of that phrase. It is as though the wine enters the very self of the person who drinks it. Of course, I hasten to add, there is a great difference in this connection between good wine and bad, and the self learns in time to welcome the one as it fights against the other. But it is precisely because the self is so actively engaged that this battle has to be fought and won, just as the battles between good and evil and virtue and vice must be fought and won. There is more at stake when it comes to taste in wine than mere taste, and the adage that *de gustibus non est disputandum* is as false here as it is in aesthetics. We are not disputing about a physical sensation, but about choices in which the self is fully engaged. The symbolism of the drink, and its soul-transforming effect, reflect the underlying truth that it is only rational beings who can appreciate things like wine. Even if taste is a non-cognitive sense, therefore, it has an aspect that is closed to non-rational creatures, and that aspect includes the one we are considering, which is the aspect of intoxication. Animals can be drunk; they can be high on drugs and fuggy with cannabis; but they cannot experience the kind of directed intoxication that we experience through wine, since this is a condition in which only rational beings can find themselves, depending as it does upon thoughts and acts of attention that lie outside the repertoire of a horse or a dog. Relishing is something that only a rational being can exhibit, and which therefore only a rational being can do.

In saying that, however, I imply that not all forms of intoxication, even for rational beings, are species of a single genus. It is therefore necessary to make some distinctions among the substances that we take in search of stimulation, intoxication or relief from the *lacrymae rerum*. In particular we should distinguish between four basic kinds of stimulant: those which please us, but do not alter the mind in any fundamental way, even if they have mental effects; those which alter the mind, but which impart no pleasure in their consumption; those which both alter the mind and also please us as we consume them and finally those that alter the mind and do so, at least in part, *by* and *in the act of* pleasing us. There are intermediate cases, but those broad categories offer a map, I think, of this hitherto uncharted territory. So I shall deal with each in turn.

1. Those which please, and which have mental effects, but which do not alter the mind.

Tobacco is probably the example most familiar to us. It has mental effects, leading to a reduction in nervous tension and a heightening in concentration and control, but it does not fundamentally alter the mind, so as to cause the world to appear different, so as to interfere with perceptual and motor pathways, or so as to hamper or redirect one's emotional and intellectual life. The pleasure involved is intimately connected with its mental effect, and although the case is not exactly like that of wine, there is a definite sense in which the taste of a good cigar, say, is relaxing, in the way that the taste of a good wine is intoxicating— i.e. the mental effect forms *part* of the gustatory quality. This is an odd phenomenon, which has its parallel in aesthetics but not, I think, in the experience of food. It arises when there is a distinct experience of *savouring* whatever it is you consume: something that, as I said above, no non-rational animal can do, and which we can do only when the mental effect of a substance can be read back, so to speak, into the way it tastes. Some sense of what this involves can be gained from considering the second kind of stimulant, which is not savoured at all.

2. Stimulants which have mind-altering effects, but which do not bring any pleasure in the consumption of them.

The most obvious examples of this are drugs that you swallow whole like Ecstasy, or drugs that you inject like heroin. Here there is no pleasure in the taking of the drug, but radical mental effects that result from doing so—effects which are wanted for their own sake and regardless of how they were caused. There is no question of savouring a dose of heroin, and the mind which is disengaged in the ingestion of the stuff remains in a certain sense disengaged thereafter. The mental effects of the drug are not directed towards the drug or towards the experience of using it: they are directed towards objects of everyday perception and concern, towards ideas, people, images and so on. You take no pleasure in the drug itself, even if there are other pleasures that result from using it. It should be obvious that this is quite unlike either the first case typified by tobacco, or the third case that I now consider.

3. Stimulants that have mind altering effects but which give pleasure in the act of consuming them.

The two most interesting cases are cannabis and alcohol. I refer to alcohol in general and not just to wine. The psychic transformation that occurs through the consumption of pot is, the experts tell us, quite far-reaching, and outlasts the moment of pleasure by hours or days. Nevertheless the moment of pleasure definitely exists, and is not dissimilar from that provided by tobacco: though it involves a loss rather than a gain in mental concentration. Likewise alcohol also has a mind-altering effect, heightening emotions, muddling thoughts, and interfering with nervous pathways; and this mind-altering effect outlasts the moment of pleasure, and is in part unconnected with it. It is precisely because the mental transformation outlasts the pleasure, indeed, that we are driven to contrast the case of the alcoholic, who has become addicted to the effect of drink and more or less indifferent to its taste, from that of the wine-lover, for whom the mental transformation *is* the taste, so to speak, and outlasts it only in the way that the pleasure of seeing an old friend survives after his visit is over. Hence the need to distinguish a fourth kind of case, the one that really interests me.

4. Stimulants that have mind-altering effects which are in some way internally related to the experience of consuming them.

The example, of course, is wine, and that is what I meant earlier in referring to the intoxicating quality of the taste. It is in the act of drinking that the mind is altered, and the alteration is in some way bound up with the taste: the taste is imbued with the altered consciousness, just as the altered consciousness is directed at the taste. This again is near to the aesthetic experience. We all know that you cannot listen to a Beethoven quartet with understanding unless your whole psyche is taken up and transformed by it: but the transformation of consciousness is read back into the sound that produces it, which is the sound of that transformation, so to speak. Hence the well-known problem of musical content: we want to say that such music has a meaning, but we also want to deny that the meaning is detachable from the way the music sounds.

While I have compared cannabis and alcohol, it is very important to be aware of the differences between them. Obviously there are significant medical and physiological differences. Alcohol is rapidly expelled from the system and is addictive only in large doses—at least to those like us, whose genetic makeup has been influenced by the millenia of wine-making. The Inuit of the Arctic Circle, and others whose ancestors never cultivated the grape, are unable to process alcohol harmlessly and become quickly addicted to it: but for the purpose of what follows I refer only to you and me. And of you and me it can safely be said that cannabis is vividly to be contrasted with wine from the physiological viewpoint. Its effects remain for days, and it is both more addictive and more radical, leading not just to temporary alterations of the mind but to permanent or semi-permanent transformations of the personality, and in particular a widely observed loss of the moral sense. This loss of the moral sense can be observed too in alcoholics, but it is not to be explained merely by addiction. Addiction to tobacco seems to lead to no demoralisation of the victim, and while people commit crimes under the influence of drugs and cause accidents under the influence of alcohol they do neither under the influence of smoking.

The temporary nature of the physiological effects of wine is of great importance in describing its emotional aura. The effect of wine is understood, by the observer as much as the consumer, as a temporary possession, a passing alteration, which is not, however, an alteration that changes the character of the one in whom it occurs. Hence you can go away and sleep it off; and the ancient characterisations of Silenus are of a creature alternating drink and sleep, with a crescendo of drunkenness between them. Moreover, and more importantly, alcohol in general, and wine in particular, has a unique social function, increasing the garrulousness, the social confidence and the goodwill of those who drink together, provided they drink in moderation. Many of the ways that we have developed of drinking socially are designed to impose a strict regime of moderation. Buying drinks by round in the pub, for example, has an important role in both permitting people to rehearse the sentiments that cause and arise from generosity (yet without bearing the real cost of them), while controlling the rate of intake and the balance between the inflow of drink and the outflow of words. This ritual parallels the ritual of the Greek symposium, and that of the circulation of wine after dinner in country houses and Oxbridge common rooms.

I don't say that cannabis doesn't also have a social function. Indeed it has, and is associated in the Middle East with a hookah-smoking ritual that produces a mutual befuddlement, briefly confused with peace, a commodity rarely to be found in the region. Each intoxicant both reflects and reinforces a particular form of social interaction, and it is important to understand, therefore, that the qualities that interest us in wine reflect the social order of which wine is a part. When Samuel Huntington writes of the clash of civilisations, meaning the conflict between the Christian Enlightenment and pre-modern Islam, he ought really to be referring to another and deeper conflict: that between wine and pot.[5] In this conflict I am on the side of wine, as were many of the greatest poets of the Islamic world.

Wine is not simply a shot of alcohol, and must never be confused in its effect with spirits or even with cocktails. Wine is not a mixed drink but a transformation of the grape. The transformation of the soul under its influence is merely the continuation of another transformation that began maybe fifty years earlier when the grape was first plucked from the vine. (That is one reason why the Greeks described fermentation as the work of a god. Dionysus enters the grape and transforms it; and this process of transformation is then transferred to us as we drink.) Although we know that human skill is involved in this transformation, it is skill of quite another kind from that of the cocktail mixer, being a skill of husbandry, and in a certain measure the result is a tribute not just to the skill of the grower and the wine-maker, but to the whole ethological process that turned us from hunter-gatherers to farmers. (Maybe there is some echo of this in the story of the drunkenness of Noah.)

When we raise a glass of wine to our lips, therefore, we are savouring an ongoing process: wine is a living thing, the last result of other
living things, and the progenitor of life in us. It is almost as though it
were another human presence in any social gathering, as much a focus of
interest and in the same way as the other people there. This experience
is enhanced by the aroma, taste and the simultaneous impact on nose
and mouth, which—while not unique to wine—have, as I have already
argued, an intimate connection to the immediate intoxicating effect, so
as to be themselves perceived as intoxicating. The whole being of the
drinker rushes to the mouth and the olfactory organs to meet the tempt-
ing meniscus, just as the whole being of the lover rises to the lips in a
kiss. It would be an exaggeration to make too much of the comparison,
ancient though it is, between the erotic kiss and the sipping of wine.
Nevertheless, it is not an exaggeration, but merely a metaphor, to
describe the contact between the mouth and the glass as a *face to face*
encounter between you and the wine. And it is a useful metaphor.
Whisky may be *in* your face, but it is never face to face as wine is. The
shot of alcohol as it courses through the body is like something that has
escaped from the flavour, that is working in an underhand way. The alcoholic content of the wine, by contrast, remains part of the flavour, in
something like the way that the character of an honest person is revealed
in his face. Spirits are comparable in this respect to cordials and medicinal drinks: the flavour detaches itself readily from the effect, just as the
face and gestures of a shallow person detach themselves from his long-
term intentions. The companionship of wine resides in the fact that its
effect is not underhand or concealed but present and revealed in the very
flavour. This feature is then transmitted to those who drink wine together, and who adapt themselves to its quintessential honesty.

The ancient proverb tells us that there is truth in wine. The truth
lies not in what the drinker perceives but in what, with loosened tongue
and easier manners, he reveals. It is "truth for others", not "truth for
self". This accounts for both the social virtues of wine and its epistemological innocence. Wine does not deceive you, as cannabis deceives you,
with the idea that you enter another and higher realm, that you see
through the veil of Maya to the transcendental object or the thing in
itself. Hence it is quite unlike even the mildest of the mind-altering

drugs, all of which convey some vestige, however vulgarised, of the experience associated with mescaline and LSD, and recorded by Aldous Huxley in *The Doors of Perception*. These drugs—cannabis not exempted—are epistemologically culpable. They tell lies about another world, a transcendental reality beside which the world of ordinary phenomena pales into insignificance or at any rate into less significance than it has. Wine, by contrast, paints the world before us as the true one, and reminds us that if we have failed previously to know it then this is because we have failed in truth to belong to it, a defect that it is the singular virtue of wine to overcome.

For this reason we should, I believe, amplify our description of the characteristic effect of wine, which is not simply an effect of intoxication. The characteristic effect of wine, when drunk in company, includes an opening out of the self to the other, a conscious step towards asking and offering forgiveness: forgiveness not for acts or omissions, but for the impertinence of existing. Although the use of wine in the Christian Eucharist can be explained as a survival of the pagan cults that Christianity absorbed under the Roman Empire, and although it has authority in the Last Supper, as recorded in the New Testament, there is another reason for the centrality of wine in the communion ceremony, which is that it both illustrates and in a small measure enacts the moral posture that distinguishes Christianity from its early rivals, and which is summarised in the prayer to "forgive us our trespasses, as we forgive them that trespass against us". That remarkable prayer, which tells Christians that they can obtain forgiveness only if they offer it, is one that we all understand in our cups, and this understanding of the critical role of forgiveness in forming durable human societies intrudes too into the world of Islam, in the poetry of Hafiz, Rumi and Omar Khayyam, winos to a man. In *surah* xvi verse 7 of the Koran wine is unreservedly praised as one of God's gifts. As the Prophet, burdened by the trials of his Medina exile, became more tetchy, so did his attitude to wine begin to sour, as in *surah* v verses 90-1. Muslims believe that the later revelations cancel the earlier, whenever there is a conflict between them.[6] I suspect, however, that God moves in a more mysterious way, and that the unforgiving nature of the Prophet in his later years reflects a growing inability to accept people as they are or to endorse their simple pleasures—a fault that is human but not, in the Christian view, divine.

The communion wine returns me to a point that I emphasised earlier, which is that the pronounced mental effects of wine are, so to speak, read back into their cause, so that the wine itself has the taste of them. Just as you savour the intoxicating flavour of the wine, so do you savour its reconciling power: it presents you with the taste of forgiveness. That is one way of understanding the Christian doctrine of trans-sub-stantiation, itself a survival of the Greek belief that Dionysus is actually *in* the wine and not just the cause of it. The communicant does not taste the wine with a view to experiencing reconciliation and forgiveness as a subsequent effect. He savours forgiveness in the very act of drinking. This is what reconciliation, mercy and forgiveness *taste like*. And since those are the attributes of God, the communicant is—from the phe-nomenological point of view—actually tasting God.

I don't say that it is easy to make sense of that, and much depends on an understanding of taste as a distinct sensory and epistemological category. However, this returns me to the topic of tastes, by way of bring-ing my argument to a conclusion.

First, tastes are not qualities in the way that colours are. That is to say, they are not, in the Aristotelian sense, attributes of substances. Every patch of blue is a blue something, if only a patch. But not every straw-berry taste is a strawberry-tasting something. The taste can be there without the substance, as when I have a taste in the mouth, but have swallowed nothing. The taste is in the mouth in something like the way the smell is in the air or the sound is in the room. Tastes belong with smells and sounds in the ontological category of secondary objects. Hence the taste of a wine can linger long after the wine has disappeared down the tube. Tastes can detach themselves from their causes, as sounds do in music, and lead an emotional life of their own. Since they are asso-ciated with, rather than inherent in, their objects, they have a facility to launch trains of association, linking object to object, and place to place, in a continuous narrative such as was famously elaborated by Proust.

Connected with that feature of tastes is the well-known difficulty we experience in describing them. Colours belong to a spectrum, and vary along recognised phenomenal dimensions, such as brightness and satu-ration. Our descriptions of colours also order them, so that we know where they stand in relation to one another, and how they pass over into each other. Tastes exhibit order in certain dimensions—for example the

sweet-bitter, bland-spicy continua. But most of their peculiarities show
no intrinsic ordering and no clear transitions. We describe them, as a
rule, in terms of their characteristic causes: nutty, fruity, meaty, cheesy
and so on. Hence the process of discriminating and comparing tastes
begins with an effort of association, whereby we learn to identify and
taste the characteristic cause. We learn to place tastes in a gustatory field,
so to speak, whose landmarks are the familiar things that we eat and
drink, and the places and processes that produce them.

This last point returns me to the earlier one concerning the epistemological innocence of wine. The "this worldly" nature of the heightened
consciousness that comes to us through wine means that, in attempting to
describe the knowledge that it imparts, we look for features of our actual
world, features that might be, as it were, epitomised, commemorated and
celebrated in its flavours. Hence the traditional perception of fine wine as
the taste of a *terroir*—where that means not merely the soil, but the
customs and ceremonies that had sanctified it and put it, so to speak, in
communion with the drinker. The use of theological language here is, I
believe, no accident. Although wine tells no lies about a transcendental
realm, it sanctifies the immanent reality, which is why it is so effective a
symbol of the incarnation. In savouring it we are knowing—by acquain-
tance, as it were—the history, geography and customs of a community.

Since ancient times, therefore, wines have been associated with definite places, and been accepted not so much as the taste of those places,
as the flavour imparted to them by the enterprise of settlement. Wine of
Byblos was one of the principal exports of the Phoenicians, and old
Falernian was made legendary by Horace. Those who conjure with the
magic names of Burgundy, Bordeaux and the Rhine and Moselle are not
just showing off: they are deploying the best and most reliable description of a cherished taste, which is inseparable from the idea and the
history of the settlement that produced it. The Ancient Egyptians, inci-
dentally, while they often labelled wines with the place of their
production, and would trade with all the best suppliers around the
Mediterranean, would classify wines by their social function.
Archeologists have recovered amphorae labelled as "wine for first-class
celebrations", "wine for tax collection day", "wine for dancing", and so
on. It is doubtful, however, that these descriptions can function as a
guide to taste. It is easy to imagine a tasting in which the punter holds

the glass to his nose, takes a sip and then says "Burgundy"; rather more difficult to imagine him saying "tax collection". Why is that?

And here we should again return to the religious meaning of wine. At the risk of drastically oversimplifying, I suggest that there are two quite distinct strands that compose the religious consciousness, and that our understanding of religion has suffered from too great an emphasis on one of them. The first strand, which we over-emphasise, is that of belief. The second strand, which is slipping away from modern thought (though not from modern reality) is that which might be summarised in the term "membership", by which I mean all the customs, ceremonies and practices whereby the sacred is renewed, so as to be a real presence among us, and a living endorsement of the human community. The pagan religions of Greece and Rome were strong on membership but weak on belief. Hence they centred on the cult, as the primary religious phenomenon. It was through the cult, not the creed that the adept proved his religious orthodoxy and his oneness with his fellows. Western civilisation has tended in recent centuries to emphasise belief—in particular the belief in a transcendental realm and an omnipotent king who presides over it. This theological emphasis, by representing religion as a matter of theological doctrine, exposes it to refutation. And that means that the real religious need of people—a need planted in us, according to some, by evolution and according to others by God—seeks other channels for its expression: usually forms of idolatry that do not achieve the refreshing humanity of the cult.

Far from supposing the cult to be a secondary phenomenon, derived from the theological beliefs that justify it, I take the opposite view, and believe that I have modern anthropology, and its true founder Richard Wagner, on my side. Theological beliefs are rationalisations of the cult, and the function of the cult is membership. It is through establishing a cult that people learn to pool their resources. Hence every act of settling and of turning the earth to the common needs of a community, involves the building of a temple and the setting aside of days and hours for festivity and sacrificial offering. When people have, in this way, prepared a home for them, the gods come quietly in to inhabit it, maybe not noticed at first, and only subsequently clothed in the transcendental garments of theology.

Now it seems to me that the act of settling, which is the origin of civilisation, involves both a radical transition in our relation to the earth—the transition known in other terms as that from hunter-gatherer to farmer—and also a new sense of belonging. The settled people do not belong only to each other: they belong to a place, and out of that sense of shared roots there grow the farm, the village and the city. Vegetation cults are the oldest and most deeply rooted in the unconscious, since they are the cults that drive out the totemism of the hunter-gatherer, and celebrate the earth itself, as the willing accomplice in our bid to stay put. The new farming economy, and the city that grows from it, generate in us a sense of the holiness of the planted crop, and in particular of the staple food—which is grass, usually in the form of corn or rice—and the vine that wraps the trees above it. The fruit of the vine can be fermented and so stored in a sterilised form. It provides a place and the things that grow there with a memory.

At some level, I venture to suggest, the experience of wine is a recuperation of that original cult whereby the land was settled and the city built. And what we taste in the wine is not just the fruit and its ferment, but also the peculiar flavour of a landscape to which the gods have been invited and where they have found a home. Nothing else that we eat or drink comes to us with such a halo of significance, and cursed be the villains who refuse to drink it.

NOTES:

1. This general question has been defined for all subsequent discussion by F.N. Sibley, in "Aesthetic and Non-Aesthetic", *The Philosophical Review*, 74, 1965, pp. 134-59. I take Sibley to task at length in *Art and Imagination*, London, Methuen, 1974.

2 See Plotinus, *Enneads*, 1,6,1; Aquinas, *Summa Theologiae*, 1a 2ae 27, 1; Hegel, Introduction to *Aesthetics: Lectures on Fine Art*, vol. 1, tr. Knox, Oxford 1981; Scruton, *Art and Imagination*, p.156.

3 See F.N. Sibley, "Smells, Tastes and Aesthetics", reprinted in F.N. Sibley, Approaches to Aesthetics, eds. John Benson, Betty Redfern and Jeremy Roxbee Cox, Oxford University Press, 2006.

4 On the theory of secondary objects see R. Scruton, *The Aesthetics of Music*, Oxford University Press, 1997, ch. 1, and "Sounds as Secondary Objects and Pure Events", forthcoming in Matthew Nudds and Casey O'Callaghan, *New Essays on Sound and Perception*, Oxford University Press, 2006.

5 Samuel Huntington. *The Clash of Civilizations: And the Remaking of World Order*, New York, Free Press, 2002.

6 The later revelations come earlier in the canonical ordering of the text—a fatal mistake, in my view, given the manifest inspiration of the Meccan *surahs* and the angry bombast of so much that is attributed to the Medina years.

Does knowing a wine
is produced from grapes of specific
terroir

or

has undergone barrell ferm or barrique aging

or

fermented with native yeasts

etc.

enhance the enjoyment, appreciat
maybe!

Can knowledge of terroir or
provenance add to pleasure

I think so

chapter two

KNOWLEDGE, WINE, AND TASTE: WHAT GOOD IS KNOWLEDGE (IN ENJOYING WINE)?

Kent Bach

It's a bit awkward for me to talk about philosophy and wine. Even though I'm very analytical in philosophy and in all but one of my other passions, I'm not very analytical about wine. I talk a lot of philosophy and I drink a lot of wine, but I don't do aesthetics, the sort of philosophy that's relevant to talking about wine, and I don't talk a lot about wine itself, even though I drink it almost nightly and have accumulated a great many bottles of it, too many in fact. Except at dinners and tastings, I don't need to talk about wine: I don't make it, market it, sell it, score it, or write about it. In fact, I'm not very good at talking about wine. I don't write tasting notes, and I can't say I get all that much out of professional tasting notes—I certainly can't tell from reading one what the wine tastes like. I'm keen to try wines of all sorts, and for me there's no substitute for tasting them myself. I recommend wines to people, but the only way I know to justify a recommendation is to pour them a glass. So, despite my reluctance to talk about wine, here I am today.

Before taking up my question, a brief autobiographical note. Until 1993 I had no interest in wine. In my ignorance and inexperience, I had no idea why other people were passionate about it, not only passionate about drinking it but obsessed with knowing about it. Then this changed suddenly, on one autumn evening in Gainesville, Florida, of all places. I was dragged to a tasting of wines from St. Emilion. The group blind-tasted, described, and numerically rated eight wines, most of which I enjoyed immensely. Despite my ignorance and inexperience, my numerical ratings were all very close to the consensus of the group. That was a revelation to this wine heathen: I was convinced that there was something I'd been missing. The clincher was the mystery wine, also wrapped in a paper bag, but not part of the regular tasting. It was a 1975 Cheval Blanc, not the greatest of vintages, as I would later learn, but more than good enough to make me a wine convert. Now I began to see the light or, rather, to sniff and taste it.

ZEROING IN ON THE QUESTION

I am asking a very specific question: what good is knowledge when it comes to enjoying the experience of drinking a wine? Can knowledge, about wine in general or about the specific wine you're drinking, help you enjoy the taste of that wine? Can such knowledge even make the wine taste better? The question is not intended to apply to people completely new to wine and without any experience at tasting it. I am asking it about people who have a basic liking for wine, have a normal sensitivity to aromas and flavours, and know how to expose the qualities of a wine to the responsiveness of their senses. Given that, how, if at all, can knowledge about a particular wine affect your enjoyment of it? Can it enhance your pleasure? Or, rather, does it provide its own kind of pleasure, cognitive or even intellectual pleasure, which accompanies the pleasure of tasting? To put the question differently, is the difference between the pleasure experienced by a connoisseur and an non-expert wine enthusiast purely cognitive or at least partly sensory?

The specific question I'm asking does not concern the many other things that knowledge about wine is good for, such as making wine, selling it, and writing about it, and understanding and appreciating the efforts of those who make, sell, or write about it. Much knowledge about wine is very practical, such as knowing how to grow and select grapes, having effective techniques for making wine, and knowing how to store and how to serve it. Practical knowledge is obviously valuable when it comes to choosing what wines to buy, deciding when to open them, and choosing which one to have with a particular dish. This requires knowing at least roughly what the wine should taste like. Precise knowledge of the taste can be handy if there's a question whether what's in a bottle is really what the label says it is or, if that's not in question, whether the condition of a wine is as it should be. And knowledge about wine, like knowledge about anything else, doesn't have to be good *for* anything to be good to have. It can be valuable in and of itself, at least if you care about wine. It satisfies curiosity, and it yields intellectual pleasure.

Knowledge about anything you're interested in is good to seek and good to get. No one would argue with that. But even though there's a big difference between the pleasure of pursuing and acquiring knowledge about wine and the pleasure of drinking wine itself, the two can of course go together. When you're drinking a fine wine, it's nice to know what kinds of grapes went into it, where it came from and when, who made it and how. Having such knowledge about a wine while drinking it might add to your understanding and appreciation of the wine, but can it make the wine taste better or otherwise add to the experience? You might be surprised to learn that the wine is 100% Syrah, that it was made in the Santa Ynez Valley, and that it came from an exceptional vintage. Of course, such knowledge may add to your pleasure *while* drinking the wine, but that doesn't mean it adds to your pleasure *in* drinking the wine. Is there any sort of knowledge that can do that? That is my question.

Why ask this question? Many people untutored in wine seem to feel intimidated by it. They think they know nothing about wine and therefore can't appreciate it. In fact, they are intimidated by wine experts—writers, collectors, sommeliers, and snobs. And, I daresay, it is not their ignorance that keeps them from enjoying wine, it's the wine they drink. The best way to make wines taste better is to taste better wines! Ignorance can keep you from knowing what wines to drink but it can't keep you from enjoying good ones when they're put in front of you. Knowing how to taste obviously helps—there's no substitute for experience at tasting—but how important is knowing about the wine, or knowing about wine in general?

ONE OBVIOUS ANSWER

Here's a plausible answer to my question. Surely the pleasure in drinking a wine is enhanced by some knowledge of the range of aromas and flavours that similar wines are capable of. And the more familiar you are with other wines, especially similar ones, the more you can appreciate what (if anything) is special about the one you're drinking. In tasting a particular wine you can ask yourself, how does this wine compare with others from the same varietal, from different vineyards in the same region, from the same producer in different years? It does seem that comparative knowledge, based on tasting experience, can enhance your tasting pleasure.

However, it is also possible that such knowledge can detract from your tasting pleasure. No matter how well you can discern and discriminate various aromas and flavours, overexposure to common combinations of them can decrease your ability to enjoy them. You could be drinking a well-made wine, even an elegant, balanced, and complex one, and be unmoved by it because you are overly familiar with its array of aroma and flavour components. I'll concede, of course, that you're unlikely to have this problem with a truly great wine, but I'll venture to say that there's no wine that anyone could enjoy drinking night after night. Also, certain wines that are a pleasure to drink don't hold up well in comparison to others. Imagine what it would be like if, before having a fine bottle with dinner, you were forced to taste an even better wine first. Having a memory for tastes can have the same effect. That's why it becomes harder and harder to enjoy good wines that you used to enjoy once you've encountered better ones of the same type.

In any case, the primary pleasure in tasting a wine surely does not consist in comparing it to other wines. If even the best wines did not taste good to you, whatever pleasure you gained from discerning the distinctive features of a given wine and comparing it to other, similar wines would be merely a cognitive pleasure, not a sensory one. This purely cognitive pleasure would not be worth pursuing by itself, any more than the pleasure you might perversely hope to gain in the course of comparing the tastes of various liquid medications or insect repellents. To be sure, it's fun to compare wines, especially interestingly similar ones, but this is a kind of cognitive pleasure. Wine connoisseurs, while enjoying the sensory pleasure of drinking a particularly fine wine that they are tasting blind, also enjoy trying to guess what grape(s) it is made from and its age and origin, and even trying to identify the wine itself. Succeeding is really fun. But these are cognitive pleasures distinct from the pleasure had in drinking the wine.

One special sort of comparison really is part and parcel of the sensory pleasure. That's the pleasure of experiencing and noticing how the wine evolves in the glass, or from one glass to the next, as it is exposed to oxygen and as its temperature changes. Sometimes it takes a while for a wine to "open up." There's a chemical explanation for what happens, but I wouldn't go into that even if I understood it. The taste of a wine can change in minutes. And it can appear to change when tasted with different dishes over the course of a meal. There's a physiological explanation for this, but I won't go into that either. So we can't exactly speak of *the* taste of the wine, and part of the pleasure in drinking it consists in discerning its evolving taste and trying it with different dishes.

Now consider the distinction between what a wine tastes like and what we like about the taste. This distinction gives rise to an interesting question in regard to our changing tastes in foods and beverages. What happens when we come to like certain tastes and smells that we didn't used to like or, for that matter, stop liking ones we once did like? Both things happen as we grow up. Many people lose the taste for sweetened breakfast cereals, and many develop a taste for spinach and even for wine. So, does the thing we used to like and now dislike taste different, or does it taste the same except that we no longer like that taste? Similarly, does the thing we used to dislike and now like taste different, or does it taste the same except that we now like that taste? It is not clear how to answer such questions.

UNTUTORED EXPERIENCE AND CULTIVATED TASTE

Some of our responses to the sensory qualities we experience seem perfectly natural, and not the result of experience. We are all familiar with truly foul tastes and the odours that go with them. As children, we were all forced to submit to certain medicines and to certain foods. As adults, we often submit voluntarily, for reasons of health or politeness. Plenty of nasty odours pass before our noses, and sometimes spoiled or otherwise awful food passes our lips. One interesting thing about foul smells and vile tastes is not merely that we can't help how we respond to them but that we react to them viscerally, sometimes to the point of getting sick to our stomachs (perhaps that is partly because smell and taste are chemical senses). Moderately bad smells and tastes don't produce such effects, but no special expertise is required to respond negatively to them.

On the positive side, it doesn't take any special expertise to enjoy and appreciate the sight of a beautiful sunset or the feel of a nice back rub. You can savour these and many other exquisite things just by taking them in. They are not acquired tastes. But so-called "adult" foods and beverages, including wine, generally are acquired tastes. Does this mean that you have to learn about them in order to enjoy them? Developing a taste for them isn't a matter of learning about them but of getting accustomed to them, as your palate matures. But, it will be objected, simply liking the taste isn't the same as cultivating a taste for them. Cultivating taste in a particular area requires noticing subtle features and detecting subtle differences. In the case of wine, this is a matter of discerning the distinctive features of particular wines and appreciating a variety of different wines (unlike a certain relative of mine, who will drink nothing but Chardonnay and only if it comes from the Carneros region of Sonoma County, California). Tasting wines of diverse types, including ones made from obscure grapes in unheralded regions, obviously helps you appreciate the range of possibilities that wine is capable of.

Does discrimination require cultivation? Take the case of colours. If your colour vision is normal, you can, believe it or not, discriminate something on the order of ten million different colours, and without any special training. You can see the colour you're looking at just by looking at it, and you can see that it looks a little different from very similar ones that are presented to you. You don't have to do anything special—you just have to look. It is another thing to be able to name the colour, but obviously there are far more colours than colour names. You may find the colour appealing, boring, or revolting, but you don't have to know why it strikes you in a certain way for it to do so. So why should flavours, wine flavours in particular, be any different? Being able to describe a wine is a nice ability to have, but do you need it to taste the wine? Being able to explain what it is about a wine that you like is nice too, but you don't need to do that to like the wine. These additional abilities are good to have and enjoyable to exercise, but they seem distinct from the ability to enjoy the wine itself. So, isn't the ability to enjoy some wine flavours and not others just like the untutored ability to enjoy some colours and not others?

Well, it will be objected, I'm relying on a bad analogy. Tasting a wine is not like looking at a uniform colour chip. All right, then, here's a better analogy. Consider what it's like to look at a good monochromatic painting. To appreciate it, you need to stare at it for some length of time. You will come to see things you didn't notice at first. Gradually certain subtle variations in the colour will appear and perhaps even certain patterns will emerge. But tasting a wine isn't really like that, unless the wine is not quite ready to drink and needs a little more swirling or a little more time in the glass. Here's another analogy, looking at faces. Most people can distinguish the faces of other people (at least of their own ethnic group) and, more to the point, can enjoy looking at them. No special training is needed for doing this. And, unlike looking at monochromatic paintings, no special effort or sustained attention is required. It does take special training or a special talent to describe or to draw faces, but these abilities are not needed to see and distinguish them. But seeing and distinguishing faces involves recognizing different geometrical forms, spatial arrays of features, and doing that is not really like tasting wines. So we need a better analogy (one other analogy, which I am not in a position to pursue, is a blind person's highly developed sense of touch). I think I have one.

ANALOGY: NOTES AND CHORDS

Compare listening to a great piece of music with drinking a great wine. A great piece of music is a complex, highly organized structure of sounds. Enjoying a fine performance of such a piece involves much more than taking in the sensuous sounds of the individual notes and chords. Just for starters, one needs to hear the melodies and chord progressions in order to sense the patterns they make up. If you are intimately familiar with the piece, you can appreciate the performer's distinctive touches to the sound qualities, voicings, phrasings, and overall shaping of the piece. But that's much more elaborate than tasting a wine. So here's my analogy. Taking a sip of wine, at least a wine worth talking about, is like hearing the sound of a sustained, musical chord. Over a few seconds, it has a beginning, a middle, and a finish, during which different qualities will reveal themselves, and you will notice them if you pay close attention. Interestingly, wines are often described as displaying "notes" of various kinds, such as notes of leather, lavender, or liquorice, maybe a little tar or graphite, along with a few obligatory fruits and perhaps some Asian spices, just to mention a few. And, although the composite taste of a wine is never described as a chord, this doesn't deter me from insisting on my unflattering analogy of the taste of a wine with a musical chord, the overall experience of a single sip of wine is comparable in duration and complexity to savouring one sustained musical chord.

However, my analogy is not entirely apt. It does not help explain why we should value wines so highly and pay so much for them. No matter how sensuous and complex a chord is, even a sustained one, it is just one momentary episode out of hundreds or thousands in an entire piece. Not much knowledge is required to hear the chord (to be sure, it would take having some knowledge, as well as experience, to identify its harmonic structure), but there is not all that much enjoyment to be had either. Certainly no one would attend a concert just to hear even the greatest orchestra play a beautiful sustained chord every few minutes, even a little differently each time. Yet one is more than content to do the equivalent of that with a glass of wine. The analogy breaks down because the basic unit of pleasure in drinking a wine comes from taking a sip, whereas the basic unit of pleasure in listening to music generally does not consist in hearing merely a chord, some exquisite chords excepted.

What does the analogy miss? What is it about tastes, aromas included, that makes experiences of them so highly valued, even though these experiences are intermittent and each is but a few seconds in length? You could complain that I have neglected the overall experience of a meal and the other pleasures that go with drinking wine, such as good food, friendly company, interesting conversation, pleasant ambiance, not to mention the effect of intoxication. But wine lovers enjoy wines in themselves. Besides, taking all these factors into account does not help explain why great wines are valued so much more highly than mediocre ones or merely good ones, even though the units of pleasure are so short in duration, as compared to those in listening to music, looking at a painting or a scene in nature, reading a book, seeing a movie, or even having sex. You wouldn't want to do any of those things a few seconds at a time and resume a few minutes later while doing other things in between.

SENSORY AND COGNITIVE PLEASURE

People who say that they can't appreciate a great wine generally haven't tasted one. In fact, no special ability is required to enjoy such a wine. All it takes is normal sensitivity to aromas and flavours (unfortunately, some people lack that) and the ability to swirl the wine in the glass, to bring the glass under one's nose to savour the wine's aromatics, and then to pay close and sustained attention as the wine passes one's lips and gets circulated in one's mouth. In my experience, that's enough for typical inexperienced tasters to be blown away by a great Bordeaux, Burgundy, or Barbaresco. When they go "Ooh" and "Ah" or go "Wow!", they're not acting.

Of course, they may not understand why they react in this way. They may be in no position to know anything about the grape(s), the region and the vineyard, the producer, and the vintage, they may have no basis for comparing this great wine with similar but merely very good wines, and they may be unable to articulate what particular aromas and flavours they are experiencing or have any notion of what experienced tasters mean by the balance, structure, and elegance of a great wine. Even so, it is not obvious that this wine does not taste as wonderful to them as it does to the expert. They may not be equipped to enjoy the cognitive pleasures that accompany tasting it, but that's not to say they aren't fully equipped to experience the sensory pleasure inherent in attentively drinking it.

The ability to identify and describe the distinctive features of a given wine does have a definite value, certainly if it is your profession to make, recommend, sell, serve, or write about wine. That much is obvious, but however enjoyable it is to exercise this ability, the pleasure one derives from that is distinct from the pleasure in simply drinking the wine. The ability to identify and describe the distinctive features of a given wine is also valuable to an amateur, and not just in selecting wines for particular occasions and collecting wines for future occasions. There is a certain pleasure in being able to remember wines one has tasted, especially great ones. Remembering what they are like, like remembering any wonderful experience, is a pleasure in its own right, but this too is a distinct, cognitive pleasure.

Wine tasting is not like bird watching and train spotting. In those other two pursuits, the pleasure is in the recognizing and identifying. With wine, the pleasure of sniffing and tasting comes first. Recognizing and identifying aroma and flavour components is secondary, and provides cognitive pleasure about the source of one's sensory pleasure.

TRACKING SENSORY DISCRIMINATION

I have been suggesting that anyone with a basic liking for wine, a normal sensitivity to aromas and flavours, and a little practice at tasting can enjoy fine wines and discern and distinguish their distinctive characteristics, and that being able to categorize and compare wines, in order to appreciate their similarities and differences, provides a distinct, cognitive pleasure. I can't prove this, but it seems to me that the burden of proof is on those who insist that expertise is necessary for fully enjoying the experience of tasting fine wines. Yes, expertise puts one in position to have further, cognitive pleasures, but these pleasures are distinct from the sensory pleasure of tasting wines. Now I have been supposing that these sensory pleasures come more or less naturally, that people can be responsive to the distinct characteristics of different wines without being able to compare, much less articulate these differences. And there seems to be good scientific reason to believe that.

Investigators in the field of psychophysics have methods for measuring peoples' powers of sensory discrimination. These are the techniques of psychometrics. It is possible, using the method of multi-dimensional scaling, to construct a quality (or similarity) space for a given individual in a particular sense modality. The idea is to determine the smallest number of dimensions necessary to model a subject's judgments of relative similarity. There are various methods by which this multi-dimensional scaling can be accomplished. For example, subjects can be presented with one sample followed by two other, somewhat similar samples, and be asked which of the others the first is more similar to: "Is this [item 1] more like this [item 2]... or like this [item 3]?" Repeating such procedures with different samples eventually provides enough data to suggest the number of respects in which the qualities in a given modality can differ from one another. The overall structure, including the number of dimensions, of a quality space represents degrees and respects of relative similarity and difference between different qualities of the type being modelled. Distance corresponds to degrees of difference and dimension corresponds to respect.

The case of colour experience is relatively clear. Just as three dimensions are needed to account for perceived differences in physical space, so three dimensions (and maybe more) are needed to account for perceived differences in colour space: hue, saturation, and intensity. Two distinct colour samples differ in at least one of these respects. With sounds the two dimensions of pitch and loudness are needed, though one can, of course, hear many sounds at once, sometimes hearing them as chords and sometimes as distinct sounds. And, since hearing is essentially the perception of events rather than objects or substances, the dimension of time is needed too, not only to distinguish otherwise similar sounds as to duration but also to reckon with the essentially temporal features of sounds. This is obvious in the case of music and speech. As to taste, it is common to distinguish the dimensions of sweet, salty, sour, and bitter, and there is also umami to contend with (never mind astringency, effervescence, or the "burning" of "hot" peppers, which are felt not tasted). The sense of smell is a great mystery. Last time I checked—I'm no expert in this field—different theorists had posited anywhere from seven to eighteen different dimensions of smell (never mind the "stinging" sensation of ammonia and other gases, which is not a matter of smell).

The total extent of a quality space represents the range of possibilities available to a given person. So, for example, human beings are visually sensitive only to the visible spectrum, which comprises a very small segment of the entire electromagnetic spectrum, and their sensitivity falls dramatically as illumination diminishes. And, of course, this range varies from person to person, and among different animals. Some people are partially or even completely colour blind, and some animals are sensitive to ultraviolet or infrared light. As to sound, dogs hear higher frequencies than people, and women tend to be able to hear higher frequencies than men. Dogs can detect scents that are far below the threshold of human detection. Some people have reduced ability to detect odours (hyposmia) or to taste substances (hypogeusia), and some can detect no odours (anosmia) or no tastes at all (ageusia). To some people a substance that has a pleasant taste and smell to normal people may taste and smell foul. Supertasters (hypergeusics) and supersmellers (hyperanosmics) can discern tiny tastes and smells to which most people are oblivious and can distinguish different ones that seem the same to everyone else. Their exceptional abilities are double-edged, depending on whether the qualities are pleasant or unpleasant. For example, some people can detect the presence of TCA (2,4,6-trichloroanisole), the main culprit behind so-called cork taint (the problem is not always with the cork), in concentrations well below most people's ability to detect.

This is not a matter of knowledge or training (of course, training can facilitate remembering and being able to identify, as opposed to merely sensing and noticing, distinct sensory qualities). People with palates and noses more developed than the rest of us don't merely know more—they sense more. In the case of wine, they can discern the presence of particular flavours and aromas, they can notice subtle changes in flavour over the course of a single sip, and they can appreciate what underlies the complexity and structure of an interesting wine. You need experience to notice what is distinctive about a particular wine—this requires comparisons with other wines and that requires having encountered and remembering similar wines. But you don't need extensive experience or expertise to notice imbalances between fruit and tannin or between sweetness and acidity.

As mentioned earlier, without any special training normal people can discriminate something on the order of ten million different colours. This number is determined by extrapolating from the number of just noticeable differences that people can detect between tested colour samples that differ but slightly as to hue, intensity, or saturation. Measuring taste and smell discrimination using the method of multi-dimensional scaling is much more difficult, because detecting tastes and smells takes longer and because tastes and smells have after-effects. It takes time to clear the palate and the nostrils (and the air). So side-by-side comparisons cannot be made, and there must be a decent interval between tastes or smells compared successively. This makes discriminations harder to make and to measure. Still, given the five dimensions of taste and however many the dimensions of smell, even if we conservatively assume only ten dimensions of taste and smell combined and only five just noticeable differences along each dimension, the total number of taste-and-smell combinations is five,[10] or almost ten million, comparable to the number of colours that people can normally discriminate.

The point of all this, whatever the numbers may turn out to be, is that, with the help of the techniques of psychometrics, it could be verified that people have a natural capacity to discern and discriminate, as with colour, a huge number of aromas and flavours. Of course, only some of these occur in the real world, and only some of those correspond to the aromas and flavours of items we consume (foods and beverages), and wines comprise only a narrow range of these. Even so, the number is still very large, and there is no reason to suppose that people with just a little training in how to taste wine couldn't, under proper conditions, discriminate a great many wines and detect a great many particular flavours and aromas in them. It is not to say that they can remember them over the long term and thereby be able to recognize, much less identify, them when they encounter familiar ones again, but that is not what I have been suggesting. My argument is very simple: People can discriminate huge numbers of aroma-taste combinations. Their affective responses to these combinations are direct, not cognitive. So, knowledge isn't needed to enjoy a given aroma-taste combination.

Even so, knowledge can guide us to greater sensory pleasures and it can provide pleasure of its own. Experts and connoisseurs have plenty of it.

EXPERTS AND CONNOISSEURS

What's the difference between being an expert and being a connoisseur? To answer that question you might ask a different one: what, if anything, does a connoisseur know that an expert doesn't? But it seems to me that that's the wrong question. Being a connoisseur doesn't require more knowledge—it requires appreciation. And, indeed, we speak of music appreciation, art appreciation and, yes, even wine appreciation. So, what is it to appreciate the music we listen to, the paintings we look at, or the wine we savour? Appreciation has both a cognitive and an aesthetic side, not that these are unrelated, and they correspond to the difference between being an expert and being a connoisseur. On the cognitive side is the ability to recognize the ingredients and how they're put together. In the case of art and music, this is a very complex ability generally requiring at least some formal training and historical knowledge, including familiarity with other works and, in the case of music, other performances, to go along with perceptual acuity. Acquiring such knowledge leads to aesthetic appreciation by enhancing one's ability to notice features and relationships that would otherwise escape one's attention. No such knowledge is required for appreciating a wine. Even the best wines are not works of art. They don't have cognitive or emotional content. Their aesthetic value is provided entirely by the aromas and flavours that they impart. Like a great work of art, a great wine has more to notice and more worth noticing than a run-of-the-mill wine, but with a great wine these are exclusively sensory qualities, and noticing and enjoying them is all that's required for appreciating the wine. It really doesn't go deeper than that. Even so, there are connoisseurs of wine.

Again, I ask, what's the difference between being an expert and being a connoisseur? With wine or anything else, one could have the knowledge required of an expert without being a connoisseur. So, for example, you could know a great deal about Persian rugs but not have a good eye for them. A connoisseur is not just knowledgeable but discerning and discriminating. That raises a further question.

What is it to be discerning and discriminating? Interestingly, the terms "discerning" and "discriminating," like the word "taste" itself, have both sensory and aesthetic meanings. In the sensory sense, being discerning is a matter of being able to notice hard to detect features, and being discriminating a matter of being able to distinguish similar qualities. These can be detected by, as the case may be, looking, smelling, or tasting, perhaps with the help of knowledge derived from experience. But a connoisseur is discerning and discriminating in an aesthetic sense. One can be a connoisseur of any of the arts or of more purely sensory things, such as cheese, chocolate, ice cream, coffee, Scotch, perfume—or wine. (Today, it is both gratifying and daunting to know that there are far more wines than ever to discern and discriminate and, more than ever before, more worth being discerning and discriminating about.)

There is more to having good taste than being able to tell differences. To see why that's not enough, imagine a beverage made from swill, called "swine." It is hard to imagine anyone wanting to experience, learn about, and comment on the different nuances from one bottle of swine to the next. Well, you could imagine tasting notes on them written by a gustatory Marquis de Sade or by the swine critic of Dickens's village Eton Swill. Or imagine there being a supertasting medical diagnostician who could use his sense of taste to perform blood tests and urinalyses directly, just by tasting samples (pretend that all the substances that a lab tests for are detectable by taste). He could do exactly what a medical testing lab does, with equal accuracy: he could sip samples of urine and blood and detect each medically relevant substance that is present and judge its concentration. This would be quite a valuable ability to have, one that would take a lot of training to develop, but despite the fact that he'd be an expert taster, we wouldn't regard him as a connoisseur of blood and urine.

COMPARATIVE PLEASURES

Wine lovers like to compare wines, especially different vintages of the same wine and different wines from the same vintage and the same region or even the same producer. This is done at so-called vertical and horizontal tastings, and it requires a good short-term memory for tastes. When, as at dinner, we open one particular bottle of a certain wine, it is interesting to compare it with previous bottles of that very wine or similar wines we've had from the same vintage. This requires good long-term memory for tastes. And that's a kind of knowledge, the kind of knowledge that connoisseurs have in spades. The more of it one has, the more pleasure one can derive from exercising it. But is the pleasure of comparing part of the pleasure *in* tasting the wine?

There is pleasure to be had in comparing the wine one is drinking with other, similar wines and in knowing what makes one better than another or what distinguishes it from others. Comparative pleasure can certainly accompany the sensuous pleasure of drinking a fine wine, and it may be the only pleasure connected with drinking a mediocre wine, if only to appreciate its mediocrity. Memory for tastes is clearly necessary for this, and no doubt being able to categorize the distinctive qualities of wines one tastes facilitates one's memory for them. Familiarity with other wines great and not so great enhances one's appreciation, positive or negative, for the wine one is drinking. Even so, I suggest, this comparative pleasure is not, strictly speaking, part of the pleasure *in* drinking the wine, although it is intimately connected with that pleasure. It's really an intellectual pleasure, indeed an genuinely aesthetic pleasure, but it is not a pleasure in tasting but a pleasure in remembering. If one has a memory for tastes, one can just well enjoy such pleasures while not drinking but just talking or thinking about wine—well almost just as well. I am not pooh-poohing these comparative pleasures; I am merely distinguishing them from the intrinsic sensuous pleasure in tasting itself.

Comparative knowledge is good to have, for both aesthetic and practical reasons. The practical reasons are obvious. It is useful to know which vintages of a particular wine or which wines from a particular place and year are worth trying again and which are better avoided.

Aesthetically, there is something a bit perverse about letting comparative judgments dictate how much one enjoys a wine. To me at least, it is much more enjoyable to look at paintings and listen to musical performances without comparing them with similar paintings or with other performances of the same piece. I used to be much more judgmental, but I came to appreciate the value of assessing what I look at or listen to on its own merits. Of course, experience helps, and that's what a connoisseur has.

I have conceded that experience is required for appreciating a fine wine, as opposed to just enjoying its taste. Compare what is involved is enjoying and appreciating a fine wine with enjoying and appreciating works of fine art, literature, music, or cinema (of course, it is dangerous to generalize here). Certainly less sustained effort and attention are required, if only because tasting a wine does not take long periods of time. One doesn't have to discern complex formal or structural features and relationships, for which sustained and repeated encounters are likely to be required. No interpretation or understanding is needed, and there is no iconography, allusion, plot, or psychological or moral import to uncover. Each taste adds to one's pleasure and, indeed, may enhance it, but the pleasure of drinking a fine wine is a momentary pleasure. When wine lovers speak of length, they're speaking of seconds, not minutes or hours, as with other pleasures. This doesn't mean the pleasure of drinking wine is any less. Quite the contrary, the great thing about the pleasure of drinking a wine, even though it consists of intermittent tastes, is that it can be so short and yet so good. That's why my earlier analogy with hearing musical chords, though somewhat apt, is inadequate.

WORDS AND FLAVOURS
It is an interesting linguistic fact that whereas we have numerous words for very specific shades of colour, our vocabulary is sorely lacking when it comes to tastes, smells, and feels. Whereas we can describe particular shades of red as crimson, scarlet, vermilion, and so on, we speak of the smell of roses, the taste of honey, and the feel of sandpaper. For tactual qualities words like "smooth" and "rough" and "hard" and "soft" get us only so far, and then we resort to describing what something feels like, that is, what it feels similar to, like sandpaper or velvet. We can describe

tastes in general terms as sweet, sour, salty, and bitter, but when we need to get specific it is more feasible to describe a particular taste by specifying what it is the taste of: the taste of chocolate, the taste of honey, or the taste of cod liver oil. We may describe substances with complex tastes as containing hints of particular tastes characterized in this way. This raises the question of whether hints and notes of particular flavours are really present in a wine or whether tasting the wine merely reminds us of particular flavours.

Being analytical about wine requires not merely discerning and discriminating the various elements in the taste of a wine but being able to talk about them. Does that ability enhance the enjoyment of wine? It certainly enhances the enjoyment of conversation about wine (it can also detract from general conversation), but does being able to verbalize what one tastes enhance one's ability to taste it, to discern and discriminate what's in it, and to enjoy it? Or does this merely facilitate one's ability later to remember and identify it and thereby compare it with other wines?

Now it might seem that being able to verbalize the qualities of a wine enhances one's ability to taste it. After all, it might be argued, attending a tutored tasting, in which a skilled wine taster provides on the spot tasting notes, enables one to taste qualities that one hadn't previously noticed. But consider what actually happens. When the expert points out distinctive qualities of the wine, is he revealing qualities you hadn't noticed or, rather, merely calling them to your attention under certain apt descriptions? Vivid verbal description can create the illusion of revealing an unnoticed quality without actually doing so. Perhaps all it does is put into words what you had already sensed but weren't able to articulate. The question boils down to this: does the wine taste different now that its qualities are singled out and labelled, or does the description ring true because it captures the experience one was already having? I'm inclined to opt for the latter answer: the description rings true not because it reveals something new but because one's experience already fits it. However, I don't think there's any way to argue conclusively for this. The difficulty is that insofar as one can sense qualities without specifically noticing them (much less describing them), it is unclear how to determine whether a newly noticed quality is newly sensed or was already sensed but not yet noticed.

It seems to me that people can be discerning and discriminating without being able to describe what they discern and discriminate. As we have seen, it is possible to test people for how extensively they can detect sensory differences, whether of colour and sound or of smell and taste (the technique of multi-dimensional scaling can be used to construct a multi-dimensional quality spaces for a particular individual and for making interpersonal comparisons among different people). Once that is done, people could then be trained, as Prof. Ann Noble has done at UC Davis, to describe what they smell and taste. They could then be re-tested to determine if this verbal learning has any effect on their quality space. Maybe this would make a difference, maybe not. I'm inclined to think not, but I can't prove this. I'm inclined to think that memory for aromas and flavours is not like memory for the sorts of cues and clues that highly trained radiologists, archaeologists, or paleontologists can discern and discriminate. For it is only within their specialized scientific frameworks that the distinctive features (visual markings and patterns) they detect by perception are meaningful. Gourmets and wine connoisseurs discern and discriminate features (aromas and flavours) not for what they indicate but for what they are.

One important consideration is that, since learning to describe aromas and flavours requires paying close attention to them, attending to them can surely enhance one's wine-tasting experience. The more one notices and the more one can go from noticing one element of taste to noticing another, the more there is to savour. If one can also remember similar wines, one can appreciate any distinctive features of the wine one is tasting (or, for that matter, realize that there is nothing distinctive about it). But perhaps one can do this all this noticing in a purely non-verbal way, by remembering what other wines were like. We shouldn't confuse the pleasure of being articulate about wine, of being able to describe the distinctive features of a wine, with the non-verbal ability of remembering what they are like, or of appreciating them without being able to say why.

CAN KNOWLEDGE DETRACT?

Can knowledge detract from enjoying a wine? Familiarity may breed contempt, even for wines, but not for a great wine. Even so, there is something about the first time with a great wine. As nice as it is to remember, the first time is impossible to reproduce. The better your memory for a wine, the harder it is to be surprised by its taste—unless it has changed or you have. In fact, one of the wonderful things about great wines is that they do change, generally for the better before they change for the worse (here I am speaking of bottle to bottle over time, not of sip to sip or glass to glass, though savouring these short-term changes is part of the pleasure of drinking a great wine). But it is hard to reproduce the thrill of tasting a great wine in its prime other than by forgetting how good it was and what was so good about it. So there is a disadvantage to knowledge. It can reduce the thrill and eliminate the surprise in drinking a great wine. Although it can generate anticipation prior to actually tasting the wine, it can also result in disappointment—a perfectly good wine can fall short of your expectations. Secondhand knowledge of the alleged greatness of an unfamiliar wine can also generate anticipation, but it too can lead to disappointment, if the wine doesn't do for you what it did for someone else or because it doesn't live up to its name—or its price.

There are other disadvantages. If you are very good at discerning and discriminating the various elements in the taste of a wine, you're in a position to be overly analytical about it and miss the combined effect of these elements. Here I am echoing the old adage that to dissect is to destroy, to which there is some truth. Also, you might fail to notice elements that don't fall neatly into familiar categories, such as those represented on Ann Noble's Wine Aroma Wheel. It is not obvious that all the aromas that can surround a glass of wine fit into familiar categories, such as (for white wines) honeysuckle, jasmine, lychee, apricot, pineapple, pear, apple, lemon, grapefruit, fig, bell pepper, asparagus, green olive, cut green grass, dried herbs, anise, clove, nuts, honey, butter, vanilla, smoke, and wood and (for red wines) violets, roses, cherry, strawberry, blackberry, berry jam, cassis, fruit candy, bell pepper, asparagus, green bean, black olive, mint, eucalyptus, tobacco, mushroom, earth, anise, black pepper, clove, butter, soy, molasses, chocolate, cedar, vanilla, smoke, and pine. We don't need to fit faces, sunsets, or bird calls into set categories to perceive, enjoy, and appreciate them, and it seems constrictive to do so. Why should the enjoyment and appreciation of wine be any different? Surely some of the aromas and flavours of some wines fall between the categorial cracks.

As I said when I began, I drink a lot of wine but don't talk about it a lot. This paper is an exception. Its main point has been very simple: most wine knowledge does not directly enhance the pleasures to be had in drinking wine. but, rather, enhances one's ability to discover such pleasures. I hope it hasn't seemed as though I have been denouncing knowledge about wine. To the contrary, such knowledge is a pleasure to acquire and to apply. But the pleasures it gives you are not sensory but cognitive. These include the pleasures in learning something new, recognizing something familiar, satisfying curiosity about the unfamiliar, and being surprised. At least I can say this: although wine is wine and knowledge is knowledge, they mix exceptionally well.

chapter three

THE OBJECTIVITY OF TASTES AND TASTING

Barry C. Smith

Most wine tasters and many wine critics will tell you that taste is subjective. It is a matter of what you like or dislike, of what is right for you. In matters of taste your opinion is sovereign. You should simply not allow yourself to be persuaded that you have not fully appreciated this or that wine: there is no such thing as getting it right or wrong. It is your opinion that counts. So oft-propounded is such wisdom that it is somewhat difficult for other views to get a hearing. However, a closer examination of the business of taste and tasting will show us that things are not so clear-cut. To begin with, the reasons people offer for saying that taste is subjective vary considerably and not all of them are compatible with each other. Moreover, the considerations most often advanced in favour of subjectivity are not always consistent with the attitudes or practices of those who advance them. (It is harder than one thinks to live up to the belief that taste is subjective.) In the end, so many different things come to be listed under the heading of subjectivity that one begins to suspect that there is no common view or single opinion about what it means to say that taste is subjective. In the light of this, just how convincing are the arguments for the subjectivity of taste? And if we can no longer give good reasons for endorsing subjectivity what should we say instead? In particular, what scope is there for thinking that there may be such a thing as the taste (or tastes) of a wine, and that judgments about taste may be objective? These are the issues I will explore in what follows. Let us examine the case for subjectivity.

What is the Case for Subjectivity?

People are inclined to say that all we can be sure of is how a wine tastes to us personally; and that how a wine tastes to one personally is a purely subjective matter. It is on this basis that we make up our minds about what we like and dislike. So, they will say, taste is subjective.

What is interesting here, is how quickly we pass from what looks like a commonplace observation to a philosophical thesis: a thesis that requires further elaboration and defence. It is also surprising that many wine tasters and wine critics are so ready to accept this controversial doctrine, especially in the light of their practice of assessing and recommending wines to others. For example, Michael Broadbent tells us that:

> After fifty years of tasting and teaching I am convinced that to talk about, let alone claim, total objectivity—"relating entirely to the external object"—in tasting is nonsense. Moreover, to be a subjective taster is nothing to be ashamed of. One can even argue that that a subjective approach—"arising out of the senses"—is the most enriching approach to fine wine. (M. Broadbent, *Wine Tasting*, p.95)

He goes on to declare that "in the ultimate analysis, 'I, the taster', am the final arbiter". Though, like most critics, Broadbent appears to be in two minds on this issue. For he tells us "The problem is, as usual, to note or convey subjective and objective impressions" (p.95). This is surely right, and yet despite this concession, Broadbent places strong emphasis on subjectivity.[1] So why does subjectivism about taste have such a strong appeal? Or to put it in a more philosophical vein: how subjective are taste and tasting?

To address this question properly we first have to understand what is meant by the subjectivity of taste. Many different claims are made under that heading and they target subtly different things; not all of them incompatible with objectivity. Talk of subjectivity as "arising out of the senses" helps to stress the experiential dimension of taste but this does not preclude tasting giving us objective knowledge of the world. After all, the senses of sight, touch, and hearing give us knowledge of the external world, so why not taste and smell also? A stronger notion of subjectivity would equate the tastes we discover with the sensory experiences we have as tasters. On this view tastes are the exclusive properties of individual tasters. A further way to construe subjectivity is to see our judgments about how a wine tastes as answerable to nothing except our current sensations. How the wine tastes just is how it tastes to me at this moment. Other notions of subjectivity have to do with the difficulty of capturing the indefinable quality of our experiences in words. Even if we could put our subjective experience of a wine into words, there would be nothing to get right or wrong about the wine, since we would merely be describing our own experiences. Finally, we have the view that judgments of taste are matters of opinion and not matters of fact; that each taster is the final arbiter, and no person's opinion of a wine is better than anyone else's. I have only my own assessment of a wine's quality to rely upon. That is because, so the thought goes, there is no standard of taste for evaluating the quality of wine, and if there were objective facts to get right there would be no divergence of opinion between expert wine critics.

These various claims concern different senses of subjectivity and to pursue the general issue, we shall need to look at each of them more closely. But first, we need to do some ground-clearing.

Taste, Tastes and Tasting

A potential distraction in all these discussions is the use of the word "taste" to indicate a certain discerning sensibility or refinement of judgment. Here is where we find ideas of good taste and bad taste, of improvement in, and of criticism of, one's taste by others. Questions of *taste*, in this sense, dominate discussions of philosophical aesthetics. *Taste* can be cultivated and educated; it qualifies for assessment and evaluation. Undoubtedly, knowledge and experience are required, but showing taste in the appreciation of wine is about exercising judgment and preference. It is controversial, however, whether there are standards of *taste*, whether we could all equally recognize them, whether there are good judges of such matters—as the philosopher David Hume thought— better able to say what counts as good *taste* and able to criticize the *taste* of others.[2] I shall return to the role of wine critics below, but for the moment let us adopt the view of *taste* proposed by art historian Michael Baxandall. Here is how he characterizes taste in *Painting and Experience in Fifteenth-Century Italy*:

> Much of what we call "taste" lies in this, the conformity between dis-
> criminations demanded by a painting and skills of discrimination
> possessed by the beholder. We enjoy our own exercise of skill, and we
> particularly enjoy the playful exercise of skill which we use in normal life
> very earnestly. If a painting gives us opportunity for exercising a valued
> skill and rewards our virtuosity with a sense of worthwhile insights about
> that painting's organization, we tend to enjoy it: it is to our taste.
> (Oxford: *The Clarendon Press*, 1972, p.34)

So with painting, also with wine![3] Increasing one's powers of discrimination, one's skills as a taster, is part of exercising *taste*, but it also requires
that there be something worthy of one's attention, something that
affords an opportunity for the exercise of a skill. This means a fine wine.

Another potential stumbling block in these discussions is the failure
to distinguish between the sensations of taste and the taste of something;
between the sensations I have when I eat a strawberry, on the one hand,
and the *taste* of the strawberry, on the other. To avoid confusion, I will
make a distinction between tastes, which I shall argue are properties a
wine has, and tasting, which is an experience a subject has. Wine tasting
is the way each of us personally encounters the tastes of a wine. The key
question will be whether the sensations we have when tasting are good
guides to the tastes of the wine.

How Convincing is the Case for Subjectivity?

Are tastes just each individual taster's sensory experiences? Can we equate
tastes with the subjective experiences of tasting? We certainly rely on subjective experiences to know how a wine tastes. For even if we know a
great deal about its objective chemical properties or vinification, we
would not know what it tastes like without tasting it. The experience of
tasting provides the only route to such knowledge. But my experience of
how a wine tastes to me need not rule out the possibility of others experiencing the same thing. Why suppose the taste I discover to be available
only to me? Surely, I discover something about the wine: its floral character, say, or its sharp acidity. These are properties I attribute to the wine,
not just to my experience. But what sort of properties are they? Not
chemical properties, for sure; we were assuming I knew those already.
Why not suppose the properties I discover through the experience of

tasting are the tastes of the wine? If so, in what sense then are such taste properties subjective?

Of course, you cannot be sure that someone else will detect the same tastes you do. But there is every reason to think tastes are there to be detected. We draw each other's attention to what we have noticed in a wine. "Do you get the pear?" we may say when tasting a white Burgundy, or "Fig?" when tasting a Rhône. Any of these descriptions may be spurned of course, but usually they help to improve one another's perceptual awareness of the commonly appreciable taste of the wine, leading to finer discriminations. Perhaps no person is a better taster than another. Their efforts are collaborative, and through such interactions their perceptions become keener, our discriminations and responses finer, and they gain more satisfaction from their responses, their decisions and choices:

> Finer perceptions can both intensify and refine responses. Intenser responses can further heighten and refine perceptions. And more and more refined responses can lead to further and finer and more variegated or more intense responses and perceptions. (Wiggins 1991, p.196)[4]

Saying that the experience of tasting is a personal one need not prevent us from saying that it acquaints us with how a particular wine tastes, or from supposing that other people can be acquainted with that taste too. Some of the flavours and aromas we notice may be so well-known that they serve as points of reference for the varietal: the smell of rose petals or lychees in Gewürztraminer, for instance. Acknowledging the role of subjective experience in tasting, by itself, provides no case for saying that that taste or tasting are subjective.

THE SENSATION OF TASTE

We assume that other people see what we see and hear what we hear, when they are in the same immediate environment. So why do we not assume that other people taste what we taste? It could be, perhaps, because taste is said to be the most subjective of the senses, requiring actual bodily contact with a substance. But isn't touch a contact sense also? But then touch allows one to explore the contours of the external world, while taste consumes and destroys its object inside us. Taste is a chemical sense like smell, requiring interactions between gases and receptors in us. Nevertheless, taste, touch and smell all contribute to wine tasting. All three are thought to be more subjective than audition and vision, which allow us to contemplate distant and unchanging objects. Visual experience enables me to see a church on the hillside. And whereas the church I see is separate from my experience of seeing it, the taste of the Chablis is not so clearly separable from the experiences I am having when drinking it.[5] Perhaps it is this closeness of a taste to the immediate experience of the taster that makes taste appear so irreducibly subjective. Must we think of tastes as being in us rather than in the wine?

To say this is to concede that people cannot literally encounter the same tastes. And an argument for subjectivity can now be constructed as follows: Tastes seem to be inextricably bound up with the personal experiences of tasters, so they cannot be part of the external world. The taste of a wine is made known to one at the place where the liquid enters one's mouth. The site of the taste is on the taste receptors, in the mouth, and on the tongue. The experience of taste occurs within me, crucially involving my conscious states. So the taste I am having is not the taste you are having: we each taste separately. Therefore taste is subjective.

The reasoning here is a little quick. The feel of a velvet fabric on my fingers is an experience that occurs to me at a specific site on my body, but this does not make the feel of the velvet available to me only. Touch allows us to discover properties of objects but leaves room for others to discover the same properties by means of *their* tactile experiences. Why not the same with taste? It may be said that taste is more focused on what goes on inside our bodies. But subjectivity cannot be characterized in terms of what is literally going inside us or else the circulation of blood around my brain would count as being subjective..

The subjectivity we are interested in—the kind that threatens objectivity—is one in which there is nothing independent of our opinions to which they are answerable. For it is only when there is room for a contrast between opinions and what makes them true that we are dealing with objective matters. A wholly subjective opinion is one that is answerable to nothing more than how things seem to the subject. So what of our opinions about wines? This may depend whether we are talking about evaluations of a wine's quality or judgments about its particular characteristics. A judgment about a wine's characteristics would be subjective if there were no gap between how things seemed to us, on an occasion, and how they were, because there was only how they seemed to us. But we do admit a gap, on occasions, between how things strike us and how they are. We distinguish, for example, between the way a wine tastes, and how it tastes to us after sucking a lemon. We are not tempted to equate the taste of a Meursault with how it tastes to us after brushing our teeth. Thus, how a wine tastes is not exhausted by how it tastes to an individual at any given moment. We distinguish between good and bad conditions for tasting, where these involve the condition of the wine as well as the condition of the taster. And we apply these distinctions to ourselves and to others. I can predict that you will fail to notice the tender raspberry fruit of Nicolas Potel's 2001 Volnay Les Caillerets if you have been eating a plate of kippers. Nor will I be surprised that a bottle of 2000 Beaucastel Châteauneuf du Pape tastes soupy given the sweltering temperature of the cupboard in which it has been kept. So, as long as there is room for a distinction between the taste of a wine and how it tastes under particular conditions there will be no reason to conclude that a taste is constituted and exhausted by the individual experience of a taster. No convincing case has yet been made for saying that tastes are subjective.

The stubbornly persistent view that when we speak about a wine's taste we can only be speaking about our response to it is based on the idea that tastes can only be experienced as sensations, and that sensations, being utterly subjective, cannot provide any basis for drawing conclusions about the world, or about other people's experiences. But this overstates the case. I can tell by the sensations on my lips and tongue that a wine has been severely chilled. On this basis I readily conclude something about the wine that enables me to predict how others will experience it. Tasting requires me to attend to my sensory experience but this does not prevent me from knowing about the world around me on the basis of my sensations. Sensations are narcissistic in telling us how things are with us, but also revelatory, telling us how things are around us. In this way, they are Janus-faced. The temperature of my skin tells me how hot or cold I am, and in normal conditions it also tells me about the ambient temperature of the room.

Why should it be any different for taste sensations? My tasting experience can tell me: whether a wine has too much alcohol because of

the slight burning sensation at the back of my throat; whether it has too
little acidity because of the flatness in the finish; whether there is an
excess use of wood by the slight irritation of the gums; whether the
tannins are still too firm by the mouth-puckering sensations of dryness
and astringency. Experienced tasters will learn more from their sensations about the texture of the wine—about whether the tannins are
fine- or coarse-grained—by paying attention to particular aspects of
their sensory experience. In similar fashion, wine-makers use sensations
of smell to detect faults or problems with the fermentation. The sul-
phurous smell from a barrel sample can tell me that the reduction has
been too severe, that the wine is starved of oxygen and will need to be
racked. So the fact that tasting sensations are the conscious experiences
of individual tasters does not thereby prevent them from providing
information about the objective characteristics of the wines tasted. The
more discerning I am, the more discriminatingly will I use my sensations to tell me something about the properties of the wine and the way
it has been made.

What we mean by Fine Wine

The character of the sensations I enjoy in tasting depends on the qualities of the wine I taste. A dull and shapeless wine cannot produce the
complex amalgam of sensations that a great wine does, however interesting and imaginative the taster. The better the quality of the wine, the
better the quality of the experience I can have in drinking it. Only a fine
or great wine will repay the attention given to it, because only a sufficiently rich and complex wine will exercise our discriminative powers in
a rewarding way.

If finer wines are responsible for finer experiences, are all the properties of fine wines available to just anyone? This is a delicate question.
To answer negatively is to risk not only accusations of elitism, but,
beyond this, a general scepticism about what experts claim to discover
through tasting. For how can there be aspects of a wine revealed to some
tasters but not others when tasting is such a direct and immediate experience? These questions bring us to the heart of tastes and tasting.

Either the aromas and flavours of a wine are there for all to recognize, or there are flavours and aromas available only to those who enjoy
particular taste sensations, who have special sensory equipment, as it

were.[7] And are normal tasters ruled out as unable to experience the pleasures of fine wines?

The assumption that gives rise to this dilemma is the view that tastes are just what is immediately experienced. The idea that there is no more to the taste of a wine than is revealed to us directly in immediate sensation leads to a credibility gap between those who claim to detect a large range of flavours and aromas in a wine and those who don't. But when we separate out initial or immediate sensations from further responses we can see a difference between the kinds of experience had by the novice and the expert, and realize that we are not comparing like with like.

Compare the undifferentiated responses of someone tasting as a matter of their immediate, overall impression of a wine, and the more componential, taste impressions of the analytic taster who mentions ripe fruit, balancing acidity, judicious use of oak, and soft-grained tannins. The analytical taster and the novice are doing something quite different. It is not the immediate or overall taste sensations the former is attending to. Instead, he guides his attention towards certain aspects of his experience, selecting some for peculiar scrutiny. To begin with, he pays a good deal of attention to impressions of smell. Novices often pay scant attention to the aromas of wine, sniffing quickly then getting down to what they take to be the real business of tasting. However, a great deal can be learned from the nose of a wine. First, the experienced taster notices the volatile aromas that arise from the glass when still, then the somewhat reluctant aromas that arise after a little agitation. He concentrates on the sequence and intensity of his olfactory sensations. Are there base, earthy notes and higher menthol notes? Is there a smooth transition or an abrupt change from the odours at the beginning to those at the end? Does any note dominate? The wine's olfactory profile usually gives clues as to its taste profile that may be confirmed in the sequence of taste sensations. A wine of age is easily recognizable by the nose. And until recently there were considerable differences between Old and New World wines. However, there are also interesting mismatches between taste and smell, giving the lie to the claim that taste is almost entirely due to smell. There may be little on the nose and yet one can be pleasantly surprised at how full and sumptuous a young wine is. The nose may be very promising but the wine be a little short. The nose can also be misleading about the taste, thus thwarting our expectations. The citrus notes can lead one to expect piercing acidity but one can be surprised by how round the wine is. The experienced taster attends to individual flavours and their intensities at different stages. Something may be present in the taste that does not show on the nose and could not have been anticipated. In addition, the experienced taster performs retro-nasal breathing to bring to life further aromas, and so see the quality and persistence of flavours in the finish. Going back and forward one can settle on a more precise identification of aromas and flavours. One can come to understand better what is going on *in* the wine. The comparison is instructive; it may tell us something about the potential development of the wine, in the glass or in the bottle. In this way taste and smell collaborate rather than collapse in tasting a wine.

As well as smell, tasting involves touch, the wine's mouthfeel, and the way it travels across the mouth. Perhaps sight too has a role to play in setting expectations.[6] Wine tasting is a multimodal experience in which taste sensations are just one component, and where attention to, and reflections on, all aspects of that experience can lead to increasingly refined judgments. There is a focus on the fruit—which kind?—the level of acidity—is there enough?—the amount and quality of the oak used—too intrusive?—and, perhaps the quality of the tannins. Each judgment requires selective attention to a particular aspect of the overall experience, and repeated attempts may be necessary to settle on the right judgment of both taste and smell. All of this goes far beyond the immediate sensations produced by sipping and swallowing. The tasting impressions on which a considered assessment of a wine are based are first sought out and highlighted by selective attention. We need to prepare ourselves and be receptive to certain kinds of experiences. We need to know what we are looking for. Tasting is not, as many think, a passive experience. We are seeking out particular types of experience, and this requires knowledge and training. Not everything about the taste of a wine is surrendered at first, or is accessible without a skilful search. A great bottle will not yield everything all at once, or to just anyone. It will reveal more if we take our time and let our experience develop like a photograph.

Now we see why we are not comparing like with like. The person who is sceptical about the elaborate descriptions given by wine connoisseurs thinks that all there is to taste is given in immediate sensation. It is just a matter of how things taste to him at a moment. And if his initial and undifferentiated experiences reveal none of the elements the connoisseur mentions, then they simply cannot be there. But on the contrary, time must be taken to build up the experience of the wine gradually. The elements for a final assessment take shape and begin to show themselves only after the novice has sipped and swallowed.

Are these further judgments and assessments open to the novice? Yes, but not without training in the art of tasting. The novice is often surprised to discover this fact about the different modalities he is employing, but after learning he becomes better able to attend selectively to each of these aspects of his experience, and to set expectations at the outset. It is perhaps the idea that we have to learn about our experience, that we have to learn to taste—or learn by means of tasting—that bemuses people and leads to scepticism. There is a kind of democracy of tasting: everyone can experience wine by tasting it; you just put the wine to your lips and drink. But thereafter the course of experience of the novice and the expert differs. For the latter, the experience is far from undifferentiated. It has to be segmented, selectively attended to, weighed, and categorized by comparisons with other experiences and memories. (The less experienced among us will do some of this but to a lesser extent.) A wine can, of course, speak to us straight away, and may even lead us quickly to something that we then focus on. But focus is what matters and the more definition a wine has the easier this will be.

The discriminations good tasters make on the basis of perceptually attended experiences require considerably more cognitive effort and concentration than is required by an immediate sensory response. "Taste invites reflection." as Voltaire put it.[8] And there is an important insight here because wine tasting is not exhausted by first perceptual reactions but also because the nature of the invitation crucially depends on those first perceptions. Many people will, alas, have had little to invite them to further reflection, drinking wines of no particular distinction that offer limited pleasure. As the great Bordeaux oenologist Emile Peynaud put it:

…there are still millions of hectolitres of neutral, shapeless, and impersonal wines about which the taster can say nothing once he has spat them out. The birth of a taster's vocabulary dates from the advent of quality wine. (E. Peynaud, 1987 p.215)

GOOD FEATURES OF SUBJECTIVITY: IMMEDIATE EXPERIENCE AND THE EPIPHANY

So far, I have been arguing that tastes are not fully revealed by our immediate sensory responses. Nevertheless—and here I wish to emphasize the importance of the immediate experience—there has to be a way to know whether a wine deserves our attention and will reward our efforts to understand it. And the invitation to pay greater attention must come in the initial tasting experience. We instantly recognize when something is worthy of reflection, when it is great. So we should not think of the immediate experience as just the novice's domain, in contrast with the reflective judgments of experts. Some wines immediately grab our attention, and reveal their stature straight away, as they do in those unique, memorable occasions in which we first become aware of the incredible poise and beauty of a great wine. One suspects that those who show no interest in carefully attending to what they are drinking have not yet had the heart-stopping moment when they first taste great wine: they have not yet had their epiphany.

As every wine lover knows, there was a time when they were unaware of the power, depth and beauty that some wines possess. Then came the epiphany. Most wine lovers will remember it: the first time they encountered a rare and astonishing wine. Until that moment they had simply drunk wine, noticing some to be more pleasing than others.

Why do we even start drinking wine? It doesn't attract us immediately; we have to acquire the taste. The reason we start isn't hard to seek. As Jamie Goode once put it: it's alcohol and it gets you drunk; what greater lure is there for teenagers than that?

There were the embarrassing pretensions of youth; the moments of soi-disant sophistication when one turned one's back on beer and said, "No, I'll have the Hirondelle, thanks." But one swallow does not a summer make and progress towards something finer was gradual. It happened at inauspicious restaurants on first dates, when one was nervously keen to impress the other party with one's savoir-faire, desperately trying to remember one's parent's wine choices in front of an intimidating head waiter.

There were student years when one drank indifferent wines, mainly for the company and the conversation. And then comes the epiphany. We always remember it: an unusual moment; the temperature of the room was just right; one was somehow more receptive, open to the unexpected; a moment when everything in the rush of experience is briefly stilled. (Am I imagining things when I say that good wine makes a different, gentle gurgling, surging sound when poured from the bottle?) You taste and at that moment you know the difference between this experience of drinking and all those that you have had before. The senses are dazzled. You are stunned by the intoxicating power of the experience; the pleasure is exhilarating and hypnotic. The velvet feel of the wine in your mouth, the lingering flavours and aromas when you swallow. It is an intensely hedonistic moment, an encounter with a fine and elegant thing. There is a desire to be still and to focus on what is happening. There is the swoon of something great entering your system. The body has no struggle in accepting this harmonious liquid—it feels good for us, like a blood transfusion with several vital elements in it. You delight in your experience, and in that of those with whom you share the bottle. The moment is fleeting, ephemeral and transitory, yet utterly memorable. And you know, at that moment, that you want more opportunities like this, not to drink this very wine again, because this is an unrepeatable experience. (As the French say, there are no great wines, just great bottles.) You want more opportunities to drink other wines as great as this because now you know great wines exist and that you are capable of responding to them. At that moment you learn something about wine and something about you. You are astonished that wine can reach such heights, provide such a complex and yet harmonious experience; and in understanding that wine can do this, you want to know more.

There is something so intense about these experiences. The quickening of the senses telling you something special is happening. The wine demands your attention: it gives you an experience so memorable that you take in and retain many of the details around you: who you were with, the room you were in, particular aspects of your surroundings, what you felt at that time. All of these things all help to create powerful taste memories. But the creation of the memory begins with a taste experience so pleasurable and uplifting that your attention is grabbed, forcing you to attend to what the wine reveals. It is an experience that cannot be repeated and will not be forgotten.

The momentary nature of these experiences is important.

Epiphanies are all about moments that change us for good and for life. We realize that the tastes of wines have dimensions and depth, and can fix themselves in the memory with such indelible precision and power that days or weeks later a taste image or memory will return unbidden. Wines with the power to do this, wines of purity, precision, and finesse are wines of *terroir*: wines of place, tradition and culture. The depth of flavour that age lends them is not only in this bottle, or that vintage—each one expressive of its season—but in the vines, the soil and the wisdom of those who have learnt how to express what nature gives them, differently, each year.[9] When we understand this we will have understood what fine or great wines are. Though we remain surprised that out of soil and sun, vines and human endeavour come wines of such outstanding beauty, complexity and balance. Even when one knows more about how wines are made it is still a staggering proposition to accept that such inauspicious elements could be cultivated into such soaring examples of richness and grandeur.[10]

The description of the epiphany amounts to a possible autobiography, yours or mine, and shows why the enjoyment and love of wine is not restricted to the precious few. It is through a transforming personal experience that each of us comes to learn of the greatness of wine. And it is due to the greatness of a wine that we have the quality of sensory experience just described. An ordinary wine cannot do this for us. Only a carefully handmade wine can lead to these epiphanies.

What is philosophically significant is the way these momentary but lasting experiences can be immediate, transitory, highly personal and yet revelatory of something beyond us: something of whose power and elegance we are made suddenly and lastingly aware.

For the experienced wine taster too, it is the immediate encounter with a wine that tells him or her whether it is worth the attention. So how do these initial experiences mark out some wines for special regard? It appears to be the immediately recognizable quality of the wine that impresses itself so forcefully upon the mind. Our judgment that something can afford us pleasure and fascination is due to a prior perception of its quality. Quality somehow impresses itself *immediately* on the mind, and only after comes our attention to the specific features and character that make it a wine of such quality. It may be surprising that I say that among the first things we are aware of is the quality of a wine.

Assessments of quality may seem to call for considered judgment. And yet the recognition of quality does appear to precede a detailed understanding of what is going on in the wine. The immediate recognition of quality also explains why an epiphany is possible for someone who lacks analytic tasting skills. The significance of these moments is due to a perception of quality that transforms our ideas about wine from that time on. In tasting an exceptional wine we are aware of something both very fine and very complex; of the purity and harmony of its many elements, of their being all there at once and in perfect unity. We are often made most aware of this by the way the different elements of a complex wine are resolved in the finish. The richness at first, then the slight austerity: the elegant final note. The sweet fruit is balanced by good acidity; the structure is there but does not disrupt the delicacy of the fruit. The alcohol does not show too strongly. Combined effects of aroma and flavour reveal a wine of real beauty. Properties of such wines, their definition, purity, finesse, unity and balance—clearly signs of quality—are given to us almost immediately and strikingly in our first overall taste impressions; though only experienced tasters recognizable as being such elements. The most important of these properties are unity and balance:

> Quality is always related to a certain harmony of tastes, where no one taste dominates another. (E. Peynaud, 1987, p.192)

Further tasting impressions, such as a wine's roundness, its weight, its length or persistence of flavours may be assessed by attending to sensory experiences in us. We note these after the initial reaction to how great or otherwise the wine is. In this way, wine tasting is a continuous evolution from initial perception, reworked and developed into a final opinion that confirms, or modifies our initial impression. Initial impressions can be misleading, of course: some wines can be false and seductive, falling apart, or disappointing under further scrutiny. The initial impression is just an impression. Final assessment requires judgment.

Claims about tastes being subjective often fail to separate these different stages of tasting. We can all easily say in the initial swallow whether we like something or not. Pleasure is something anyone should be able to recognize straight away. But saying what it is about the wine that is so pleasurable, what is good about it, and what makes it preferable to another is less easy. This requires practice and concentration: weighing things in the mind as one holds a little wine in the mouth. Nevertheless, the immediate impression of an exceptional wine already signals the difference. The bouquet is more beguiling, the feel in the mouth more luxurious. All of this prepares us for the greatness of the wine.

Does the expert's knowledge also make a difference in tasting? Surely it does. Knowledge comes into play as soon as we reflect on what we are experiencing. One realizes something about the wine that was not obvious at first. Thus knowledge doesn't simply add to the overall experience of tasting, it changes the intensity of one's tasting impressions. It can lead to better focus, through which we revise our initial impressions. The expert knows that the immediately apparent bitterness of a Viognier is part of the essential apricot kernel taste of the wine; so is its viscosity. Coming to understand this grape and its typical expression, may lead one to appreciate a style of wine that would have at first been off-putting were one expecting something similar to say a Chardonnay. Through knowledge of what is aimed at we can acquire a taste for what we did not at first appreciate. [11] In this way knowledge changes the way a wine tastes to us, affecting our experience and enjoyment of the wine.[12] Not only should we reject the idea that everything there is to the taste of a wine is available to just anyone, we should also reject the idea that anyone is always ready to taste anything. Knowing what we are tasting, and knowing what to look for in tasting it, may have a great impact on the quality and pleasure of the experience. Initial impressions are seldom neutral. Accuracy in tasting is often set by prior knowledge and expectations. Notice, though, that knowledge does not guarantee the extraordinary recognition skills some have in blind tasting. This is an exceptional ability and partly depends on large amounts of prior experience of, and memory for, wines not tasted blind.

WINE TASTING: DESCRIBING, COMMUNICATING OR SHARING THE EXPERIENCES

We have rejected the line of reasoning that says all there is to the taste of a wine is given by our immediate, undifferentiated responses, and the claim that all that wines have to reveal will be equally accessible to just anyone at any time. But there is a further consideration in favour of subjectivity that exerts a considerable pull; namely, that in tasting there is some pure and irreducible residue of subjective experience that cannot be put into words or shared with anyone else. Notice that this kind of subjectivity is entirely compatible with our experience revealing real properties in the wine, so we have come a long way from the stronger claim that tastes *are* the subjective experiences of tasters. On this more liberal notion of subjectivity there is the qualitative feel of an experience: what it is like to taste the last mouthful of 1986 Château Margaux while looking down on the Île St. Louis. Can anyone else really know what that experience was like? Can every aspect of those sensations be put into words and conveyed to others? Perhaps this is the stubbornly subjective part of wine tasting that can never be dismissed.

Several things are run together here that need to be kept apart. There is whether we can describe the taste of wines, whether there is some way to communicate what it is like to drink them, and whether others are able to share the pleasure we take in drinking them. These are three separate issues. If I could describe the taste of Château Margaux to you, you may still not know what it was like to drink it. Conversely, if you share the bottle with me, you may enjoy the same heady experience without either of us being able to describe the taste of the wine. Nevertheless, we want to speak about the exceptional bottles we drink, want to note the tastes we find in them, and hone our powers of discrimination.[13] What we lack is a precise vocabulary to describe tastes and smells. It is a common problem that our experience of these characteristics outstrips our language and we struggle to find any way to describe them. I may want to tell you about the subtle range of flavours in a 2001 Clos de Tart, but capturing its tastes in words may defeat me. I could speak of the firm structure cloaked in fruit, the purity of expression, the slight *pruneaux* taste, the rustic, earthy notes, the supple roundness in the mouth, the touch of *réglisse* in the finish. It all helps but none of it uniquely pinpoints this wine's taste. A factor in this difficulty is the subtle combination of flavours in good wines. Well-made wines with age take on a complexity of flavours that blend and harmonize. The components having been somewhat distinct, finally knit together and are less clearly separable than before. We lack names for these complex yet beautifully harmonious tastes. Similarly, we may search in vain for the words to convey the particular aromas we attend to before drinking. Here I disagree with Peynaud when he says:

…it is easy to describe what one senses provided one has made sufficient effort to notice it. (Peynaud, 1987 p.215)

We constantly face the problem of how to label the elements we can distinguish in tasting. We can attend to, and recognize, them, but we do not name them. This is also true for pain sensations. We are not used to describing such things.

How then do we indulge our shared love of wine? And how do wine critics succeed in writing about wines? There are ways to overcome the limits of literal description. We often use similes, as when we say the wine tastes of stone fruits, or honey, or smells of asparagus, or rose petals. We are saying the wines smell and taste *like* these things, not that these are elements of the wine. Riesling has the smell of kerosene and limes but it does not contain them. A well-aged Bordeaux will smell of antique furniture polish, but there is none in the wine.

We need to make a distinction here between the intrinsic and extrinsic properties of tastes and smells.[14] Consider smells. When we say a flower smells fragrant we can say it *is* fragrant. Though when we say a wine smells *of* leather we are not saying it *is* leather. Kerosene and limes are extrinsic properties of the Riesling's bouquet. Similarly, if a wine tastes acidic, or sweet or tannic, these are intrinsic tastes of the wine, while its tasting of liquorice, of raspberries, or of vanilla, are simply extrinsic properties: things the wine tastes *like*. That intrinsic taste properties are real properties of a wine is not compromised in the least by the fact that they may only be detected by creatures like us with our sensory apparatus. All this means is that it is through the subjective experience of tasting that we gain personal access to what is objectively there in the wine. It doesn't mean it only exists for each of us.

By distinguishing the tastes in a wine and our experiences of them, we can see that sometimes we talk about one, and sometimes about the other. Wine writers work this way, mentioning either properties in the wine or their characteristic effects on the experiences of tasters. They may speak about a wine's having firm tannins, or prefer to talk about the mouth-puckering feel. Through such experiences tasters can correctly identify what they drink as a tannic wine. Their subjective experiences are a good guide to the objective properties of the wines. The properties they detect, in the case of tannins, are not just the wine's polyphenols.

Tannin is a texture but it also has a taste. Wine writers speak of savoury tannins, of the difference between fruit and wood tannins, of bitter and astringent tannins, and of aromatic tannins. By talking about the quality of the tannins we are speaking about the tastes of the wine we perceive in tasting.

The case of tannin is straightforward. It has a distinctive experiential profile. But the rarer tastes will be harder to identify through our experience of them, and the experiences may be less easily sifted and discriminated by the novice. The best we can do to convey a wine's flavour is to try to highlight the nuances of our experience. The trouble is that they are notoriously difficult to put into words. Yet this is what most of us have to go on in attending to the tastes of the wine we are drinking. How, then, can we convey to someone else what it is like to drink this particular wine? Sometimes, metaphor is the answer. As poets and novelists know, metaphor serves very well to allude to these elusive features of our subjectivity, the changing moments in consciousness. Metaphors are the writer's stock in trade for conveying different aspects of our inner lives to others.[15] So too, gifted wine writers often resort to metaphors to allude to features of their tasting experiences, How successful they are depends on how apt the metaphor is. Good wine metaphors set off chains of associations that give us clues about our own likely experiences. We know what to expect when a wine is described as "monumental". We are being told something about the wine and how it will strike us. Jancis Robinson provides an excellent example in her tasting notes for a 1945 Château Pétrus: "Like velvet. But with a pattern on it." In these few words she conveys something majestic about the wine *and* something about the experience of drinking it. In similar vein, Andrew Jefford, talking about a rich and ripe Moulin à Vent, writes that the fruit "comes helicoptering into the mouth." Very different wines, but both ones we want to taste on the basis of these metaphors. More expectations are set by these surprising words than by the frequent talk of "Asian spices and pain grillé notes"—much beloved of Robert Parker in describing Bordeaux.[16] Metaphors are exceptionally good at capturing aspects of subjective experience, but as acts of creativity they demand exceptional skill and ingenuity. Some will be better at this than others.

To resort to conveying something about our experiences need not preclude us from giving information about the wine, since to convey something accurately about our experience of tasting a wine is to convey something about the wine. Its objective properties are known to us through the distinctive experiences the tastes of the wine give rise to in us. The same is true of colours. The colour of objects is known to us through our experience of those objects in normal lighting conditions. We take an object to be red when it looks red under normal conditions. We do not take everything that *looks* red *to be red*: the lighting conditions may be abnormal. So it is only under certain conditions that our experiences serve as guides to the colour of things. It is reasonable to suppose that normally colour-sighted people have similar experiences when looking at things in good light. If I know you are looking at a red door I know the kind of subjective experience you will be having.

In similar fashion, the tastes of a wine are identified by the sensory experiences they produce in us in good conditions. And if I know the taste of a particular wine—by the experiences it gives rise to in me—I may know the experiences you are likely to have when tasting it too. This thought makes sense of the care we take in choosing wines for others, and why we look forward to tasting the wines they select for us. There is something important here not to be missed. When I taste a wine of extraordinary beauty I want to share this experience with someone else. I may have a specific person in mind. Due to the tasting experiences we both had when tasting together, I may know that you will appreciate the exquisite poise and elegance of this wine. By reference to the bottles we drank together, the qualities we have noticed and commented on, we know each others' subjective responses. The common pleasure we take in these wines connects us to one another at a basic level. Our perceptions, pleasures and preferences coincide. And as these things form part of who we are, part of our inner lives, we learn that we are to this extent alike. By responding similarly to the fineness and beauty of this 1996 Méo-Camuzet Vosne Romanée Aux Brûlées, we understand something very elemental about one another. We understand something about the wine and about each other. When someone else recognizes the pleasure we take in things, we know there are others who have that pleasure too.

This deeply social aspect of wine helps to explain the intense feelings that accompany the experience of tasting a great wine, and how it connects us to people, places and things at a particular moment. The desire to share part of ourselves with another, to share the intensity of delight we feel, is an important part of our social natures, and great wine, affords us this opportunity. [17] The wines we drink in company unite us with others, and in this way we retain a fleeting moment of intense experience as a fixed point in our dealings with one another.

However satisfying such moments are, it is also disappointing to recognize people with whom we cannot share such experiences. Why are they not stirred by this remarkable wine? Are they just unmoved, or is it that they do not taste what we do? To concede as much may seem to put pressure on the view that what we taste are real and objective properties of the wine. Though it may simply mean that we have to recognize that there are different populations of tasters, and that they will not all have the same range of tastes available to them.

Conversely, does similarity of response among a population of tasters indicate that they are getting something objectively right about a wine, or does it only indicate agreement in opinion? If people fail to have such experiences, is it right to say they missing something? Perhaps there is just a restricted intersubjectivity—a mere matching, among some individuals in their subjective reaction to wines. But such a view offers no explanation of why they all have such similar responses. Why does their experience take the form it does if not in response to the features and qualities of the wines they are tasting? Their experience can only have the degree of complexity or interest the wines afford them. For how could we draw one another's attention to aspects of a wine's taste, and value the accuracy and precision with which people do this, unless we were doing more than just commenting on our own experiences? Unless it were simply a matter of suggestion—which would have limited success— there must be something in the wines these individuals are tasting that gives rise to these common responses. Why not say it is the tastes in the wines that give rise to the variety of experience we enjoy as tasters?

OBJECTIVITY AND REALISM ABOUT TASTES
The length of a wine, the persistence of flavours in the mouth, the aromas one detects by retro-nasal breathing. Sensations of this sort are often reliable guides to features of the wines we taste and to what others are likely to find in them. (There are seldom disputes over whether a wine is "short" or "long".) From tasting impressions, we assemble a view of the qualities and characteristics of the wine we taste. These judg-

ments concern real features of the wine even though they are based on our experiences as tasters. To say this is to defend a form of realism about tastes.

Tastes are properties a wine has that give rise to certain experiences in us; and they cannot be reduced to, or equated with, those experiences. If tastes were no more than subjective experiences it would be literally false to say that a wine was long, or rich or sumptuous. These would be mere projections of our responses onto the wine, and it would be as mistaken to say these things about the wine as it is for children to think that disgustingness is a quality of broccoli just because it tastes disgusting to them. A subjectivism which regarded attributions of tastes to wines as projections from our experiences would have to deny that some of our taste impressions could be more accurate than others. This would make no sense since all claims we make about tastes as features of the wine would be mistaken. But we do distinguish between sensory experiences that are good guides to the taste of a wine and those that are not. There are optimal conditions for tasting that have to obtain for our experience to relate us to the real taste of a wine. The optimal conditions are both internal and external to us: the temperature and odours in the room, the condition of the bottle, the shape of the glass, the time of day, what one has just eaten or drunk, one's level of attention and one's mood are all important in creating conditions in which to appreciate what is there to be discovered in a wine.[18] Realism about tastes makes room for such a distinction between how things strike us and how they really are—between the appearance and reality of tastes. Subjectivity about tastes does not. It suggests that not all experiences of tasting are on a par, or equally valid: one's tastes sensations at each moment are the sole arbiter of how something tastes. But tastes are not exhausted by our sensory experiences: to taste a wine after eating watercress is not to experience what the wine really tastes like.[19] If other people fail to respond enthusiastically to tasting a very fine Château Palmer, a likely explanation is that they are not in the right tasting conditions to appreciate the wine properly. Similarly, if our reaction to a wine surprises them, they may ask us to entertain the idea that we are not in the right condition to taste correctly.

The gap that realism opens up between tastes and our experience of them gives tastes a life of their own. They are not constituted or exhausted by the tasting experiences we have, and may exist independently of us. This is surely what we want to say. A trophy wine may be traded at higher and higher prices until it disappears into the cellar of a speculator, never to be tasted by anyone. But we still think of it as having a taste and we wonder what it was like. Of course, we could think of its taste in terms of the experiences that would be available to someone were they to taste it. But what would give any such taster the glorious experiences they would have in tasting it—except the tastes the wine itself has?

But why say that it is the tastes rather than the chemical properties a wine has that gives rise to these experiences? The answer is that it is not the chemical properties themselves but how they taste that matters. Which of the many chemical properties in wine we promote depends on which ones gives rise to the desired responses in us. They may be quite diverse and there may be no way to identify them save by our experience of them in tasting. The knowledge and skill of the wine-maker is to select and promote a heterogeneous collection of chemical properties of a wine, and choose them because of how they taste. Tastes are real properties of wines even though they bear an essential relation to the subjective experiences of creatures like us. We cannot think about or identify them save in terms of our subjective experiences, but they exist whether we experience them or not. They are there to experience. They are not in us, they are in the wine, while the pleasures they give rise to are in us not in the wine.[20] Tastes are what enable wines to produce certain kinds of pleasurable (and unpleasurable) experiences in us.

Sometimes our sensations reveal the tastes of a wine directly, sometimes they only indicate these properties at one remove. Not every feature of a wine's taste is directly given in experience. For example, we seem to "taste what isn't there" on occasion, as when we taste that a wine is hollow in the mid-palate, or that it lacks acidity, or structure. We look for a something in our tasting experience, and when it is missing from our experience we conclude it is missing from the wine. Experienced tasters can tell that a wine is closed: that we cannot get at all the flavours it has. Similarly, we may taste that a wine is too young to drink at present, tasting how things are now, and judging how they may be later. A nice example is given by Andrew Jefford, writing about Château Latour 2000 in 2004 (note again the use of metaphor):

> At the moment, it is a kind of velvet bomb quietly ticking. Inside it,
> curled up like nascent ferns, lie the densely backed black fruits that char-
> acterize young Bordeaux. (*The World of Fine Wine*, Volume 1, 2004,
> p.58)

Tastes extend beyond our experience. We encounter them, or recogniz-
ably fail to do so on occasion. Through the experience of tasting we feel
for their shape and dimension. They are not matched to simple sensations: they can be many-layered. They develop in time and at times elude
us. Our experience of tasting (including sensations of touch and smell)
can point to qualities not presently accessible in a closed or a young
wine, just as vision and hearing can point to things over the horizon or
out of earshot. Tastes are what tasting under the right conditions gets at.
From tasting impressions we assemble a view of the qualities and characteristics of the wine we taste. What should we say, though, about
tasters in equally good conditions who disagree about what they taste?
Should these disagreements lead us to abandon objectivity? Not necessarily.

Take the case of phenol-thio-urea. In most populations it tastes
bitter to about twenty-five per cent of people and tasteless to the other
seventy-five per cent. Should we say that the seventy-five per cent are
mistaken? It seems right to say they are missing a bitter taste that phenol-
thio-urea has. But suppose that the seventy-five per cent became the
dominant population and that eventually there were no more of the
people to whom it used to taste bitter. Should we say it no longer has a
bitter taste? Why say that? After all, there was no change in the substance, only a change in those tasting it. Instead we should say we can no
longer perceive the bitter taste phenol-thio-urea has. In other cases too,
where there are different populations of tasters, perhaps some populations will be able to perceive some tastes but not others, with different
degrees of overlap between the populations. A wine may have more tastes
than any given taster, or population of tasters, can discern. They may
exist in the wine awaiting detection by a discriminating palate. Hence
the right view is to embrace pluralism about tastes and assert the co-exis-
tence of such tastes in the same wine. Take the example from *Don
Quixote*, by David Hume in his famous essay, "Of the Standard of
Taste".[21] Here, two wine connoisseurs are drinking from a hogshead of

wine. One says the wine tastes of leather. The other says it tastes of iron. They contest each other's descriptions while drinking more and more of the wine. When they reach the bottom of the barrel they discover a key on a leather thong. The right conclusion to draw should be that both were right and there is a plurality of tastes in the wine. The connoisseurs did not really disagree: there was no genuine conflict. They were mistaken in criticizing one another's opinions since they were both right about a taste the wine had. The taste of iron and the taste of leather were both in the wine. Notice that this is not to subscribe to relativism about truth. Relativism would lead us to say that each was right to deny the other's opinion: that truth was relative to a point of view, and that from the point of view of the one who tastes leather it is true (relative to that point of view) that the wine does not taste of iron. But pluralism denies this. It has tastes of leather and iron. Each taster is only sensitive to one of them. Pluralism and realism are the best options to explain these facts.

Realism about tastes makes room for each person's tasting judgments to provide objective assessments of a wine: good tasters are those who get matters right. In assessing a wine, our judgments are not simply answerable to how things are with us, and to our natures, or our perspectives as tasters. Judgments of taste go beyond our sensory experience to how things are in the wine itself. Whether we like what we find there is another matter.

But what about assessments of the quality of a wine? Should the properties by which we classify wines as mediocre, exceptional, delightful, outstanding and hedonistic equally be seen as properties of the wines to which our judgments are answerable? Or are they just matters of intersubjective agreements within populations of tasters? Interestingly, there is little disagreement when a wine is awful. But saying what makes a wine good or better than another can lead to deep disagreements. Can some or any of these judgments about quality be getting something objectively right?

Perhaps the properties of quality these judgments reflect are related to easily identifiable properties like being tannic or having persistence. However, take the property of balance in a wine. Balance can be thought of as the unity and harmony of its parts, comprising fruit, alcohol, acidity and tannins in red wines. Each of these properties can be detected by good tasters, but what about a judgment that no one element dominates any other: and that they are harmoniously combined? Is this just a subjective impression of the taster? Surely not; balance is something that is difficult to achieve and for which wine-makers strive, even if it is a property that it takes human tasters to discern. Even when a wine is balanced, there may be several points at which the alcohol levels, the acidity, the fruit and the tannins could have been brought into harmony. One taster may be blind to one level because of under- or over-sensitivity to some of these elements, and yet be able to appreciate its balance had the wine had slightly more alcohol, or acidity or wood. This is not to say that just any combination will produce balance: balance is difficult to achieve and there are still objective facts about when it does and does not occur. But there may be more points at which a wine could be balanced, and some tasters will recognize one of these points while other tasters recognize another.

What of properties like finesse: the subtle way a wine produces its elegant effects on us? It too can be treated as an objective property in the wine, albeit one identified solely by the quality of experiences it gives rise to in us. In philosophical parlance, such properties are secondary qualities: the sort of qualities only detectable through characteristic experiences of creatures like us. At this point, some of my fellow philosophers will insist that such properties amount to mere dispositions of the wine—at certain times and under particular conditions—to produce a certain pleasurable taste experience in normal perceivers. By "normal" they do not mean "those who get matters right," they mean what is statistically normal among a population of tasters who are not hypo- or hyper-sensitive to one or more of the basic taste elements or alcohol. What is statistically normal in a given population is often cultural. Cultures raised on a spicy cuisine, or diets that include or exclude dairy products, or which are constantly exposed to Coca-Cola and sweet foods, may have different thresholds of sensitivity to different basic taste elements of sweetness, sourness, bitterness, etc or their combination, even though the basis for the sensitivity thresholds will themselves be physiological. Perhaps within these cultures there will be statistically normal perceivers and it is by reference to them that we can establish whether someone is a reasonably reliable taster. From what a person purports to find in a wine under good conditions, we can tell whether he/she is a good judge of the wine's properties in that population. We may even find out, to our cost, that we are slightly out of the normal range of the surrounding population, just as many men find out that their colour judgments are not discriminating enough for clothes shopping. However, if you always claim to find wines acidic, or sweet, then I know you may not be in the statistically normal range. (As Peynaud showed, different sensitivity thresholds to these features can be measured.)

Do we have to say that a wine's balance, finesse, purity, along with more descriptive characteristics like roundedness, weight, or structure consist in its having dispositions to produce different experiences in diverse populations of tasters? Why say this, rather than saying that these properties are in the wines? It is not just that we have particular responses to the wine: we respond in precisely the way we do *because* our experiences are responsive to characteristics of balance, finesse and roundness, and so on, in the wine. We are appropriately sensitive to these features in a good wine. It is true that our concepts of properties such as body or suppleness or balance are, as philosophers say, response-dependent: we cannot conceive of such properties save in terms of the kind of responses they give rise to in us. But the properties our concepts apply to are there in the wine: it is these characteristics we recognize or fail to recognize on occasions, Finesse, balance, purity and definition are the sorts of properties that *call for* the responses of pleasure and recognition we have.

If the tastes of a wine only consist in dispositions to produce effects in us, which ones should count? A wine tastes less agreeable when combined with certain foods, or tasted at the wrong temperature. Are we to countenance all these dispositions to taste different ways to different people under a variety of circumstances—as tastes the wine has? All the variations would have to be included if we thought of tastes as interactions between us and the wine.[22] Why stop at one set of conditions as the crucial ones concerning our interaction with the wine? Why not include them all? To do so would lead to a proliferations of tastes and offer no definitive criteria for talking about *the* tastes of a wine. And yet we are more inclined to think of getting the best out of the wine by creating the optimal conditions to experience the flavours and aromas it has. We think of a fine wine as having integrity, precision and purity. In taste it is not the kaleidoscope of interaction effects we are after. With a wine of *terroir* we will consider it to have a very definite profile of flavours and aromas that characterize it uniquely. And by thinking about that taste (or those tastes) of the wine as the tastes it has, we can then see the various experiences we can have under different, non-optimal, conditions as the way that taste is masked or distorted by interfering factors. On this picture there is the taste a wine has and the way it tastes when presented to us. We can often sense (by tasting or by smell) what has to be changed (temperature, for example) to get closer to the real taste of the wine—to access its optimum expression of flavours.[23]

Wine Critics and Divergence in Opinions

Finally, if tastes are real, objective properties of wines, then what is the role of the wine critic? Are they always the best judges of the character and quality of wines, and should we subscribe to their opinions? Resistance to this idea comes from many quarters: from doubts about critics' abilities given their differences of opinion; from refusal to have one's own opinions about taste overruled; and not least from wine critics themselves who tend to stress the subjectivity of taste. However, critics do not claim that tastes amount to no more than their subjective experiences of wine: if they did their writings would simply be narrations of their experiences, amounting to nothing more than autobiography. Such a view would make a nonsense of their recommending wines. It is because their experiences of drinking wine—undoubtedly subjective experiences—tell them about something about the character and qualities of the wine that we can benefit by what they write. Thus critics take their experiences to reveal something about the wines they taste and to have implications for the experiences of others. They use their tasting experiences as guides to how others may enhance their drinking pleasures. However, wine critics will insist that their recommendations and opinions cannot overrule the personal preferences of individuals; a view shared by the public. But does this view challenge the objectivity of taste judgment? Can a critic really tell us a wine we do not like is exceptional, or that a wine we do like is of poor quality, or little interest? The answer is yes, for there is a difference between the quality of a wine and people's personal preferences. A wine may not be very interesting or very well made but some people may prefer drinking it to drinking something more complex. Titian is a better painter than Jack Vettriano but that does not prevent some people from preferring the latter to the former. Bach is a better musician than Barry Manilow but some people will prefer to listen the later.[24] These personal preferences cannot be criticized, people have the right to choose what they wish: it is up to them. But it is not up to them, or a mere matter of personal inclination, to determine who is the better painter or musician, or which is the better wine. There are standards by which we can judge a wine, or musical score, or painting to be better than another, and these reflect discernible properties of those objects, though it may take practice and experience to recognize them. Once our perceptions and discriminations are sufficiently refined we can appreciate the reasons for evaluating wines as we do.

The issue of preference, or *personal taste*, as I will call it, is very important in wine. I may have no personal liking for Chenin Blanc and however enthusiastically you may describe the qualities of the very best Savennière, I will remain unmoved. Critics are right to praise the virtues of a Coulée de Serrant, to prize and value it highly as a fine and exceptional wine, but as a matter of personal taste I will always prefer a premier cru Chablis from Dauvissat or Raveneau. Wine critics understand that they cannot overrule an individual's personal tastes and it is in this limited sense that they take taste to be subjective. They still make recommendations and they are predicting a certain experience for those who that take their advice. They also know that the wines they select and admire are not to everyone's taste. The moral is that we must find the right critic to advise us, the one whose personal tastes or preferences are more nearly aligned with ours. In this way, we can use critics like fine scientific instruments to test and select those wines that will give us exceptional pleasure. A good critic or taster will be able to identify and recommend the best wines of a given kind or style even when he or she does not favour that style of wine. Having the ability to assess and describe wines is one thing; having certain personal tastes is another. That we, and the wine critics, have *personal tastes* does not imply that *all* taste is subjective.

A popular reason for doubting critics' competence in assessing wine is their lack of success, on occasion, in identifying a wine by blind tasting. Is it guesswork or precise judgment, people wonder,, that which enables critics to get it right on occasion? And if they lack the ability to identify the wines they are drinking why should we trust that they know what they are talking about? Should we take them to be reliable tasters at all?

There is a widespread mistake in popular thinking here. Why should we suppose that appreciating a beautiful painting depends on first being able to identify it either as Piero della Francesca or a Fra Angelico? Why suppose that a music critic can only respond critically to a piece of music when they can identify the composer?[25] A highly developed musical appreciation does not await the precise identification of a particular piece of music. Why should it be different with wine? Winemakers have been noted, on occasions, not to recognize one of their own wines when it is presented blind at a dinner party. Why should this matter? Perhaps this makes them able to assess the qualities of the wine more fairly and objectively.

However, if wine critics really are good judges of taste why are there differences of opinions among them? Novice tasters may doubt their own powers of discrimination but they will wonder why, if there are objectively correct judgments to be made, wine critics disagree about the qualities of certain wines. After all, they are trained to recognize flavours and aromas, and have tasted widely. If they can reach different opinions about a wine's character and quality is there such a thing as getting matters of taste right? Are judgments of taste just matters of opinion rather than matters of fact? This line of thought puts in doubt the claim that there is something in the wine to which critics' judgments are answerable. For if the judgments of experts is unimprovable, how can they be responding to the taste of the wine and yet arriving at different conclusions? Surely, these judgments are answerable to something in each of them, not just something in the wine; and this would make their opinions to a large extent subjective, with one opinion as good as any other.

Nevertheless, when we say that critics vary in their opinions about a particular wine we need to be cautious. It may be the case that critics diverge from one another in their assessment of a particular wine. But divergence is not always disagreement or conflict. There are cases where we might want to say that each critic is detecting and reporting a different taste the wine has and that it has both of these tastes.

We also need to know whether the difference in opinion between

critics is about the merits of the wine, how appealing it is, its comparative standing with respect to other wines, or about the actual flavours or
features it has. Differences in opinion with respect to preference or
overall assessments of quality may leave untouched an underlying agreement about the properties and characteristics of the wine so assessed.
Personal tastes may make the difference and yet there may be considerable overlap and agreement between tasters about what they are tasting,
i.e. about what a wine tastes like.[26] Being objective in one's judgments,
getting something right, may be a matter of stating, with considerable
accuracy, what a wine is like, what it tastes like. Beyond that there are
many differences in opinion about what is most appealing about a wine,
what gives most pleasure. These disputes over and above a certain standard of quality are perhaps due to personal preferences, and then again,
preferences may be due to particular sensitivities of particular populations of tasters to the certain aspects of a wine: to its alcohol, or acidity,
its tannins or the use of oak in a wine. It should be possible to separate
out these differences and thus reach some objective agreement on the
properties of a wine. Different critics may pick out different tastes, some
may be more sensitive to one taste than to another. So why not avail ourselves of all these opinions so long as they do not conflict?

We have now arrived at a view of tasting as an objective exercise that
relies on our subjective responses to the real and many tastes a wine has.
Astute critics or *cavistes* may lead one to refine and develop one's perceptual experiences and responses. Some of them may be more sensitive
to one range of tastes than another, and to the different points at which
a wine can be brought into balance, so we have to find the best guide to
the tastes in which we take particular pleasure. There is objective knowledge to be had here. But the chance to know one's own tastes, to develop
one's palate and discriminate more and more finely depends on the
opportunities for drinking that are presented or can be sought out, and
these depend on both the advice of critics and the skill of winemakers.
The danger is where too many people rely on just one critic, whose tastes
and preferences comes to dominate the wine market because of commercial pressures and financial speculation. The emergence of
super-critics who favour big, ripe fruit, high alcohol wines with high
extraction and the use of new oak—a simplified and easily replicated
world-style of wine-making—may lead to a simplification in tastes or in

measures of quality. The market may welcome these simplifications, where giving scores replaces the careful descriptions and the slow acquisition of knowledge. For those who trade, but know little about wine, this may be vitally important. But it is also potentially distorting, and there is a great risk that something will be lost, not just in judgment but also in opportunities to taste. Wines will be made to give quick and easy pleasure, and to collect the ratings that traders and their clients will understand. Over-reliance on a single critic's preferences, by buyers, traders, or consumers may lead to the erosion of discrimination and difference, the loss of a sense of a place and of culture: the *terroir* that sums up the history and geography of a people who have laboured in particular vineyards to express wines of individual character that were given their personality by nature. Such wines, like people, behave differently at different ages, and to get to know them in all their variety and diversity makes us richer for the experience. When critics, willingly or not, come to dominate the style of wine that is preferred by the markets, and hence produced by more and more wine-makers, they are dominating our tastes and as a result limiting our experience and opportunities. When this occurs, we will have fewer evocative memories of the sort that Proust knew could at times bring back a whole world: a walk up to the hill of Corton, a late evening tour through the villages of the Côte de Nuits. Fewer and fewer of us will delight in discovering the multiple layers of taste simultaneously present in a bottle of Vosne-Romanée. These experiences can give us intense feelings, can bring us closer to others. We must seek them out and not lose sight of them. Besides, however many wines of a similar style and easy pleasure people drink, they will eventually seek out something new, something different. People and their palates are easily bored and markets are never static. People want interest and diversity, and it is to be hoped this will still be available to them. The *local* matters. Wines of *terroir* are worth fighting for. Go on tasting as well and as widely as you can, enjoy the best experiences available to you. This advice need not mean an oenological tour of the world: the vineyards of Bordeaux and Burgundy contain enough diversity and interest to last a lifetime. We should get to know them, for they are wines which at their best produce an intensity of experience and require a delicacy of response. It is by tasting these wines that we refine our exercise of taste. By understanding them better we gain greater satisfaction and the reward of better and better experiences. And through the intoxicating pleasure these great wines afford us we learn to recognize what is there for all experience.[27]

REFERENCES

Baxandall, Michael (1972), Painting and Experience in Fifteenth-Century Italy (Oxford: Clarendon Press)

Broadbent, Michael (2003), Wine Tasting, 9th edition (London; Mitchell Beazley)

Brochet, Frédéric (2001), "Tasting: chemical object representation in the field of consciousness", http://www.academie-amorim.com/us/laureat_2001/brochet.pdf Denham, A.E. (2000), Metaphor and Moral Experience (Oxford: Clarendon Press)

Hume, David, "Of the Standard of Taste", from the Essays, Moral, Political and Literary (1776) reprinted in David Hume: Selected Essays, (1998) edited by S. Copley and A. Edgar, (Oxford World's Classics)

Kosmeyer, Christine (1999), Making Sense of Taste (Ithaca, NY: Cornell University Press)

Locke, John (1823), The Works of John Locke, New Edition, Vol. X. (G. Shaw and Son)

Lyas, Colin (1998). "Art Criticism", in E. Craig (ed.), Routledge Encyclopedia of Philosophy (London: Routledge)

Peynaud, Emile (1987), The Taste of Wine, translated by Michael Schuster (New York: J. Wiley)

Reid, Thomas (1758), Essays on the Intellectual Powers of Man, edited by D. Brookes (Edinburgh: University of Edinburgh Press)

Schaper, Eva (1983), "The Pleasures of Taste", in Pleasure, Preference and Value, (1983) edited by Eva Schaper (Cambridge: Cambridge University Press)

Wiggins, D. (1987), "A Sensible Subjectivism", in Needs, Values, Truth (Oxford: Blackwell)

NOTES:

1   See also Hugh Johnson telling us that he does not "think that taste should be a great cause of argument. We each have our own taste". Though he goes on, "as long as we account for it and make it available for other people to enjoy, that's all we can do." (*Decanter* interview Oct.2005). Jancis Robinson tells us, "I know that all wine tasting is a subjective business" (*Decanter* interview March 2006). The Michelin guide *to The Wine Regions of France* states that, "Taste is subjective, individual, and yet experts seem to understand each other, know what to look for, and recognize the same sensations their fellow experts find." (p.58)

2   In his famous essay, *On The Standard of Taste*, Hume tells us that good critics, or judges of taste must show delicacy of judgment, be free from prejudice, able to draw on a wide range of experience for comparisons, pay due attention, and be unclouded by mood.

3   I am indebted to Louise Page for bringing this quote to my attention and suggesting the analogy with wine.

4   Here I am deeply indebted to David Wiggins' paper, "A Sensible Subjectivism". I do not know if he would approve of the uses to which I am putting the subtle and wise things he says there.

5   For a good account of how the hierarchy of the senses has been presented through the ages see Kosmeyer 1999.

6   There are of course super-tasters and those with gustatory disorders such as agueusia who lack all sense of taste. But the issue addressed here goes beyond these cases.

7   The French psychologist Frederic Brochet (2001) conducted experiments with experienced wine tasters asking them to describe the characteristics of a white and a red wine. The next day he gave them the white wine coloured by a tasteless red dye. The same tasters now used descriptors of the red wine to characterize the white wine. We may see this as showing that sight is also a component of "tasting".

8   Voltaire's view is discussed at greater length by Eva Schaper (1983).

9   No better example is there of such expression of vintages and *terroir* than the great wines of Burgundy. In different vineyards, different parcels, different growing seasons, the gifted wine-maker will adapt to what is there and help transmit these expressions of difference in wines that show power and restraint. The elegance, harmony and purity of the wines, and the skill of the wine-maker allow them to retain their personalities *and* differences.

10   John Locke was struck by just these facts about Château Haut Brion on his agricultural tour of France:
     "It grows on a rise of ground, openmost to the west, is pure white soil, mixed with a little gravel [...] One would imagine it scarce fit to bear anything." (John Locke 1677 from Observations on Vines, In *The Works of John Locke*, Vol. X, p.329)

11   Although as a maker of Scotch once explained to me: if you have to acquire the taste you don't really like it.

12   Here I am at odds with Kent Bach (see Chapter Two) who thinks that knowledge of a particular wine cannot affect your enjoyment of it.

13   "Great wine has that marvellous quality of immediately establishing communication between those who are drinking it. Tasting it at table should not be a solitary activity." (Peynaud, 1987 p.214)

14   The distinction in this form is due to P.M.S Hacker in *Appearance and Reality* (Oxford: Blackwell 1987) to which I am also indebted for his discussion of secondary properties.

15   See A.E. Denham, *Metaphor and Moral Experience* (Oxford: Clarendon Press, 2000).

16   That said, Robert Parker, does provide near exhaustive coverage of the world's greatest wines–Burgundy excepted–and has a remarkable ability to predict the future quality and character of wines tasted from barrel.

17   When considering whether wine is an aesthetic object the comparison is usually made with the contemplation of music or painting. But neither of these provides the right analogy, I believe. The right comparison with tasting a great wine is more like to be the rather 1960s idea of a happening: a one off event in which everything came together and where all the details conspire to create the exalted moment of experience.

18   Mood is important because it connects or divides us from others and may divide us from better parts of ourselves.

19   In the Middle Ages monks regarded watercress as a substance with medicinal powers that purified the blood. People who drank to excess could be put on a diet of watercress for a week. Whatever the wisdom of this remedy it is true that wine and watercress do not mix.

20   This the view the Scottish philosopher Thomas Reid held: "I cannot say what it is in a sapid body that pleases my palate but there is a quality in the sapid body which pleases my palate and I call it a delicious taste" Chapter 1 Section I, *Essays on the Intellectual Powers of Man* (1758).

21   From Hume's *Essays, Moral, Political and Literary,* (1776) reprinted in *David Hume: Selected Essays,* edited by S. Copley and A. Edgar (Oxford World's Classics 1998).

22   Even if we claim that tastes are interactions between the wine and the taster, the issue of how subjective or objective they are remains open. If our reactions to a given wine differ then tastes will be, to that extent, subjective; whereas if, as normal tasters, we respond in similar ways, under similar conditions, tastes will be objective, or at any rate, inter-subjective. Therefore, nothing about the current issue is settled by taking the interactionist view.

23   For a robust defence of the dispositional view against these objections see Deroy's chapter in this volume.

24   This point is well made by Colin Lyas.

25   Of course, someone may confuse two painters or composers that are so different that it reveals a certain incompetence in judgments of similarity that undermines the credibility of that person to judge. However, even in blind tasting critics will not mistake an Alsace Riesling for a Puligny-Montrachet.

26   In a famously sharp-edged dispute between Robert Parker and Jancis Robinson about the merits of 2003 Château Pavie the protagonists' highly contested statements were concerned with the relative standing or overall quality of that wine. However, the clear disparity in their verdicts tended to obscure the level of agreement there was between them about the actual characteristics of the wine. The very same qualities in the wine, identified by Parker and singled out for praise as signs of the pleasure to be afforded by drinking this wine in the future, were criticized by Robinson as symptoms of excess and a lack of respect for Bordeaux-style wine making.

27 A previous version of this paper was presented at the University of London's Institute of Philosophy conference, on "Philosophy and Wine: from science to subjectivity" Dec. 2004., and I would like to thank members of that audience for the discussion that followed. I owe a considerable debt to Michael Dwyer for his excellent editorial suggestions. I am also very grateful to Jean Hewitson for so many helpful discussions of these topics, and to Ophelia Deroy for acute critical advice and comment on previous versions of the paper.

chapter four

WINE AND THE BRAIN

Jamie Goode

WINE TASTING: FOCUSING ON THE PERCEPTUAL EVENT

The central focus of any philosophical study of wine is the perceptual event that occurs when we 'sense' the wine that is in our glass, by sniffing it, or putting it in our mouths, or a combination of these two processes. The goal of this chapter is to explore the nature of this perceptual event from a biological perspective. That is not to say that (largely reductionist) science is the only legitimate way of framing questions about taste; there are limits to the sorts of questions that the scientific method can address. But what biology has to say about the perception of wine is of great use, because its insights can usefully constrain our thinking. I've titled this chapter "wine and the brain", because here I am assuming that the perceptual event of wine "tasting" is one that occurs in the brain, and that it is one and the same as the electrical communication between neurons occurring here as we process the signals generated by our sensory apparatus when we encounter wine. To biologists, this suggestion—that conscious events are explainable in terms of neuronal activity in the brain—is uncontroversial: if they are aware of the mind-body problem at all, biologists frequently assume it has been solved. But I'm not a scientific fundamentalist, and I recognise that the reductionistic language of neurobiology is just one way of approaching the complex subject of conscious awareness, and that it doesn't necessarily exclude other descriptive approaches.

Some caveats are in order. Inevitably, a broad-ranging chapter such as this touches on several disciplines. Consequently, I've tried to keep the science here as accessible as I can without dumbing it down or otherwise misrepresenting it. Second, I'm dealing with several complex branches of

science, some of which lie outside my realm of expertise. I'll try my best
to get it right.

I need also to add a word on terminology. Although the term "wine
tasting" is technically inaccurate (we are referring to the combination of
several different sensory inputs here, chiefly smell, taste, touch and
vision), I shall continue using it simply because there isn't a better
description for the practice of assessing and comparing wines. And while
"smell" stands largely as a sense on its own (you can smell a wine without
tasting it, although there will be some visual input), taste doesn't: you
can't taste a wine without smelling it. Much of the sensory information
when wine is in our mouths comes from the senses of olfaction and
touch, which can't therefore be dissociated from the sensations coming
from the taste buds. Thus I prefer to use the term "flavour" to describe
this multiple sensing of wine in the mouth which results in a seamless,
unified perception of wine.

A NEW THEORETICAL FRAMEWORK FOR WINE TASTING
While many of these issues are as yet unanswered, or only have partial
answers, what we already know of how the brain processes flavour suggests that we should revise the theoretical framework we use to approach
wine tasting. Most significantly, I'm going to argue (perhaps controversially) that the way rating or scoring wine is currently practised is based
on a false premise: that when a critic rates a wine, they are assessing the
wine, and that any score thus produced is a property of this wine. This
is incorrect. We need to make the subtle yet important paradigm shift of
seeing a critic's assessment as a rating of that critic's perception of the
wine. To put it another way, the critic is actually describing a conscious
representation of their interaction with the wine, and therefore the score
or rating is a property of that interaction and not the wine itself.

My goal here is therefore to explore the nature of that representation, how it is constructed in the brain, and how this might lead to
differences between individuals' perception of the same wine.

TASTING WINE
Uncork a good bottle, pour yourself a glass and then take a sip. We call
this process wine "tasting", but this is actually a fairly misleading term.
In this interaction between you and the wine, the impression you form

is a conscious experience that involves the fusion of inputs from at least four different senses, coupled with some sophisticated brain processing. It's a unified "representation" that can't easily be dissected into its component sensory inputs, which we commonly try to do with taste and smell.

INTRODUCING THE CHEMICAL SENSES

Philosophers reading this book will likely be familiar with Thomas Nagel's famous paper posing the question of what it might be like to be a bat. The world would seem very different to an entity relying on a sophisticated sense of touch, which operates like sonar, for spatial navigation. Along similar lines, any readers who have ever walked a dog will be aware that for them, the world of smell is as important and dynamic to them as the visual world which we are so familiar with. In contrast, we humans live in a vastly diminished smell world, having traded our olfactory acuity for enhanced colour vision—an evolutionary change that took place some time during primate evolution. Many of the genes encoding olfactory receptors in our genome are now redundant. Rather than being important for orientation, social organisation and mate choice, as it is for many mammals, our use of the chemical senses, taste and smell, is largely restricted to food choice—a reduced but still vital role.

Taste and smell begin with receptors in the mouth and nasal cavity that turn chemical information into electrical signals, which can then be processed by the brain. The tongue and soft palate have taste buds containing receptors for five modes of chemical stimuli: sweet, salty, bitter, sour and umami. The nasal cavity contains olfactory receptor neurons which express, between them, around 2,000 different receptors, each tuned to recognise different volatile odorants. (How they actually do this is one of the last remaining great mysteries in biology, and the subject of a thought-provoking popular science book by Chandler Burr, *The Emperor of Scent.*)

But it's wrong to think of our sensory systems as complicated measuring instruments, which give a read-out of the taste and aroma molecules that they encounter. This is a common misconception: that wine perception is a result of a combination of such linear inputs. This simplistic view of taste and smell leads to a range of misunderstandings and apparent anomalies when it comes to wine tasting.

Instead, what the brain does is to model the world around us. Our sensory systems are bombarded constantly by a mass of information, which, if attended to uniformly, would swamp our perceptive and decision-making processes. So the brain is able to extract from this sea of data just those features that are most relevant. This is done by a procedure known as higher-order processing.

Let's look at this another way. We often think that our sensory system is revealing to us the world around us in an accurate and complete way. But in reality, what we experience is an edited version of reality that is based on the information that is most relevant to our survival and functioning. For almost all purposes it does no harm for us to think of the world around as revealed us to be "reality"—indeed, life would become quite complicated if we operated any other way—but for the purposes of this discussion it's useful to realise that the version of reality we experience is an edited and partial one.

This can be illustrated in a number of ways. Think again about your household pets, if you have any. As I mentioned earlier, dogs live in a smell world that is almost completely closed to us, and which is just as vivid to them as the visual world is to us. Rats and mice, like many small mammals, get almost all the information they need about their environment from a combination of sniffing and using their whiskers: they are nocturnal, and vision isn't so useful at night. Now switch on your radio or television, or take a call on your mobile phone: it's clear that the air is full of information that we can't access unless we have a device to decode it. Third, take a look at the visual illusion in Figure 1, known as the café wall illusion. It's just one of many tricks that "fool" the visual system. These sorts of illusions give us clues about the sort of higher-order processing that is taking place, and demonstrate that what we "see" is not always what is there.

The higher-order processing in the visual system is the best understood for any of the senses. Scientists have worked out how visual processing extracts features of the environment that are most likely to be relevant. For instance, our peripheral vision is sensitive to motion: moving objects immediately stand out, because neurons are tuned to respond to them. This motion detection ability is much stronger in the periphery than it is in the central visual field. Look at your computer

Figure 1.

monitor (as long as it is a conventional cathode-ray tube and not a flat screen), and then look away. As you look away, the screen of your monitor appears to flicker in your peripheral vision; you weren't aware of this while you were staring at it. Faces are also likely to be significant cues, so our visual systems have special brain mechanisms for face processing. This is the reason why so many advertisements and magazine covers rely on human faces, even where the face isn't particularly relevant to the publication.

Although it is less well studied, this sort of higher-order processing is also important in flavour detection. We are bombarded with chemical stimuli all the time and the brain has to filter this information so that only the important bits get through. It seems that much of the brain is dedicated to producing a suitably edited view of reality, just as the staff in a newsroom work hard all day sifting through the output of their journalists to produce a fifteen-minute news bulletin for broadcast that evening.

GATHERING DATA
So we come to the key question. How is it that electrical currents from nerve cells are translated into a unified conscious experience in the brain? Science is a long way from being able to address this complex question directly. But a relatively new technique, functional magnetic resonance imaging (fMRI), has transformed brain research in recent years by allowing researchers to visualise the brain in action. During an MRI scan, a

subject is placed inside a large cylindrical magnet and exposed to a massive magnetic field. A sophisticated detection device then creates three-dimensional images of tissues and organs from the signals produced. fMRI is a twist on this theme, where the technique is used specifically to measure changes of blood flow in the brain. When a group of brain cells becomes more active, they need more blood, and this generates a signal in the scan. Although there was initially some controversy about whether a direct correlation exists between the blood flow detected in an fMRI scan and actual brain activity, the consensus in the field is that this is indeed the case. (This raises a more complex question, alluded to in the introduction, and beyond the scope of this chapter: can our conscious thoughts be reduced to an electrical signal in the brain? Is the brain activity viewed by MRI one and the same as the conscious thought we are having? Most biologists would assume this; few would have ever questioned the implications of this assumption, or realised that it was an assumption.) The power of fMRI is that it can show how we use our brains when, for example, we think of chocolate or move our middle finger; the limitation is that to be able to detect these signals reliably, subjects are required to lie inside a large metal cylinder with their heads completely still.

Because of the practical and experimental difficulty of these sorts of studies, it's an area where there's still much uncertainty. However, even the limited data obtained so far are highly relevant for wine tasting and are important if we want to provide a robust theoretical basis for human interaction with wine.

Let's pick up on the theme of flavour processing in the brain. The senses of taste and smell work together to perform two important tasks: identifying nutritious foods and drinks, and to protect us from eating things that are bad for us. The brain achieves this by linking food that we need with a reward stimulus—it smells or tastes "good"—and making bad or unneeded foods aversive. To do this, flavour perception needs to be connected with the processing of memory (we remember which foods are good and those which have made us ill) and emotions (we have a strong desire for food when we are hungry that then motivates us to seek out a decent meal). Because seeking food is a potentially costly and bothersome process, we need a strong incentive to do it. Hunger and appetite are thus powerful physical drives. They are also finely tuned. It is striking that we are able to eat what we need and not a lot more or less: even a slight imbalance, over decades, would result in gross obesity or starvation.

Taste begins on the tongue, where we have some 5,000 specialised structures called taste buds, embedded within lumps called papillae. Each taste bud contains 50–100 sensory cells responding to one of five different primary tastes. These sensory cells convert this chemical information into electrical signals, which then pass through to the primary taste cortex in the brain. This is located in a region called the insula. Taste provides us with relatively little information compared with the sense of smell, more commonly referred to in scientific texts as "olfaction". Whereas there are just five basic tastes, we can discriminate among many thousands of volatile compounds ("odorants"). Our olfactory epithelium, located in the top of the nasal cavity, contains olfactory receptor cells, each of which express just one type of olfactory receptor. This information is also turned into electrical signals by these receptor cells, which is then conveyed to the olfactory cortex via a structure known as the olfactory bulb.

At this stage, with the information that exists at the level of the primary taste and smell areas of the brain, it is likely that all that is coded is the identity and intensity of the stimulus. Alone, this information is of relatively little value. But what the brain does next is this clever higher-order processing mentioned above—it extracts the useful information from this mass of data, and begins to make sense of it. This is where we turn to the research of Edmund Rolls, a professor of experimental psychology at the University of Oxford, who has studied a region of the brain called the orbitofrontal cortex. fMRI is one of the tools used in his work.

The work of Rolls and others has shown that it is in the orbitofrontal cortex that taste and smell are brought together to form the sensation of flavour. Information from other senses, such as touch and vision, is also combined at this level, to create a complex, unified sensation that is then localised to the mouth by the sense of touch—after all, this is where any response to the food or drink, such as swallowing it or spitting it out, will need to take place. Rolls has also demonstrated that the orbitofrontal cortex is where the reward value (the "niceness", known more grandly as "hedonic valence") of taste and smell is represented.

That's another way of saying this is where the brain decides whether what we have in our mouths is delicious, dull or disgusting. Another fMRI study has shown that the brain uses two dimensions to analyse smells, intensity and hedonic valence. The amygdala responds to intensity while the orbitofrontal cortex is the region that decides whether the smell is good or bad.

CROSS-MODAL PROCESSING

Some nerve cells in this brain region respond to combinations of senses, such as taste and sight, or taste and touch, or smell and sight. This convergence of inputs, known as cross-modal processing, is acquired by learning, but it is one that occurs slowly, typically requiring many pairings of the different sensations before it is fixed. This suggests an explanation for why we often need several experiences with a new food or wine to be able to appreciate them fully. It is also at this level where stimulus-reinforcement association learning takes place. This is the situation where, for example, you are faced with a new food (stimulus) which tastes good, but then it makes you violently sick (association). Next time you pop some of this in you mouth, you immediately spit it out in disgust. It saves you the bother of being sick again, and is therefore a protective mechanism. (However, this aversive mechanism is of somewhat limited power: a student may drink seventeen pints of lager on a Friday night, throw up in the gutter, feel rotten the next morning, but return to drinking lager the next evening.)

SENSORY-SPECIFIC SATIETY

One aspect of Rolls' research on the orbitofrontal cortex that has direct relevance to wine tasting is his work on sensory-specific satiety. This is the observation that when enough of a particular food is eaten, its reward value decreases. However, this decrease in pleasantness is greater than for other foods. Putting it more simply, if you like both bananas and chocolate, and then eat lots of banana, you can't stomach the thought of another banana but you will still fancy a chocolate. This clever brain trick makes us desire the particular sorts of foods that we need at a given time, and helps us to balance our nutritional intake. By fMRI Rolls has shown that in humans the response in the orbitofrontal cortex to the odour of a food eaten to satiety decreases, but the response to another odour that has not been eaten doesn't change. The subjects' perception of the intensity of the smell of the consumed food doesn't change, but their perception of its pleasantness (hedonic valence) does. In another study, he showed that swallowing is not necessary for sensory-specific satiety to occur. When I quizzed him about this, Rolls was cautious about speculating (as many scientists rightly are), but agreed that this could have some effect during a wine tasting where a taster is repeatedly encountering the same sort of taste or smell. At a large trade tasting it is quite common to taste as many as 100 wines in a session. If these results of sensory-specific satiety are extrapolated to this sort of setting, then it's likely that the brain will be processing the last wine you taste differently from that of the first, assuming that there are some components to the taste or smell in common—for example, tannins, fruit or oak.

This all makes perfect sense at a practical level. When you haven't eaten for a long time, even simple foods can taste great: their hedonic valence has been altered by your state of hunger. I love raspberries, but they would lose their appeal if I had already eaten five punnets of them. I'd still recognise them as raspberries, though. My brain is altering how attractive I find various flavours according to other information it is receiving.

TRAINED TASTERS EXPERIENCE WINE DIFFERENTLY

In 2002, researchers from the Functional Neuroimaging Laboratory of the Santa Lucia Foundation, headed by Dr Alessandro Castriota-Scanderberg, put together a simple yet elegant study addressing a key question: do trained tasters experience wine differently from novices (Castriota-Scanderberg et al 2005)?

They took seven professional sommeliers and seven other people matched for age and sex but without specific wine tasting abilities, and monitored their brain responses while they tasted wine. But getting someone to taste wine while they are having their brain scanned is no trivial feat. "The experience was pretty uncomfortable," recalls Andrea Sturniolo, one of the sommeliers involved. "I was under a tunnel with four plastic tubes in my mouth, totally immobile." Through these tubes the researchers fed subjects with a series of four liquids: three different wines, and a glucose solution as a control. Subjects were told to try to identify the wines and form some sort of critical judgment on them.

They were also asked to judge when the perception of the wine was strongest: while it was in the mouth ("taste"), or immediately after swallowing ("aftertaste"). "The experiment lasted a good fifty minutes," says Sturniolo, "which seemed endless." He added, "certainly they were not the ideal conditions to carry out such a delicate experiment, but as these conditions were identical for all participants, I think the results are reliable."

So what did the scans show? Some brain regions—notably the primary and secondary taste areas, in the insula and orbitofrontal cortex—were activated in both sets of subjects during the "taste" phase. But during this initial period, another area was activated only in the sommeliers, and this was the front bit of a region known as the amygdale-hippocampal area. In the "aftertaste" phase the untrained subjects also showed activation of this amygdale-hippocampal area, but only on the right side, whereas in the sommeliers this zone was activated on both sides. In addition, during the aftertaste the sommeliers exclusively showed further activation in the left dorsolateral prefrontal cortex.

Not surprisingly, given its importance in the processing of flavour, the orbitofrontal cortex is one of the regions activated in the brains of both trained and non-trained wine tasters in this study. What about the other areas—the ones that were highlighted specifically in the sommeliers?

First we have the amygdale-hippocampal area. This is a zone that plays a key role in processing motivation (the amygdala) and memory (the hippocampus). According to study leader Dr Scanderberg, "the finding of an early and consistent activation of the amygdale-hippocampus complex in the sommelier group suggests a greater motivation for the recognition process." This may indicate that the sommeliers were expecting a reward and thus pleasure from the wine tasting process. The other key area is the left dorsolateral prefrontal cortex, which is a zone involved in the planning and use of cognitive (thinking) strategies. The sommeliers' unique activation here is consistent with the idea that only experienced tasters follow specific analytical strategies when wine is in their mouths. The researchers speculate that these strategies might be of a linguistic kind, associating words with specific flavours. We'll return to this important concept later.

In parallel with fMRI studies on musicians that have shown that music activates different areas of trained musicians' brains than those of casual listeners, it seems that the sommeliers are experiencing something different from the average person when they taste wine. "There is clear evidence that the neural connections of the brain change with training and experience," says Dr Scanderberg. He explains that, "there are two apparently contradictory ways that the brain adjusts its structural network in parallel with the increasing expertise of the subject." The first, and most common, is to assign a specific function to a smaller cluster of cells higher up in the brain's hierarchy. For example, during rehabilitation of stroke patients it is common to see a particular task activate a much smaller, but higher-up region in the brain at the end of rehab than it did at the beginning. The second strategy is to recruit more brain areas to help with a complex task. Experienced wine tasters seem to follow this second strategy, pulling in new brain areas to help with the analysis of sensory stimuli.

The implications for wine tasting are clear. I'm assuming here that having chosen to read this book you may well be someone who has drunk a fair bit of wine over the years. Do you remember one of the wines that first really appealed to you? If you were to go back in time now and taste that wine again, yet with your current wine drinking history, then you'd actually perceive something quite different as you sipped that wine the second time around. Your brain has been changed by drinking all that wine, and we aren't talking alcohol-induced neural degeneration. By paying attention as you've been drinking, just like the sommeliers in this study, your response to wine differs from that of untrained subjects. This also underlines the importance of the learning component in wine appreciation. People versed in one culture of wine may need to re-learn about wine when exploring another. Even if you have years of expertise in Australian reds, for example, you may have to start from scratch when trying to appreciate German Riesling.

WORDS AND WINE: HOW WE FORM REPRESENTATIONS OF THE TASTING EXPERIENCE

Moving fields slightly, Frédéric Brochet, a cognitive psychologist, has conducted important research that is highly relevant here (see Morrot *et al* 2001, Brochet & Dubourdieu 2001, Brochet 2001). He has studied the practice of wine tasting as carried out by professionals. His claim is that the practice and teaching of tasting rests on a fragile theoretical basis. "Tasting is representing," says Brochet, "and when the brain carries out a "knowledge" or "understanding" task, it manipulates representations." In this context a "representation" is a conscious experience constructed by the mind on the basis of a physical experience, in this cases the taste, smell, sight and mouthfeel of a wine. Brochet uses three methodologies in his work: textual analysis (which looks at the sorts of words that tasters use to verbalise their representations), behaviour analysis (inferring cognitive mechanisms from looking at how subjects act) and cerebral function analysis (looking at how the brain responds to wine directly through the use of fMRI) (see Brochet 2001).[1]

TEXTUAL ANALYSIS: STUDYING THE WORDS THAT TASTERS USE

Textual analysis involves the statistical study of the words used in a text. Brochet used five data sets, consisting of tasting notes from *Guide Hachette*, Robert Parker, Jacques Dupont, Brochet himself, and notes on eight wines from forty-four professionals collected at Vinexpo. Employing textual analysis software called ALCESTE, Brochet studied the way that the different tasters used words to describe their tasting experiences. He summarises his six key results as follows. (1) The authors' descriptive representations are based on the types of wines and not on the different parts of the tasting. (2) The representations are "prototypical": that is, specific vocabularies are used to describe types of wines, and each vocabulary represents a type of wine. Putting this another way, when a taster experiences a particular wine, the words they use to describe it are those that they link to this sort (or type) of wine. (3) The range of words used (lexical fields) is different for each author. (4) Tasters possess a specific vocabulary for preferred and non-preferred wines. No taster seems to be able to put aside their preferences when their representations are described. Brochet adds that this result, the dependence of representations on preferences, is well known from the fragrance world. (5) Colour is a major factor in organising the classes of descriptive terms used by the tasters, and has a major influence on the sorts of descriptors used. (6) Cultural information is present in the sensorial descriptions. Interestingly, Brochet states that "certain descriptive terms referring to cognitive representation probably come from memory or information heard or read by the subject, but neither the tongue or the nose could be the object of the coding." (Brochet 2001)

BEHAVIOURAL ANALYSIS: PERCEPTIVE EXPECTATION

In the next set of experiments, Brochet invited fifty-four subjects to take part in a series of experiments in which they had to describe a real red wine and a real white wine. A few days later the same group had to describe the same white wine and this white wine again that had been coloured red with a neutral-tasting food colorant. Interestingly, in both experiments they described the "red" wine using identical terms even though one of them was actually a white wine. Brochet's conclusion was that the perception of taste and smell conformed to colour: vision is having more of an input in the wine tasting process than most people would think. Brochet points out a practical application of this observation, which has been known for a long time in the food and fragrance industries: no one sells colourless syrups or perfumes any more.

In a second, equally mischievous experiment, Brochet served the same average-quality wine to people at a week's interval. The twist was that on the first occasion it was packaged and served to people as a Vin de Table, and on the second as a Grand Cru wine. So the subjects thought they were tasting a simple wine and then a very special wine, even though it was the same both times. He analysed the terms used in the tasting notes, and it makes telling reading. For the "Grand Cru" wine versus the Vin de Table, "a lot" replaces "a little"; "complex" replaces "simple"; and "balanced" replaces "unbalanced"—all because of the sight of the label.

Brochet explains the results through a phenomenon called "perceptive expectation": a subject perceives what they have pre-perceived, and then they find it difficult to back away from that. For us humans, visual information is much more important than chemosensory information, so we tend to trust vision more. Brochet uses these results to explain Peynaud's observation that "Blind tasting of great wines is often disappointing."

VARIATION IN REPRESENTATIONS

A further study in this series examined how the qualitative ratings of a series of wines differed among a group of wine tasters. This group of eight tasters were asked to rank eighteen wines which they tasted blind in order of preference. The results differed widely. With a similar methodology to that employed by the Italian researchers, Brochet then used MRI to assess the brain response of four subjects to a series of wines. One of the most interesting results obtained with this technique was that the same stimulus produced different brain responses in different people. In terms of brain area activated, one was more verbal, another more visual. Also, when a subject tastes the same wine several times, the images of each tasting are somewhat different. Brochet concludes that this demonstrates the "expression of the variable character of the representation." The representation is a "global form, integrating, on equal terms, chemo-sensorial, visual, imaginary and verbal imagination."

Dr Charles Spence from the Department of Experimental Psychology at Oxford University has also gathered relevant data on this sort of crossmodal sensory processing. I asked him about how his studies might apply to wine. "Here in my lab we do indeed do a number of studies looking at how what people see influences their perception of the flavour identity and intensity." says Spence. "However, unfortunately we can't give people alcohol, because of danger of litigation, so we do most of our studies with coloured soft drinks, looking into which colours are particularly effective in modulating flavour perception. It turns out that one of the reasons why red colouring turns out to be such a powerful driver of what we experience (both in terms of smell and taste) is that redness typically equates with the ripening of fruits in nature." Spence thinks that both semantics and experience are also important. "Expectations or labels about what something might be can play a key role in how you interpret an ambiguous or bivalent odour," he adds. "Surprisingly, expertise doesn't seem to help with the red wine colour effect. I have seen experts completely fooled, perhaps even more than novices. The thing is that many of these multisensory interactions occur pre-attentively. In other words, given the overload in the amount of sensory stimulation that is constantly bombarding each of our senses, our brains try to help out by binding what we see, hear, taste, etc. automatically, and only giving us awareness of the result of this integration. Hence, attention also fails to impact on many of these crossmodal illusions" (C. Spence, personal communication). Spence also has something to say about the importance of learning, which he thinks plays a very important role. "I have not seen this studied for the case of wine tasting but for other combinations of taste and smell, your previous experience (e.g. in terms of cultural differences in exposure to certain foods, or to certain combinations of tastants and odorants) critically determines how your brain will bind the different sensory cues. The brains of Westerners, for example, are especially geared up to binding sweet tastes in the mouth with almond like odours, but not salty tastes with almond odour. Go to Japan and the reverse is true, as Japanese people never experience the combination of sugar and almond, but instead get a lot of exposure to almond and salt taste in pickled vegetables and condiments." (Personal communication).

VARIATION AMONG TASTERS

Taste psychophysics is a field of study that concentrates on how physical taste stimuli are perceived by the mind. Linda Bartoshuk, Professor of Surgery at Yale University, is one of the leading experts in this field. In her work on the psychophysics of taste she has addressed the difficult question of how we can compare sensory experiences among different individuals (see e.g. Bartoshuk 2000, Lucchina *et al* 1998, Duffy *et al* 2004).

Are two people drinking from the same bottle of wine having a common experience? "In my view, this is one of the most interesting questions in sensory science," responds Bartoshuk. "It taps into an important philosophical issue: since we cannot share experiences directly, is there a way to make comparisons across individuals (or groups) indirectly?" (Personal communication) One of Bartoshuk's contributions to this field is that she has devised a reliable scale for making intersubjective comparisons that makes use of cross-sense comparison. Let me explain.

Part of the problem of comparing taste experiences among individuals stems from genetic differences. "The best known of these genetic mechanisms is that involving PROP (6-*N*-propylthiouracil)," Bartoshuk explains. "This compound and its chemical relatives contain a group that stimulates a specific bitter receptor in the taste membrane." Non-tasters of PROP carry two recessive alleles of a gene that has recently been localised to chromosome 7; tasters carry either one or both alleles. "My lab discovered a large variation among tasters; those with the most taste-buds are called supertasters and those with fewer are called medium tasters," states Bartoshuk. "Supertasters live in a neon taste world; taste sensations are roughly three times as intense to them as non-tasters." But it is not just taste that is affected by these genetic differences. "Since taste buds are surrounded by nerve fibres carrying oral burn/pain, supertasters perceive more oral burn from stimuli such as alcohol, and supertasters also perceive more intense oral touch sensations." Tannic structure in wine is perceived by the sense of touch, so this is highly relevant here. Bartoshuk continues, "perhaps the most important attribute of the sensory experience produced by wine tasting is retronasal olfaction. When we sniff odours from the outside world, this is called orthonasal olfaction. When we put things in our mouth, chewing and swallowing pumps up volatiles up behind the palate into the nasal cavity. This is retronasal olfaction". Supertasters, it seems, perceive more intense retronasal olfaction, presumably because they perceive more intense oral sensations.

Given the individual differences in taste perception, how does Bartoshuk make sensory comparisons among individuals and groups? Initially, she used responses to varying dilutions of salt solutions (NaCl) as a taste standard, but she found that this varied with PROP tasting status. The answer was to take advantage of the surprising observation that experiences from different sensory modalities can be matched for perceived intensity: a contrived sort of synaesthesia. Putting this more simply, using appropriate standards from an unrelated sense that shows less individual variation than taste, such as the brightness of a light or the loudness of a sound, can make between-subject comparisons in taste intensity possible. For example, in one experiment, non-tasters matched the bitterness of black coffee to the brightness of low-beam headlights at night, while supertasters matched it slightly above high-beam head-lights at night. A deliberate, voluntary synaesthesia such as this enables us to break free of the noise and confusion brought about through genetic differences in taste, making possible our recourse to descriptions from other senses from where it seems we live in closely similar worlds. Without the use of an appropriate standard from another sense, scales labelled for taste intensity produce invalid comparisons across groups and individuals.

CONCLUSIONS

While there's a lot still to be learned about how the brain constructs our experience of wine, it is already clear that this is a complex area that we often try to simplify. It is our attempts to simplify the concepts underlying wine tasting and to iron out the very real inter and intra-individual variation that leads to problems in the interpretations of results from tastings. There is a lot more to the wine experience than just smell and taste: the basic information from these chemical senses is supplemented in a very real way by other inputs, for example from vision, touch and memory. Added to this, the higher-order integration of all this input is a flexible and complicated processing stage that then forms our unified perception (or "representation") of the tasting experience. The important results of Brochet and others show that factors such as whether or not we are tasting blind make a crucial difference to the nature of this representation, and that representations of the same wine differ quite markedly among tasters. Furthermore, the past experiences of tasting will change the nature of our current experiences. Information of this nature should help us in our understanding of the scientific underpinnings of the wine tasting process, and help in the design of tastings. For example, panel tastings, where consensus is sought, look doomed to failure. It is likely that further studies using similar techniques to those described here will give us a greater understanding of the rather complex business of tasting and describing wine.

Perhaps it would also be useful in these discussions to distinguish between different types of wine tasting practice. Sensory analysis is widely used in the wine industry. It attempts to remove all the sorts of external cues that can affect perception, and iron out any inconsistencies among tasters, for example by agreeing on a common vocabulary for tastes and smells. In this form of tasting, participants are trying to analyse what is in the bottle—they are attempting to act as measuring devices, and the focus is very much on the nature of what is in the bottle. Quite different, though, is the sort of tasting done for fun, where the objective is to drink the wine, rather than analyse it. Of course, with many tasters, a degree of analysis will take place as they drink, but in this instance the context and the experiences and preferences of the taster will play an important role in shaping the perceptual experience.

In closing, I'll throw out some tentative ideas that I haven't been able to develop here because of space constraints. First, I think that we already have enough evidence here to warrant a paradigm shift with regard to rating wines. What critics are scoring is not some intrinsic property of the liquid in the bottle, but a perceptual representation that is to some degree specific to them. Does this mean that we can't have a shared experience when we taste the same wine? While it's helpful to acknowledge the individual nature of these representations, we also need to bear in mind that one of the remarkable properties of the human mind is its ability to exploit shared space, thanks to language and the development of writing and other recording technologies. The laptop I am writing this chapter on is effectively acting as an extension of my brain. It gives me the ability to take my thoughts, in word form, and then develop them over an extended period of time. Most importantly, I can then share these thoughts with others, and in turn access extensions of their mental landscape in a similar fashion. With wine tasting, our sharing of experience through a common culture of wine enables a degree of calibration of perceptual representations to occur. In particular, we develop a language for sensory terms—a way to encode and share our representations. The language we use for describing wine is intrinsic to not only sharing those ideas, but also to forming them in the first place. By possessing an extended vocabulary for taste, smell and flavour sensations, we are able to approach wine tasting in a structured fashion, and in a way that generates a detailed verbal description of the wine being analysed. It follows that the nature of this vocabulary will shape the description of the experience, and even the experience itself.

References

Bartoshuk LM 2000 Comparing sensory experiences across individuals: recent psychophysical advances illuminate genetic variation in taste perception. Chem Senses. 2000 25:447-60

Brochet F 2001 Chemical object representation in the field of Consciousness. Dissertation for Grand prix of the Académie Amorim. http://www.academie-amorim.com/us/laureat_2001/brochet.pdf

Brochet F, & Dubourdieu D 2001 Wine descriptive language supports cognitive specificity of chemical senses. Brain Lang 77:187-96.

Castriota-Scanderbeg A, Hagberg GE, Cerasa A, Committeri G, Galati G, Patria F, Pitzalis S, Caltagirone C, Frackowiak R 2005 The appreciation of wine by sommeliers: a functional magnetic resonance study of sensory integration. Neuroimage 25:570-8

Duffy VB, Peterson JM, Bartoshuk LM 2004 Associations between taste genetics, oral sensation and alcohol intake. Physiol Behav 82(2-3):435-45

Lucchina LA, Curtis OF 5th, Putnam P, Drewnowski A, Prutkin JM, Bartoshuk LM 1998 Psychophysical measurement of 6-n-propylthiouracil (PROP) taste perception. Ann N Y Acad Sci 855:816-9

McClure SM, Li J, Tomlin D, Cypert KS, Montague LM, Montague PR 2004 Neural correlates of behavioral preference for culturally familiar drinks. Neuron 44(2):379-87

Morrot G, Brochet F, Dubourdieu D 2001 The color of odors. Brain Lang 79(2):309-20

The Pepsi challenge and what it tells us about wine tasting

Read Montague, a neuroscientist at Baylor College of Medicine in Texas, devised a fascinating experiment (McClure *et al* 2004) that has implications for wine tasting. It stemmed from a series of TV commercials in the 1970s and 80s where individuals were subjected to the 'Pepsi challenge'. In this test Pepsi was pitted against Coke blind, with subjects not knowing which was which. They invariably preferred the taste of Pepsi, but this wasn't reflected in their buying decisions. Montague wanted to know why.

So he re-enacted the Pepsi challenge with volunteers. The difference was that this time their brain activity was being scanned by an MRI machine. On average, Pepsi produced a stronger response in the ventral putamen, a region thought to process reward. In people who preferred Pepsi, the putamen was five times as active when they drunk Pepsi than it was in Coke-preferring subjects drinking Coke.

In a clever twist, Montague repeated the experiments, this time telling subjects what they were drinking. Remarkably, most of them now preferred Coke. The brain activity also changed, with activity in the medial prefrontal cortex, a region that shapes high-level cognitive powers. The subjects were allowing what they knew about Coke—its brand image—to shape their preferences. Remarkable.

The implications for wine tasting are clear. When we don't taste blind, our preferences are liable to be shaped by pre-existing information we have about the wine. Try as hard as we might to be objective, this isn't possible. What we know about wine will mould how we perceive the wine, and will even shape how much we enjoy a particular bottle. This brings another fascinating level of complexity to wine tasting.

NOTES:

1   Chemical Object Representation in the Field of Consciousness Frédéric Brochet
     2001 grand prix of the Académie Amorim
     http://www.academie-amorim.com/us/laureat_2001/brochet.pdf

chapter five

THE POWER OF TASTES RECONCILING SCIENCE AND SUBJECTIVITY

Ophelia Deroy

She uncorked it and put it to her lips. "I know something interesting is sure to happen" she said to herself, "whenever I eat or drink anything, so I'll just see what this bottle does".

(Lewis Carroll, *Alice in Wonderland*, Chapter IV)

However complicated and puzzling philosophers may appear when talking about wines, they don't depart that much from ordinary people: both feel concerned by the same range of issues, raising questions and doubts about the way we come to perceive and characterize wine, the reliability of our evaluations and the relative importance of the art of tasting. Am I objective when I say that this wine tastes like ripe pineapple, or do I just indulge in association of memories, condemned to remain purely personal? Do I try to find rare tastes or fine adjectives to conform to a social ritual, in an arbitrary and perhaps pretentious way? But, even if socially codified, do these practices and ways of talking about wine transform the experience we have of it? And what about so-called experts and other impressive connoisseurs that influence our judgments—and purchases—by convincing us to take their opinions as a reference point?

These questions are raised by philosophers as much as between friends or colleagues at the end of a dinner party. The philosophers' answers will probably differ on the kinds of arguments they accept and the kinds of conclusions they expect to reach. Yet both groups, when questioning the way we perceive, appreciate, and come to know wine, take for granted what there is to perceive, appreciate and come to know—i.e. an alcoholic beverage obtained from fermented grapes. This idea might be complemented by additional knowledge and information, gathered sometimes by chance, sometimes through the itinerary of the amateur, from vineyards, salons or brief talks with professionals. Cellarmen, talkative wine-makers or passionate friends may all be eager to share their knowledge. Thus one comes to know that differences in wine are explained by differences of grapes or that fermentation, even if it is a "natural" process, occurring sometimes without external intervention, requires controlled conditions, great care and expert assistance to produce a drinkable wine that satisfies appellation standards. In the end, without expecting too much, we can attribute to anyone with a minimum knowledge about wine the default opinion that wines taste as they do because of their composition; or more precisely, because of their chemical composition.

The wine connoisseurs' knowledge appears to be a refinement of this—the ability to name various grape varieties and identify different primary aromas, distinct from secondary and tertiary ones added by vinification and *élevage*. Mourvèdre, Carignan, Barbera or Zinfandel contribute differently to a wine's taste: one of the numerous interests about wine is to appreciate these differences, to be able to identify specific characters and discover more of them. What it means to make progress in our wine tasting, and what it is to know the difference made by makers, labels, vintages or Parker points, are subjects worthy of inquiry but not ones I wish to discuss here. Instead of observing the way wine knowledge develops, I am interested in the basic assumptions on which most of its development relies—namely, that everything is explained by the chemical composition of wine.

What do we really mean by saying that taste is in the wine? Is it located in it? Does it then impress us? Whether we simply receive it or react to it in a specific way makes a huge difference to what tasting reveals. And if taste is a property of a wine's chemical composition, why should it be distinguished from it? However, if taste occurs in us, as it seems, shouldn't it be located in us, and treated as a property of us? How can taste be really shared then? Perhaps taste lies somewhere in between a wine's chemical properties and the taster? But what strange sort of property could it be? Are there laws of taste than account for the way this or that wine tastes to anyone in every possible circumstance?

The problem here reminds us of the long philosophical quarrel about the secondary qualities, i.e. colours, smells, tastes, feelings of cold and hot, famously distinguished by John Locke from the primary qualities of shape, extension and solidity. The latter characterize physical reality, independent of us, and the corresponding ideas are thus considered to be objective and the proper domain of science, whereas the former are linked to our subjective impressions, and correspond only to the powers things have relative to us. They are secondary for they depend on the way we react to things that are there first.[1]

This distinction, all the more fundamental since modern science is built on its assumption, raises important questions about our knowledge, and challenges our opinion about the objectivity of taste.[2] But it also concerns the proper object of our tasting: what is there in the wine that corresponds to, or causes, our tasting experience? Is there a way to decide whether wines really have the distinctive properties that they appear to us to have? And what sort of properties are they?

These are important issues for discussion, and quite new ones, given that smells and tastes have been noticeably despised by philosophers and aesthetes. A better understanding of their complexity has much to teach us about sensory qualities. But first, I would like to see why these questions can be raised specifically in relation to wine.

CULTIVATING TASTE WITHOUT SCIENCE

> Wine is regarded by the French nation as a private good, as its 360 kinds of cheese. It is a totem-beverage, analogous to the milk of the Dutch cow or to the tea ceremoniously absorbed by the English Royal Family. (Roland Barthes, *Mythologies*, 1957)

Although we know that taste is a chemical sense,[3] or are aware that the wines we now enjoy owe much to chemistry (so that we fortunately drink wines very different from those consumed in classical times, by monks in the Middle Ages or by eighteenth-century aristocrats), science has almost no role in *our* tasting. We care not at all that the slight mushroom aroma of the Vosne-Romanée Méo-Camuzet 1994 we drink may be due to the presence of 1-octen-3-ol and its cherry taste to benzalde-hyde. Actually, the question that is worth posing about wine and science would rather be: why do wine amateurs show so little interest in chem-istry?

Our practices may be so conservative and traditional that we prefer to ignore the more modern aspects of wine-making. Are we so self-deluded to suppose images of *terroir* and oak barrels are more picturesque than those of chromatographic analysis and aluminium tanks? The former are clearly more popular with the public and are exploited by wine advertising, but they also enjoy a cult-like devotion among wine aficionados. Choosing wine instead of garish cocktails gives us the feeling that we are participating in a deeply-rooted culture, instead of running after a febrile and hyped modernity. But there is a kind of conflict here. If wine is such a natural product, then it doesn't need science or improvement. But if it is so natural, then it should also obey scientific laws, and be less richly surprising.

Contradictions and tensions in our images of wine may be the sign that there is something going on that has to do with the mythology or "totem" worshipping Roland Barthes pointed out in French culture. But there may be more to it than that. Our ignorance and putting aside of wine's technical aspects is acceptable provided we do not need chemical analysis[4] to enjoy drinking: what we taste and enjoy are indeed flavours, smells and aromas, not molecules. And not only does it seem irrelevant to our pleasure, it also seems to conflict with it. Chemistry breaks the charm of surprises in tasting, reducing it to the causal mechanism of shapes of molecules and sensitivity of receptors. Who could bearably substitute for the stream of epithets and metaphors, so delightful and specific to our half-poetical drinking moods, the barbarian names of molecules, all in -yde and -ol endings?

Chemical knowledge is not needed to taste wine and is not even of the first importance to make or "grow" it, as Paul Draper nicely puts it, by an analogy with the education of children (see his chapter in this volume). What is needed is mainly patience and care, and scientific expertise seems quite external to the matter. It is required only as a check or when problems occur. Chemists, as much as educational specialists, are not supposed to tell people what to do but to help them to perform what they are trying to do. Chemists can confirm that the alcohol by volume of a wine is less than sixteen per cent, that no dangerous bacteria are developing and they may, at best, suggest hypothetical solutions to solve problems noticed by tasting or previous analysis. They cannot substitute for the art of winemakers, which remains irreplaceable in at least two respects. First, there is the art of appreciating, by which the ripeness of fruits, the tastes of fermentation, the way the young wine develops and other relevant qualities are estimated and on which processes are finally decided. Secondly, there is the ability to form an idea of the future of the vintage, of the kind of wine it could be, where this influences selection, assemblage and growing choices.

Chemists can neither substitute for the inexhaustibly surprising wealth of *terroirs*, soils and climates—otherwise fine wine would already be being produced in laboratories and wine flavours obtained by synthesis. Thus, when Château Rieussec, a Sauternes, is poured into your glass and smells of ripe pineapple and honey, it is not because it happens to contain some ethyl butyrate and phenylethylic alcohols; it contains ethyl butyrate and phenylethylic alcohols because they have smells of pineapple and honey, and the wine-maker has cultivated them. A proper account of wine could not do without the subjectively perceptible qualities, which science and positivism ignore and elsewhere try to eliminate. Chemical indicators are taken into account afterwards and only as a confirmation or negative assessment. In France public health bodies and the Appellation Commission[5] exist to check the absence of any undesirable elements or the minimal agreement with a range of criteria (being less than 16% alcohol by volume, for instance) but they have nothing to say about the positive qualities of the wine, such as the qualities of taste or balance. In professional tasting sessions and competitions, chemical analysis plays only a secondary role, being used to confirm expert's judgments. No chemical diagnosis can decide in itself the quality of a wine. Wine thus comes with serious ambitions—putting our pleasure before science, and trying to submit the laws of chemistry to the edicts of our sensitivity.

Rating the art so high above the science thus does not rely only on a romantic or picturesque idea of wine growing, however pleasant and central this idea may be. For instance, a wine cannot be modified too many times without acquiring a recognisable taste that suggests it has been over-worked. For this reason, some laws forbid the selling as "wine" of a beverage that has been worked on more than three times. Inscribed then in our definition of wine, related to its essence and part of our experience of it, is the fact that it results not only from technology and synthesis, but also remains a natural product. We appreciate the matter, not just the form or style of making.

BLENDING SCIENCE AND WINE
At this point, it is important to distinguish between two things: on the one hand, the fact of knowing chemistry, which seems quite irrelevant to having a proper experience of wine, and, on the other hand, the facts described by this knowledge, which may be less easy to ignore in the determination of this experience. I can live without knowing how blood circulates and without being aware of the way the immune system works, but I cannot live without my blood circulating and my immune system working properly. I can enjoy wine without being aware of wine chemistry, or even chemistry in general, but this does not mean that chemical molecules do not play any role in my experience.

Which science?
By "the science of wine", we do not mean the knowledge possessed by sommeliers and expert tasters, who aim at deference toward the wine, but rather that of laboratory scientists whose analysis involves treating wine roughly, both in the handling and in their reductionist account of it.

A scientific account of wine has it as a liquid composed of molecules, and molecules are no more sweet or perfumed than they are white or red. They are characterized by their shape and structure, analysed in terms of forces exercised between atoms and sub-particles. The microparticles combine in the wine and then combine with the sense receptors to cause the taste we experience. The proper task of chemical analysis is to separate and classify molecules, and this can now be performed minutely for wine. The history and progress of oenological science is a fascinating topic, running from Pasteur's experiments in the 1850s to Emile Peynaud's works on malolactic fermentation in the 1950s, and going on with the latest research in departments of the most prestigious universities.[6] The content of a glass is not only the result of the history of the land, but also of the history of science and technology.

The study of the sensory and cognitive mechanisms involved in taste and olfaction also undergo constant change and leads to astonishing progress. It reveals how wrong we were to conceive these senses as more primitive than sight or hearing. Wine constitutes an exceptional field to explore. The experience it gives is incredibly rich, integrating smells and tastes into complex flavours. Moreover, it has always appeared worthy of discussion, over and above its purely nutritive aspect, so that it offers a fantastic repertoire of sensory reports and of linguistic resources we use to characterize smells and taste. Perhaps "no other food but wine has such an intimate relationship to language [...] It is the only product that *demands* people to comment on it".[7] Being so "spiritual", wine is a good subject for the sciences of mind.

What can we ask of science?

The fact that science evolves quickly in these areas, and still has much to explain about how wine tastes, should not be taken immediately as a sign of any weakness or limit in competence. It is true that it has limits: for instance, whereas having reached a causal account of the differences in the colour of red wines by mechanisms implying molecules called anthocyanins, present in grape skins, scientists still have difficulties in explaining differences of colour in white wines. The skins are not macerated and thus cannot contribute to colouration. (Anyway, as is known, white wine is not made just of white grapes.) It doesn't mean that there is no physical property that explains it but rather that this one is still unknown to science.[8] One may reasonably hope that in the near future, colours and hues of white wines will be related to physical properties of molecules or to the property of their composition. After all, it has taken time to discover that colours relate to surface reflectance. Colours of non-opaque liquids like wine constitute a special case and theories have only just recently enabled us to deal with the case of red wines. There is great confidence that the soft yellow hues of Chardonnay and Sauvignon wines will be explained in turn.

Is what we say about hues the same for everything else? Does this raise hopes that for any term used to describe wine, we can assume that there is a physical correlate that science will be able to account for in its turn? Not at all. Scientific accounts are legitimate and illuminating, but it doesn't mean that we will ask them to explain everything. We have to be clear which properties we are talking about and how we identify them, before we look for their true nature and turn to them in our scientific hypotheses about wine.

First, our descriptions of wines are sometimes erroneous, misplaced or metaphorical, as Adrienne Lehrer points out (chapter six). Some odours or characteristics are purely imaginary or verbal, and nothing real can be expected to correspond to them in wine. For instance, science will not look for, nor find, some objective property of "feminine" wines. There is no way to believe, in an Aristotelian scientific fashion, that they would have "more wet" or "more fragile" links. A philosophical lesson can be drawn here: it is dangerous to draw an inference from an occurrence of a word, or predicate, to the existence of a property. This reminds us that the world is not merely a reflection of what we say about it. Thinking that the wine gets to be what I say or think it is would be as great a miracle as its turning it into blood just by claiming it is blood.

Secondly, we also use subjective terms, for which it seems difficult to find an objective correlate. This may be said of evaluative terms, as when we claim that "this Volnay Les Santenots 2001 is delicious", "The Charmes-Chambertin 1998 is better than the 1997" or that "Gruaud Larosse suits red meat very well". It is difficult to assume an objective property of "being good" that would be a common characteristic present in every chemical structure of these fine wines, let alone a characteristic that could be measured and quantified so as to provide the objective truth of comparisons such as "be better than", or that would allow refinements, as in "being good with red meat". Could there be a chemical characteristic correlated with "being good" and another one with "being good with red meat"? Would it be the same as "being good with cheese"? This does not mean that our evaluations do not refer to objective characteristics of the wines but that, if they do, these cannot be accounted for in terms of basic chemical analysis. They deserve a distinctive and careful examination,[9] as do many words we use about wine such as "clean" or "sharp".

We all agree that we do not expect science to explain straightforwardly our evaluative practices. Yet, in the case of wine as in many others subjects, it is quite hard to say when the evaluative stops and when the purely descriptive starts. We often use half-descriptive, half-evaluative terms for which we both expect and yet cannot easily find objective correlates. What counts, objectively, as "overripe" or "too young"? There is, it may be argued, an objective quality (ripeness, or age) for which there exists a precise account in terms of chemical compounds, and this one is qualified by an evaluative term. What is problematic here then is not the existence of an objective phenomenon, for instance, the increase of sugars in ripe grapes, but the subjective distinctions introduced over and above these when deciding on qualitative differences. The fact that our personal evaluations of ripeness differ does not entail that there is no real phenomenon they refer to. They target the same thing, albeit in different ways.

Doesn't all this leave too little room for scientific expertise? Not at all, considering that smells and tastes, the most important characteristics of wine, remain fair objects of inquiry. Being qualities does not prevent them from being quantitatively or scientifically assessed. Yet oenological science has a lot to do here, in combination with philosophy, to provide a finely grained approach to qualitative aspects of experience. This extends to more specific features of wine, which are treated as objective and descriptive: this is the case of basic ones such as "long" or "balanced", or, more controversially, ones such as being "closed". Different questions may therefore be addressed by science: is there any systematic and reliable correlation between our most objective judgments about wine and a quantifiable compound in the wine? How are the differences in perception to be explained: by elements in wine, or by the individuality of tasters?

WHAT CAN BE OBJECTIVELY RETRIEVED FROM OUR IMPRESSIONS?

Some examples may help us to get a better grasp on what is going on when a predicate is said to capture an objective feature of the wine. It relates something that occurs in us to something in the wine, but not necessarily in a simple or crude way, as if a definite state of the wine, or its chemical profile as captured by scientific analysis, was solely responsible for our experience.

What a "closed" wine may be

The term "closed" is perhaps one of the most puzzling ones we use about wine: it takes time to understand what it means and even more time before daring to use it. It seems (at least to me) a sort of prophetic judgment, reserved to sibylline viewers of wine, to be able to know (or guess) that "there is something here that isn't here yet". This is also the kind of adjective which it seems easy to mock. It is more polite to our hosts to say of a renowned wine that it is closed instead of disappointingly flat. People kindly engage in such prophecies: "Things will be better tomorrow", "Oh, I am sure that your daughter will be pretty when she grows up". In these cases, we do not simply say something about the way things actually are, but we claim to sense now how they will or could be in the future. Many will agree that we overstep the boundaries of prudence here and go beyond what we can legitimately claim to know. This could be Humean lesson about our tendency to predict things we cannot really know.

In fact (and Hume wouldn't disagree here), even if our use of the adjective "closed" is a case of such a tendency, it does not condemn it. We gamble on everything, everyday, so why not wines? When people fill their cellar with five or six cases of a 2002 Bordeaux, after tasting it and considering it to be closed or very promising, are they not gambling on what it will be like in ten years' time? Wine is often associated, in popular imagery or arts, with gambling houses and games. Latour or Cézanne's card players would not look credible without a bottle of wine on the table. There may be something deliciously adventurous in thinking that when we taste a wine that seems closed today, we take a chance on it improving further, and gamble on when it is time is to open it. We enjoy the risk.

However there may be a need to enter into apology, or into the vindication of drinking as an aesthetic of life. We do not bet on wines, at least not as such, and our purchases, as much as the use of predicates for describing the future of wines, are underwritten by objective facts. This suggests that there could be an objective correlate when someone truly judges a wine to be closed.

Imagine, for the sake of the argument, that Jane and Paul taste a 2002 Saint Emilion. They disagree on whether it is closed, in other words, they both agree that it is dull now but disagree on how it could evolve. Paul thinks that it will remain as dull as it is now. It is just flat and dull. There may be every reason to side with him: after all, what reasons are there for us to think that it will change, as Jane claims?

Despite a proverbial tolerance for the subjectivity of tasting, we tend to be unhappy about disagreement over a wine. We would rather give a plausible reason to someone when they say things about wine, and not just negative ones as given by Paul. After all, this could also help us to reject the pretentiousness of the term "closed", and to say something objective about wine.

We could thus start inquiring into each taster's reputation and experience, to see whether they are expert in the use of vocabulary. But, still for the sake of the argument, we could learn that Jane has tasted lots of Saint Emilion from many different vintages. We could thus believe that in her 2006 tasting she is able to compare the 2002 with another one, let's say a 1996. She might remember than the 1996 was better after seven years than after four, and she could project that idea onto the 2002. It is dull in 2006 but should have nicer aromas in 2009. She comes thus to look for signs or precursors of them, swirling her glass in an expert way. "Closed"—she says, and we may come to trust her.

But we should be prudent here about relying on reputations, memory and claimed expertise. First, and especially for wines, reputations may easily be dismissed as socially constructed and not that reliable.[10] Second, if we turn to the core objective skills and experience, olfactory and gustatory memory is shown to be highly complex and fragile, probably unable to warrant in itself such complex comparative judgments. To perform Jane's, we must assume that (1) she remembers the taste of the 1996 Saint Emilion, as it was in 2000 when she first tasted it, (2) that this memory was vivid enough in 2003 when she tasted it a second time and (3) is still the same one she remembers today when she tastes the 2002. This is a complex relational judgment, difficult to engage in. She has also to perform a broad comparative judgment, deciding among all the memories of wines her tasting evokes which one is really the closest to this 2002. Experiments[11] have shown that our comparisons about wine are highly unreliable: most people have difficulties in distinguishing not only between many vintages but between only three glasses, not even memorized but all present and available for tasting. Presented with three glasses of red wine, they cannot say whether they are all different, or the same wine poured in different glasses. (Try the experiment at home.)

Perhaps Jane has exceptional judging skills, and is gifted at taking careful notes and remembering. Experience of wines is complex, and developed in many ways. And remarkably, some people come to develop an amazing memory of wines, together with the art of comparing and ranking them.[12] But the problem with them, as with Jane, could be that they do not explicitly or consciously make the comparisons or judgments we reconstitute. When Jane says that the wine is closed, she does not make an inference or complicated, comparative judgment. She does not open her notebook: she just feels the wine to be closed and knows it the moment she says so.[13]

In the case of "closed", there is a common way to decide that also seems more objective and reliable. It does not assume exceptional skills, and does not require professional wine tasters (even if they often agree on which wine is closed and which is simply dull, with their agreement supporting the idea that there is something objective here). Nor is it a matter of blind tasting, usually chosen so as to eliminate questions of politeness and prestigious labels. Instead, it consists in violently shaking the glass of controversial wine (with the hand covering the top: wine stains) to see whether it gives off new, stronger smells. In doing so, the oxygenation is enhanced. On this basis, one decides whether the wine is closed or not. If this is what "opening" a wine is, then "closed" is more accurately defined as "not having a sufficient reduction-oxygenation balance". Yet, science shows that wine maturation consists mainly in reduction processes, whereas the role played by oxygen is still controversial (see the cork versus caps issue). There is thus some objective correlate to judgments about closed wines that science helps to establish. This also suggests that Jane can taste a real difference between this closed wine and another one to which Paul may be insensitive. "Closed" judgments detect something about wine; yet they don't close questions. Speaking of closed wines in that sense, we may actually consider that the wine is promising, siding therefore with the champions of cork who consider that oxygen plays a role in the ageing of fine wines. Or we may be simply critical that the making has not managed to get a good redox potential. Taken as a prophecy, our judgments about the closed wines are somewhat ambivalent.

"First notes, second notes": does the order of our tasting reveal something about wine?

Another example may help us weigh up the advantages of a scientific approach. Science teaches us that aromas and smells are correlated to structural, spatial properties of molecules within wine and in sensory receptors. But our experience of wine does not juxtapose tasting spots, but results in a kind of musical line, characterized by a harmonious succession of aromas and flavours, each with its own way of developing, lasting and fading.

This is particularly true in smelling wine and less for smelling in general, where differences in intensities are interpreted (as it may be the case for sounds) as differences in spatial localisation and distances. I may be guided by the growing intensity of a bread smell to the bakery. When I smell a glass of Pinot Gris, the difference in intensity between notes of faint lime, pine and rose petals is not interpreted as signs of their being more or less distant. The glass remains obviously at the same distance from the nose. The image of a wine given by its smell is rather bi-dimensional and dynamic, something more like drawing a curve, than a three-dimensional picture—even if the latter may correspond to some of our experiences of perfumes or to animal orientation by olfaction.

A wine amateur speaks about "first" and "second" notes in smells, or "attack" and "finish" in taste, but is this translation in successive terms objective? Does it correspond to some genuine successive phenomena in wine or is it only the correlate of the way our perception proceeds?

This problem may seem specific to smells. When I hear noises or sounds, my sense of hearing enables me to know whether they were contemporary or successive (as in polyphonies or symphonies). Conversely, I interpret two successive views taken of a building, for instance a front view and a side view, as being of coexisting parts of the same object. Naturally, I correlate the successive order of images with the limitation or conditions of my perspective. For both hearing and viewing, we seem to possess an immediate non-problematic interpretation of whether the temporal order of our sensations has an objective correlate in the world.[14]

Going back to smells, it thus seems legitimate to ask whether the successive order of smells that makes them as easily describable as musical lines, is actually a reliable source of information about an objective ordering of phenomena. As in previous examples, what is questioned is not the fact that I smell (or hear, or see) X and then Y, but whether the object of my perception is really "X, then Y" or rather "X+Y", which I cannot grasp simultaneously. After all, the notes of lime and rose that I smell, if they correlate with spatial properties of the molecules in wine, all coexist in the wine. (Especially as it is reasonable to consider that no new molecules appear in the wine when I turn the glass.) This Alsace wine has flavours of lime, rose petals and flavours of pine that I come to appreciate successively. Thus our speaking about "first" and "second" notes would be simply a matter of our access to wines.

But a further inquiry into the chemistry of wine may change our conclusions: the differences of time are explained by scientists in terms of volatility. First smells correspond to the more volatile molecules, which, once dissipated, may let the less volatile ones (the second smells) express themselves. So the frequent first smell of alcohol, sometimes very strong in high degree, powerful wines from the Languedoc, South Africa or Chile, invite patience. The subtler, fruity smells are to come. A molecule is all the more volatile when its temperature for evaporating, or getting in a gaseous state, is low, and these differences in volatility are mainly explained by atomic weight. The ordering of smells has thus a kind of objectivity, and getting smells of lime before the pine ones is the sign of a more expert nose, closer to the real properties of the wine.

What "acidic" and "balanced" wines may be

One may start to understand the difficulties we have in correlating the usual predicates with objective properties. When people say that a wine is closed, or firm, it is difficult to know what they refer to, even when they use the same words as the scientist. To say for instance that a wine is acidic, may not mean that the absolute pH balance in the wine is higher than normal (i.e. 7) but may refer instead to its manifest acids. The pH acidity will not capture the acidity that is tasted. We could think that we have to find another way to measure the latter. Yet this supposes knowledge of the individuality of a taster, which is highly complex.

A supplementary difficulty is that perceptual judgments, being complex, are also relational: how acidic or tannic a wine is depends on how much alcohol it contains, and how high the quantities of the other elements are. We judge a wine to be less tannic if it has high alcohol and high acidity; the same wine appears more tannic when cooler, and more acidic at higher temperature; it tastes surprisingly different depending on what we eat: compare tasting a Sauternes with a Roquefort against, say, a crème brûlée. This makes it very difficult to get a unique stable experience of a wine.

One has to be careful here. The fact that our judgments are relative does not conflict with their having objective correlates. They may rely on intrinsic properties that constitute firm features of reality, as previously seen, but not necessarily some definite state, or exactly the same ones that are accessed by chemical analysis. The problem is even more complicated when dealing with properties of wine that are, in themselves, relational. By relational properties we mean (by contrast with simpler properties or "qualities") a property whose definition implies the existence of a relation and mentions the different things it relates. In wine, properties like balance are obviously like this: it amounts to a relation between acidity, sweetness and alcohol in the wine. These elements may be separately measured and assessed, but there is no unique chemical profile to say at what relative point or strengths of acid, tannin, alcohol, a wine reaches balance. This is not a linear phenomenon, and thus cannot be predicted or looked for uniquely by chemical analysis.

These three cases show how careful one must be in tracing the correlation between common predicates and chemical properties. They also suggest what role science can play within our practices of tasting. It need not challenge them, but offers a way to filter and classify them.

What about flavours?

Are things simpler when we turn to tastes and smells? We know that these are correlated with the structural properties of molecules,[15] but how, and in what sense? Philosophy and the cognitive sciences have for long addressed such questions about our experience of colours. Yet even if colours can be accounted for in relation to—to put it crudely—surface reflectance,[16] the debate continues. Are colours properties of objects or of our sensations? Do objects really have them, or are they relative to us? If they are no more than surface reflectances, how do we explain that the same red colour is caused by different types of reflectance? Why should some kind of reflectance, such as the one responsible for red, be felt closer to the ones correlated with orange than with blue? After all, they are all different. And why does the same object appear in different colours in different circumstances?

All the questions about colours must also be addressed about smells and taste. But they must be adapted, in two different respects: first, it is scientifically necessary to modify them as smells and taste do not exactly match the optical phenomena; and secondly, it is philosophically essential to question the domination of colour perception in accounts of perceptual or secondary qualities. Debates focused on colours have been used to decide the status of all kinds of secondary qualities, perhaps as an effect of the early development of optics, or perhaps because of the privileging of visual information. Nevertheless, we can and should also account for the rich experience smell and taste give us, no matter how complicated they are. Indeed, as Aristotle warned us:

> It is less easy to give a definition concerning the sense of smell… for it isn't clear what sort of quality odour is, in the way that was clear what sort of quality sound or colour was. (Aristotle, *De Anima*, 421 a 7-11)

Since Aristotle, a strong scientific interpretation has been given to odours or tastes. Basically, it could be summarized by the phrase: "to each molecular structure its odour, to each odour its molecular structure". This statement is actually a "two in one" thesis, each part of which raises difficulties.

Let us consider the first part of the thesis. "To each molecular structure its odour" is contradicted by the fact that some molecules are odourless, although they cannot be shapeless. Having a shape is a necessary but not sufficient condition for being odorant: the molecule has also to be volatile enough and not to weigh more than 300 Daltons. Each odour is indeed correlated with numerous properties of matter and cannot be simply eliminated and replaced by the mention of a single chemical aspect, like spatial arrangement. This makes the scientific analysis all the more complex, and all the more modest in its ability to offer a clear, firm and definite basis for telling what is really going on in wine.

This is just an actual limit and the physicist could trust in further progress to provide answers. But what it more seriously attacks is a certain way of doing or conceiving of physics, that we could call the "mechanicist" view. According to this perspective, all properties are reducible to shapes and arrangements of molecules. This may be an attractive view: shape is a structural or categorical property that remains constant through time, and can be measured once and for all. When a general change is observed, it must be reduced to changes of composition or chaining between basic particles whose shapes remains constant.

But weight and volatility vary: variation may be subtle but they vary nonetheless. They depend on conditions. Temperature, for instance, greatly influences the taste wine has, without necessarily changing its molecular constitution.[17] We experience different flavours, or the same flavours in different ways, when Pouilly-Fuissé is fiercely chilled or cool. The changing smells cannot just be attributed to us, nor eliminated and explained by unchanging definite states of matter. They cannot be measured once and for all.

Yet, this is not the only point against the mechanistic slogan: the second part of the thesis, "to each odour its molecular structure" also needs to be qualified. The smell of vanilla, for instance, may be realised in different ways, i.e. obtained via different molecules: either by vanilline, or ethyl vanillate, or vanillic acid.[18] It is a case of what philosophers call multiple realisability: the possibility of the same property being implemented or realised in different structures. This is more common than the technical definition suggests: we "multiply realise" all the time. Playing chess, for example, may be realised in different ways: on a 3D chessboard, mentally, or on a piece of paper, or a screen. The way the play is realised does not change the game itself. It is always playing chess. In the same way, the way an odour is realised does not make it a different odour, it does not change it.

Let us go back to the case of vanilla. Pure vanilline is the molecule present in vanilla pods, and develops also in wood—noticeably oak. Yet it is not really the one responsible for the tertiary vanilla aromas you can appreciate in some wines, especially in Rioja or certain Californian wines. The molecule present in wood cannot easily be present, as such, in wine for it reacts with it and results in vanillate ethyl. It is this second molecule, of a different shape, that seems mainly responsible for the smell of vanilla in wines.

One may then say that this is a problem for theoretical chemistry, not for wine tasting and wine chemistry. From the presence of the vanilla smell one cannot in general safely infer the presence of a specific molecule. But one can in the case of wine: it is ethyl vanillate. The identity thesis between smells and molecular arrangement seems still valid within the enclosed, protected domain of wines. This suggests how careful we have to be when, by developing specialized sciences, and narrowing the object of our inquiries, we actually look at some principles or theses that are not true of nature as a whole.

Anyway things are not so simple: vanillic acid also smells of vanilla. More importantly, it can be present in wines. This acid may even occur naturally in wines made in aluminium tanks as it develops from the wooden fibre present in grape stalks. Thus a vanilla smell is not necessarily the sign of a wood *élevage*, and the claim "it smells of vanilla, thus it has spent time in oak" is often—but not always true.

One may start to understand why this all matters to our judgments about wine, and to appreciate the other consequences that follow from it. First, we are able to acknowledge that the vanilla smell is something different from the smell present in vanilla. The smell of vanilla pod is a specific instance of a vanilla-smell. It is just more important because the name of the plant has been adopted as a generic term. This happens with many technical devices where a specific brand name is taken for a generic. Wine may thus have a real vanilla smell, without having to contain the molecules present in vanilla. Smells and flavour are named after substances, but are not absolutely attached to them in a "one to one" correlation. This paradoxically makes our recognition of smells in wine less metaphorical or imaginative than people have supposed. It is a supposition with which I disagree, hopefully, with good reasons. I may detect a vanilla odour in a wine, but this should not be mistaken for getting at something that is equally present in vanilla itself. This is not what I propose when saying "it smells of vanilla". Finding "vanilla smells" or "rose petals smells" is not a matter of being pretentious.

Another consequence follows: if there were a strict cause and effect correlation between smells and the structures of molecules, I could, as a taster, always infer from the presence of a smell to the presence of a molecule. I could track its origin or trace the history of its presence. As a wine-maker, I could make wine by selecting a kind of molecule and be sure of obtaining the corresponding smell. I could be certain to eliminate any vanilla smell by choosing not to mature in oak. But as we have seen it is not so simple.

Some further factors tell against what we may call this reductionist perspective. Take the effects of alcohol on taste. You taste a 1997 Chateâuneuf du Pape and find it has wonderful tannins and a nice raspberry flavour. If it was distilled, and you had to taste the residue that contains the odorant and tasting elements, you will find it disgusting and will not recognise raspberry at all. The part of the experience we get by our discriminative tasting and attention may not correspond to the parts obtained by chemical decomposition. Nothing says that what is possible for us to distinguish through perception and attention necessarily exists in actual separate states.

RAISON D'ÊTRE OF OUR TASTING PRACTICES

However troubling the factors just dealt with may be for a reduction of smells to molecular structure, they help in justifying our tasting practices. Thus, it is normal that we are so often surprised by the taste of wine from one moment to the next. At other times we will experience different sensations and another bouquet. It makes our experience a legitimate source of discussion and sharing. As a conclusion, I would like to suggest how the previous inquiry into the scientific aspects of wine and the objectivity of our judgments combines with the rich subjective aspects of our tasting.

BOUQUET AND EMERGENCE

As we have seen, tasting the residue separately from the alcohol has nothing to do with tasting both of them together. And appreciating a wine's balance is not like appreciating its distinct acidity, sweetness and bitterness. This suggests that appreciating a wine is global rather than analytic. What we smell or taste is not just the sum of distinct smells and atomic tastes, but their integrative transformation into a whole. Thus when we speak of a harmonious bouquet of flavours, we mean a continuous and integrated taste which can't be reduced to any juxtaposition or succession.

But how can we account for this character of a wine's taste, while agreeing on the relevance of a scientific account of distinctive smells? Probably by acknowledging another property, namely the "wine taste" that emerges from the different properties of wine, revealed either by chemical analysis or analytic tasting practices. We say something "emerges" here because it is an irreducibly new property of the whole beverage, over and above the properties of its components. Science can at times deal with emergent properties, and does so in the case of biological properties emerging from the physical ones.

This conclusion about wine may seem hazardous: it states an *a priori* limit to analytical methods of judging wine and challenges as much the compositional analysis in terms of molecules as the amateur analysis in terms of distinct smells of fruits and flowers, sweet and acid tastes and other discrete features. But this may be the wrong way to state the problem. What is challenged is not the local relevance of analysis but its ambition to exhaust the nature of what there is to a wine. This may be the ambition of scientism, yet it is not necessarily the one of science itself. It is certainly not the wine-lovers' desire either. By contrast, they do not want to have an exhaustive grasp of a wine's composition, nor wish to be sated by experimenting on a single sample.

A related point, that gives reason to our coming back again and again to a wine we like, is that we do not experiment on states of wine but on its dynamics. Wine is a highly evolutionary substance that changes throughout its life: in the fermentation tanks, in the oak barrels in which it takes on tertiary aromas, in bottles while kept in dark cellars, and when oxygenated and poured in a glass, wine keeps on changing. Tasting, by contrast with "having a drink", is a question of taking time and attending to what wine is doing at a certain moment, not what wine it is, what qualities it could possess, whose wine it is. I guess that many people would be more comfortable with the wine lexicon, if they realised that what the words track are evolutions, changes, directions and possibilities. As Alice would say, we look for "what this wine is doing", rather than what it is. Wines, no more than people, have definite characters[19] that we come to know about. This depends on the circumstances and their deeds.

Strangely, this is the point where scientific accounts and wine tasters share a common perspective against accounts provided by appellation commissions, commercial labellings and certain kinds of expertise. Some descriptions have to state what there is in the wine, some can state what it does. Contrary to what we think at first, the latter characterises a wine more objectively whereas the former give at most a partial grasp of it and lead to many clichés.

WINE POWERS AND NORMAL TASTES

There is an immediate problem in considering what wine does (its "powers") instead of its stable properties. The question will naturally be "it does what to whom?" There seems to be an indissoluble tension between the claim for objectivity and the characterisation of properties as powers. Powers require reference to an experimenter on whom the power acts, and thus may reintroduce the threat of subjectivity.

However, the apparent tension is overcome by referring to "normal" perceivers, i.e. to perceivers whose sensory apparatus works and is not damaged. Just as we do not take the colour-blind as guides to define the colours of things, or as guides to matching shirts and ties, we should not take as our guides tasters suffering from a cold or who have an acknowledged smelling disease (asnomia) to define wine tastes. Normally, a Bordeaux smells of red fruits and wood to tasters, even if they then disagree on its smelling of blackcurrant or raspberries. Sauternes taste sweet, and Chardonnay does not. These are the ways wines are normally perceived. Even individuals most sceptical about "wine tasting rituals" would agree on a certain range of indubitable distinctions, on certain objective smells and tastes certain wines really have.

Nonetheless, there may be a problem as normal flavour is defined by its being the one perceived by normal tasters. How, then, are "normal tasters" defined if not by their ability to perceive normal tastes? The circularity seems hazardous, as it would be awkward and unhelpful to state that "Burgundy tastes of red fruit to normal tasters" and "normal tasters are the ones to which Burgundy tastes of red fruits". This is not the kind of trivia we are interested in when we inquire into the nature of wine.

But is this apparent circularity that threatening? It seems a rather common characteristic of cultural practices that they don't really begin with a baptismal act, but arise from random or isolated acts that have succeeded in being transmitted, sometimes through transformation and improvement. They have been adopted, validated and modified through history. Our ideas of normal tastes and normal tasters are correlated. This means that they reinforced each other through subsequent experience and interactions, not that they rely on nothing at all. This is why normal taste may evolve. When Bordeaux winemakers decided to stress tertiary aromas, previously considered undesirable and too "woody", the idea of the "normal" taste of Bordeaux changed. Those who now count as normal tasters for Bordeaux wines become those with the ability to notice the new taste and secure the agreement of their peers.

Thus wine tasting is partly a cultural practice that has evolved through history. This does not make the taste of wine something constructed out of nothing—but something powerful enough to set in motion a rich practice, structured enough to allow for discussion and agreement.

The general criticism of circularity deserves further analysis and more points could be made, but it seems more important here to consider the specific challenge wine poses to the definition of normal perceivers and normal perceptual quality. Regarding colours, normal or official colours are the ones perceived by average people, whereas in the case of wine, its normal qualities are the ones perceived and described by experts. Isn't it paradoxical to consider that normal taste is actually experienced only by a (happy) few tasters? Why don't we say that normal taste is the most commonly experienced, and consider the expert's taste as a non-normal one, a sort of esoteric taste?

Again, there is only an apparent tension here. One can think of the normal taste of a wine as the way it would taste to anyone taking her time to taste it in the best conditions, such as the ones experts have. This is to say that the normal taste is not different from the most complete and purest taste of wine. There is nothing esoteric about it: all there is to taste is accessible. Yet it could not actually be accessed unless one is in certain conditions. These conditions are dictated by the wine itself, not arbitrary codified by culture.

An important lesson to be drawn is that the smells and tastes favoured in our descriptions, and considered as normal, are not exactly the most frequent ones. There may be no such thing for wines, given all the different conditions in which they are served and appreciated, and the variability of people's tasting apparatus. Normal tastes draw the limits of all that could be tasted.

The normal conditions may appear too difficult to realise and can seem rather abstract or ideal. The wine has to be tasted alone, before eating but not that far from a meal (for even appetite may change the saliva, and thus the taste), somewhere between room and cellar temperature. But, in fact, they consist in the most easily obtainable and repeatable conditions, and also in the ones that seem to enable one to appreciate the most important range of differences within the wine. Hot wines, as we know, do not express many different tastes, nor taste very different from one another. Thus it is a pity to warm a good Bordeaux; without mentioning the crime of adding sugar and cinnamon. Wine experts recommend tasting a wine in certain conditions in order to get more out of it.

PREDICTING AND BEING SURPRISED

There is another benefit in saying that wine has a "power to give rise to the experience of sweetness" rather than saying than "it is sweet". As previously mentioned, to have the power to do something to the perceiver means that the experience of sweetness will be had or not depending on whether the conditions are met. It also suggests that it may be revealed in different ways. Elasticity for instance is a power, or a disposition to be stretched: rubber is elastic whether or not it is stretched. And its elasticity may be manifested when it is lengthened and also when it contracts. There are many ways for the same rubber piece to be stretched or to contract. The fact that they never occur does not effect how elastic or not the piece of rubber is.

Applied to wine, the model can account for its potential tastes—we know that wine would taste different after a mouthful of chocolate mousse; we know that it could taste different to someone else. These tastes cannot always be enumerated. First, we do not know precisely what they are. How would this wine be with a foie gras, or if it was a bit warmer? I may have ideas about it, but if I am so eager to taste it with foie gras, and if I wait for the glass to get warmer I will have the precise experience in question. It would be a limitless task to list every different condition for tasting, yet this does not mean that wine flavours do not fall under a certain general descriptions.

FINE QUALITY AS THE POWER TO BRING ABOUT A CONSENSUS

Preferring powers of wine rather than states does not blur our image of wine. In a way, it is more compatible with our practices and with rigorous scientific methods. Of course, there are points where it may get more controversial. For instance, if so many things depend on conditions and "normal" tasters' profiles, it seems difficult to distinguish between fine and bad wines. Science does not, though we do, assess wine quality all the time. Our practices are not only about appreciating what a wine does—as with Alice—but how well it does it. When tasted in the best conditions, what make the taste of a grand cru better than a vin de table's taste?

The distinctions between particular dispositions provide a criterion to differentiate between fine and common wines. Indistinct smells and flavours are generally characteristic of bad wines. There is then something confused, and frustrating in the experience. Does this smell of orange or of grapefruit? Both perhaps, or none: we do not grasp what the really distinctive feature of this wine is, and cannot relate our different sensations to different features of it. The better the wine is, the more complex the experience of it will be; but also the more this complexity shows distinct directions, revealing different things are going on there. It seems then that the adjectives we use are imposed by the wine: the discrete features we acknowledge account for the sharply distinct things the wine shows. In tasting fine wines we often come to recognise flavours we wouldn't have thought a wine could have. Yet they reveal themselves to us in a striking and powerful way. I wouldn't have thought that a ripe pineapple smell was so distinct before being able to recognise it in Château Rieussec, and hearing people around me agreeing with my judgment. Wines are better if they do many things, in an expressive way.

This also explains why a fine wine will secure most agreement. If the wine is bad, it has few dispositions that are manifested in different ways, and our accounts of it are too conflicting and variable for us to learn much, except that, as we then say, this wine is confused. Ongoing disagreement and silent drinking are both signs that the wine is flat or bad.

CONCLUSION: STILL "CLOSED" CONSIDERATIONS OF WINE PROPERTIES

The domain of wines, smells and tastes is thus a promising field for a deeper inquiry into the nature of "secondary qualities". It could illuminate philosophical debates. In turn, these considerations give sense and clarity to our tasting practices, such as the ambivalent place granted to chemical analysis or the official taste promised by labels.

These considerations point to further inquires. First, it may be possible to obtain a more precise view of particular wine properties, such as those responsible for allergic reactions or those that cause headaches, facial flushing, etc. and for some of the ones that give rise to pleasure or disgust. Secondly, the scope could be expanded from the examination of this or that particular wine to consideration of the commonalities among kinds of wines, taking in questions about vintages, *terroirs*, appellations, etc. Having a better look at the dispositions of a particular wine, we may wonder what it shares with other wines of the same kind, and we may appreciate whether it is representative of the *terroir* or appellation. What is it in all of these wines that gives sense to the classifications and enables us to recognise them as Burgundies or Côtes du Rhônes? Is there any "real essence" corresponding to appellations, châteaux or vintages? Is there any better, or more natural, classification of wines, such as the New World classification by grape varietal, rather than the complicated and protected names of Burgundy and Bordeaux? What does objectively relate a 1998 Charmes-Chambertin to other Burgundy wines, more than to a Californian Pinot Noir?

All these perspectives, however general they may seem, may help us to understand what makes for the singularity of a given wine, and for the uniqueness of wine among other beverages.[20]

REFERENCES

Barthes, Roland, *Mythologies*, Paris: Seuil, 1957, transl. New York: Hill and Wang, 1972.

Brochet, Frédéric, "Tasting: chemical object representation in the field of consciousness",

http://www.academie-amorim.com/us/laureat_2001/brochet.pdf.

Casamayor, Pierre, and Moisseeff, Michaël, *Les arômes du vin*, Paris: Hachette, 2002.

Châtelain-Courtois, Martine, *Les mots du vin et de l'ivresse*, Paris: Belin, 1984.

Coutier, Martine « Tropes et termes: le vocabulaire de la dégustation du vin », *Meta*, 39/4, 1994, pp. 662-675.

Doty, Richard (ed.), *Handbook of Olfaction and Gustation*, 2nd edn, New York: Marcel Dekker, 2003.

Goode, Jamie, *Wine Science*, London : Mitchell Beazley, 2005.

Hacker, Peter Michael S., *Appearance and Reality: a Philosophical Investigation into Perception and Perceptual Qualities*, Oxford, New York: Blackwell, 1987.

Hinnewinkel, Jean-Claude, *Les terroirs viticoles, origines et devenirs, Bordeaux*: Féret ed. 2004.

Johnson, Hugh, *A Story of Wine*, London: Michael Beazley, 2004.

McGinn, Colin, *The Subjective View: Secondary Qualities and Indexical Thoughts, Oxford*: Oxford University Press, 1983.

Peynaud, Emile, and Blouin, Jacques (1996), *Le goût du vin*, 3rd edn, Paris: Dunod, 1996.

Shepherd, Gordon M., "Outline of a Theory of Olfactory Processing and its Relevance to Humans", *Chemical Senses*, 30, 2005, pp. i3–i5.

Turin, Luca, and Fumiko, Yoshii, *Structure–Odour Relationships: a Modern Perspective, in Doty* (ed.), pp. 275-94.

NOTES

1   This is ambivalent: "first" may mean "necessarily", for no experience of secondary qualities is possible in their absence, and "essentially", as they account for what the thing really is, whereas secondary qualities are accidental and may vary without the identity of the thing being lost. The Lockean distinction (*Essay Concerning Human Understanding*, especially vol. II, viii, 10) has given raise to numerous discussions and interpretations.

2   On these issues, see Barry Smith's chapter, this volume.

3   Smell and taste are chemical senses, meaning that they are reactive to molecular determinants (the exact nature of which is still debated). The linking or interaction of molecules and our sensors induces a complex chain of reactions, leading finally to their encoding and producing information in the relevant perceptive areas of the brain (the olfactory cortex but also the higher cortex). Complex models have of course been elaborated, but for our purposes a basic picture will suffice, as agreed by scientists and common sense. For a more detailed account of olfaction and taste, and a glimpse at competing interpretations, see Doty (2003) , Shepherd (2005) and about wine, see Goode ((2005) and this volume).

4   This is a distinct and more restrictive question than the one raised by Kent Bach about whether we need *any kind* of knowledge or even any *resort to language* to enjoy wine. Yet the two may be related.

5   The INAO (Institut National des Appellations d'Origine) formed in 1947 is the successor of the Comité National des Appellations d'Origine (CNAO) created in 1935. It states the standards for the famous AOC (Appelation d'Origine Contrôlée). The concept of AOC and the juridical assessment of the regional quality standards are not that recent: they were launched to protect the wines of Porto in the middle of the eighteenth century. For a more detailed account, see Hinnewinkel (2004).

6   On history of wine and its production, see Johnson (2004); on contemporary science of wine, see Goode (2005).

7   Châtelain-Courtois, 1984, p. 5. About the development of wine vocabulary, see also Coutier, 1994.

8   Actual investigations seem to expect explanations involving phenol or iron components, but no definite result has yet been reached, at least as far as I know.

9   On the objectivity of the notion of "fine wine", see Barry Smith's and Steve Charter's arguments in this volume.

10   On this point, see the rich account by Origgi, this volume.

11   See Brochet experiments (2001) and Goode (2005).

12   Is there a reliable method of developing olfactory, and, more specifically, wine memory? Obviously we try, by keeping labels, writing personal tasting notes, or remembering bottles that accompanied a particular meal. The question is worth asking, and its solution would be of interest both for scientists and amateurs eager to develop their skills.

13   Of course, she may proceed to unconscious inferences. There is an important issue here, to know what the judgment implies and on what it relies. However I think that one has to be careful with such charitable principles that give too much to tacit process and unformulated characterizations.

14   Things are a bit more complex however: I modulated my interpretation of two
      sounds heard simultaneously according to the distance of the supposed sources,
      and, as shown by the famous example of a moving train next to ours, passing from
      the order of my perception to the order of events relies on a complex set of hypothe-
      ses.

15   Given the difficulties raised by this theory, doubts about it have been expressed, but
      they remain marginal. See Turin and Yoshii (2003).

16   There is obviously a problem about the way these are to be interpreted: does it
      mean that tastes are purely identical to the structural properties of molecules, are
      nothing over and above them, and thus eliminable? Or does it mean that they may
      be "reduced" and explained in terms of these properties? The distinction could be
      refined, but there is no need to enter in such technicalities here.

17   Temperature of course plays a role in some molecular transformations, as in those
      occurring during fermentation and later in maturation. That's why cellar tempera-
      ture matters so much and explains how wines can be damaged by irregular or high
      temperatures.

18   See Casamayor and Moisseeff (2002) for a fascinating catalogue of aromas in wine,
      explaining their sources and characteristics and giving methods for recognizing
      them.

19   Despite what our vocabulary suggests: many wine words compare wine to people
      (they are strong, feminine, have tears, legs, etc.). But, as the idea of people having
      definite characters is challenged and qualified by current psychology, so should the
      idea about wines.

20   Thanks for very helpful comments and suggestions to Michael Dwyer, Barry C.
      Smith and Claudine Tiercelin, and thanks to Yann Lioux and Nicolas Potel for
      sharing with me their knowledge and enthusiasm about wine.

chapter six

CAN WINES BE BRAWNY?: REFLECTIONS ON WINE VOCABULARY

Adrienne Lehrer

Wine descriptions have been the topic of interest, investigation, and humour. Concerning the last, many people are familiar with James Thurber's cartoon of a group of people drinking wine, in which the host tells his guests, "It's just a naive domestic Burgundy without any breeding, but I think you'll be amused by its presumption." Such an attitude has led some to wonder whether wine descriptions, at least those that employ metaphorical language, really have any meaning at all.

The linguistic theory that lies behind the descriptive part of the vocabulary has two parts which are closely related: (1) the intra-linguistic component, which is how words (and other linguistic terms) are related to each other and (2) the application (reference, denotation) which is how linguistic terms connect to the world. Both parts are necessary for a semantic theory. And although the two are closely connected, neither can be completely reduced to the other. The intra-linguistic component I use is the theory of semantic fields, developed by Trier (1931) and Lyons (1977). An important part of the field theory is a set of lexical relationships. The ones most important for wine vocabulary are synonymy, antonymy, class inclusion (hyponymy), and various other types of association.

BASIC WINE WORDS
Basic wine words are those that can be directly applied to properties of the wine and include words for colour and appearance (which I will not

discuss), bouquet and aroma, taste and mouthfeel. In addition, there are words for the way in which these properties combine, for example, balance. Finally there are a large number of evaluative terms, some of which are not confined to wine descriptions. However, much of the wine vocabulary is value laden. A *light wine* is neutral or good, but a *thin wine* is bad, and a *watery wine* is even worse. In my experience and experiments, wine drinkers who like a wine will never use *thin* or *watery*, but those who dislike it might.

The pure taste words are quite simple and limited: *sweet, sour* and *bitter. Salty* is rarely used. Subtypes of *sour* include *tart, acidic, acetic,* and possibly *tangy,* which may also involve a feel as well. Related to *sweet* is its antonym *dry* and several hyponyms of *sweet: cloying* and *sugary.* As is obvious, *sour, bitter, acidic, acetic, cloying* and *sugary* are negative in evaluation, while the others are neutral or positive, depending on the norms for any particular wine and the drinker's personal preferences.

There are relatively few pure smell words, among them *scented* and *fragrant.* Almost all the other aroma words are based on a substance: blackberry, asparagus, tar, coffee, chocolate, etc. Since taste and smell are so intimately connected, the term *flavour* can be used to cover both. These flavour words are straightforward, however, and Ann Noble has listed and categorised them in her wine aroma wheel (Noble, 1987, 1990). Many have positive or negative connotations, also relevant to wine type and personal taste.

The most interesting words for a linguist are those relating to mouthfeel, which involves two general classes of words: 1) *body,* characterised most generally by the antonymous pair *full-bodied* and *light,* and 2) other tactile sensations like *hard* or *prickly.* The physical correlates of *body* are the dissolved solids and the alcoholic content of the wine. This aspect of wine description uses metaphors from the semantic field of size, shape, and weight. *Full-bodied* wines can be *heavy, big, fat, flabby, thick, solid* and *deep.* These words, in turn, have associations and yield terms such as *strong, sturdy, solid, powerful, forceful, beefy* and *robust.* On the *light* side we find *small, little, thin, weak* (all negative) *delicate,* and *fragile. Flat,* another dimension word, has two technical meanings: 1) the wine lacks sufficient acid and (2) a sparkling wine has lost its bubbles.

The antonymous pairs *smooth/soft* and *rough/hard* serve as general words for other tactile (mouthfeel) sensations. Pleasant-to-touch substances are used for smooth wines, such as *velvety* and *silky*, plus other positive associations like *soft*, *gentle* and *tender*. In the *rough/hard* category, in addition to *hard* and *rough*, we find *sharp*, *harsh*, *firm* and terms relating to astringency, such as *astringent*, *tannic* and *puckery*. Other than *firm*, these terms are negative.

The acids in a wine can produce a tactile sensation, and there are several positive words to describe this feeling, including *prickly*, *lively*, *zestful*, and *crisp*. *Acidic* can be placed in this category as well as in the taste category.

We have seen that some standard wine descriptors like *big*, *hard* and *smooth* can be understood by their conventional associations to descriptors that relate directly to perception and sensation. These associations allow people to understand more distantly related terms like *masculine* and *feminine*. Masculine wines are heavy, big, strong, and maybe harsh, while feminine wines are soft, light, perfumed, elegant and delicate.

Many wine words concern *age*. *Young* and *old* are not just wine descriptors, of course. Although any wine a few months old is young, and any wine made a century ago is old, generally these and related words are used in a context relevant to the type of wine and the norms for when a particular wine should be drunk. Many of the age words depend on natural growth, development and change, such as *green*, *unripe*, *ripe*, *mature* and *immature*. In addition, descriptors based on the human life cycle can also be used, especially for wines that are too old, as in *decrepit*, *senile*, *dying* and *dead*. However, wine drinkers judge age, not by how many years ago a wine was made or bottled, but by how it tastes, and this is an inference based on smoothness or roughness, ripeness, acid, and other properties that develop as the wine changes.

Other common wine terminology is closely connected with evaluation, for example, balance and complexity. *Balance* refers to the proportion of various components in a wine: sugar, acid, tannin, etc. Positive descriptors include *balanced*, *harmonious* and *round*. *Unbalanced* and *unharmonious* are negative, along with terms that specify particular faults (*flat*, *cloying*, *sour*). *Complexity* refers to a wine's various components and flavours. Complex wines, that is, those with several flavours that interact and emerge during the drinking process are highly valued; *simple* wines are not bad, but they are uninteresting to wine gourmets.

SOME NEW (AND OUTRAGEOUS) METAPHORS

The semantic field of personality terms has been imported into wine descriptions. Words I found in wine literature of the 1970s include *personality* and *character*, and more specific descriptors like *serious*, *disciplined*, *austere*, *severe*, *forward* and *assertive*. Some of the newer ones are *shy*, *sly*, *reserved*, *reticent*, *generous*, *mean*, *polite*, *bold*, *in-your-face*, *loud*, *brash*, *sassy*, *ostentatious* and *flamboyant*. Many of these personality terms can be grouped into two antonymous sets, which we can label as *generous* and *forward* vs. *polite* and *shy*. *Generous, forward* wines "give out their flavors freely" (Stevenson, 1997:575); *brash, ostentatious* and *in-your-face* are more extreme. In contrast, *polite, shy* wines are harder to "get to know" and the wine drinker has to pay close attention to the taste and aroma.

Many of the descriptors from human personality domains are used mainly in wine evaluation. These include *charming, diplomatic, friendly, classy, laid-back, easy-going* and *approachable*. Except for Thurber's cartoon, I never encountered *pretentious* as a wine descriptor, although I came across one wine described as *unpretentious*.

Sometimes meanings are stipulated by a wine writer. For example, Parker (1998: 1404) contrasts *intellectual* with *hedonistic*.

> Certain styles of wine are meant to be inspected and are more intro-spective and intellectual. Others are designed to provide cheer delight, joy, and euphoria. Hedonistic wines can be criticized because in one sense they provide so much ecstasy and they can be called obvious, but in essence they are totally gratifying wines meant to fascinate and enthrall—pleasure at its best.

Hedonistic is obviously a term of high praise, but in addition I would interpret it as a *forward* and *assertive* wine. *Intellectual* and *introspective* wines, on the other hand, are *shyer* and more *reticent*.

Another set of new descriptors comes from the semantic field of artefact production. Wines are made, of course, but recent additions to the vocabulary include *crafted, sculpted, tightly-built* and possibly *polished* (all of which are positive). The word *manufactured* is, however, negative. A manufactured wine is made "not in a vineyard but by a chemist" (*Wine Spectator,* Jan 31, 2001:82).

Many of the newer words for describing mouthfeel come from the domain of expressions related to the human body. (*Body* is already a semantic extension, but this meaning no longer seems metaphorical.) The term *structure*, along with *backbone* and *frame* are used. For example, Sogg writes "In red wine the backbone mostly comes from tannin" (*Wine Spectator* 2001:139). Other words may be influenced by our current interest in fitness, giving us *brawny, fleshy, stout, muscular, beefy, big-boned* and *chunky* for heavy wines, and *lean, sleek, sinewy* and *svelte* for light ones.

An interesting set of words are elaborations on the properties of balance. Positive descriptors include *integrated, well-defined, focused, formed* and *assembled*, and negative ones, the opposites, are *disjointed, unfocused, muddled, uncoordinated* and *diffuse*. "Wines that are focused have flavors that integrate. Also the scents, aromas, and flavours are precise and clearly delineated" (Parker, 1998, 1403).

Textiles provide other metaphors. *Open knit* or *loose knit* can be added to other fabric descriptors, like *silky, satiny* and *velvety*. The interpretation, however, is related to integration.

Related to the age words, but focusing more on readiness to drink, are *open* and *closed*. Whereas *open* wines are ready for drinking, a *closed* wine is one that "is not showing its potential, which remains *locked in* because it is too young" (Parker, 1998: 1403). *Tight, tightly wound* and *tightly coiled* are also used for "immature and underdeveloped" wine (Robards, 1984: 35). Another recent word is *precocious*, referring to a wine that matures quickly. Recent uses of *forward* also have this meaning, a different sense from that described above. The opposite of both is *backward*, meaning "slow to develop" (Robards, *ibid.*). Closely related to *backward* is *dumb*, in the sense of *mute*, which Parker defines as "closed, but more pejorative. Closed wines may need time to reveal their richness: dumb wines may never be better" (1998: 1403).

ISSUES IN THE PHILOSOPHY OF LANGUAGE

Although many of these wine words are cute and amusing, they have implications for various topics discussed by philosophers of language, for example, truth conditions, metaphor, synonymy and interpretation. I will put aside some controversies that are important to many philosophers of language, such as which parts of meaning and interpretation belong to semantics and which to pragmatics and concentrate only on what a phrase like *svelte* wine can mean in a wine conversation.

There are three issues raised by the data on wine descriptions. 1) Who determines what words mean? 2) How are we able to interpret these metaphors? 3) What are the implications for synonymy?

EXPERTS, KINDS OF

Putnam (1975) has proposed a theory where there is a division of labour such that some speakers (experts) have the authority to determine the meaning and application of certain words. Others in the language community, if they use these words, will try to deploy them like the experts, or at least accede to the judgment of those experts. Let's look first at the speakers and writers who talk about wine.

First of all there are the oenologists—the wine scientists for whom a precise vocabulary is used and understood in the same way by other oenologists. Their vocabulary is both larger in some ways and more restricted than others. It is larger in that many more technical terms from chemistry and related fields are used; it is restricted in that trendy, novel, metaphorical words are considered inappropriate for scientific publications. This is the group Putnam would consider as expert with respect to wine words. Most modern wine-makers probably belong in this group as well—at least those who learned their trade in a university.

The second group of experts consists of individuals in the wine trade, sommeliers, wine drinkers who have learned about wine through reading, attending seminars on wine, drinking wines, and. finally, wine writers. The wine writers generate most of the new terms. They try to communicate with a whole range of wine drinkers from those who are very knowledgeable to novices. But in addition, as writers they want to write interesting and colourful prose. For example, if one is evaluating and describing thirty Merlots from California, commenting on the body in each, it is boring to read *wine A is full-bodied, wine B is light, wine C is very heavy*, etc. Therefore, the prose can be enlivened with synonyms, near synonyms, metaphors and a variety of other associations. If all the writers who use terms like *unfocused, polished* and *intellectual* agree on the properties denoted, then these are or can become conventional wine descriptors, and the writers become the experts on these words. Some words can have their meanings stipulated, such as those by Parker, quoted above. If other writers pick up on them with the same sense, then these words, too, join the wine vocabulary. Other experts will understand these new words whether or not they use them because they read wine literature. This second group of experts will defer to the scientists, especially on technical terms. But they are unconcerned with the fact that scientists disapprove of their flamboyant vocabulary.

The last group, novices and other less experienced wine drinkers, may try to learn how to use these terms the way the experts do without realising that there are different kinds of experts. When such individuals encounter a sentence like *Wine A is feminine*, they are often puzzled, but when I link *feminine* to *light, perfumed* and *delicate*, they quickly see the relationship and catch on to decoding process. Then they can discern what a *masculine* wine must be. (In terms of expertise, there is a very wide range between expert and novice.)

Putnam's theory works reasonably well for wine talk. Yet it is oversimplified because there exists a chain of "respect", from the novices, who defer to the expertise of wine writers and wine sellers, who in turn defer to the scientists (Lehrer & Wagner, 1981). People connected by chains of respect give rise to a consensual use of words resulting from convergence toward the appropriate consensual weight to assign to wine drinkers, sellers and scientists in their use of wine descriptors. This may result in the scientists receiving so high a consensual weight that all defer to them concerning some descriptors, *corked*, for example, whereas scientists would probably receive no greater weight than others for their use of *delicious*. Deference to experts or the refusal to defer depends on context and other factors influencing the assignment of weights (Lehrer and Lehrer, 1994).

UNDERSTANDING METAPHORS AND EVALUATING TRUTH

A method for interpreting wine metaphors is not necessarily appropriate for understanding Shakespeare's sonnets or Wallace Stevens' poetry. Semantic field theory is useful in understanding how and why whole sets of new words suddenly enter the lexicon of wine description. According to field theory, the vocabulary of a language is organised according to conceptual clusters, for example, kinship, animals, cooking words, or emotion words, and within each field the lexical items are structured according to an inventory of lexical relationships (synonymy, antonymy, hyponymy, incompatibility, etc). When a word from one semantic domain, for example, personality or body type, is applied to another domain, such as wine, then other words in that field can tag along and will retain their same relationships. For example, if *muscular* can be applied to wine, then *svelte* can be, too, and it will be employed as an opposite for wine as it is for body type.

Utterances (or sentences) can be evaluated for truth, after they are interpreted. How would one evaluate the truth conditions of an utterance like *Wine A is brawny*? If *brawny* is interpreted *full-bodied*, which is a synonym of "heavy" in wine discourse, either by convention or by associational links, then if Wine A is indeed heavy, the sentence is true. With some predicates, like *heavy*, things are more complicated because *heavy* is a scalar term. So a wine could be evaluated in terms of various norms: for all wines, for red wines, for Merlots, for Merlots from California, from a particular year, winery, etc. Therefore, any utterance must be indexed for the relevant context (and other things as well). In my research on how people apply words to wines, often miscommunication arises because different wine-drinkers are using different norms.

Some writers on metaphor have argued (or asserted) that metaphors cannot be paraphrased, or that if they are, the point of the metaphor is lost. I would certainly agree in the case of poetry, but wine description *is* description. Whether or not a wine description like *brawny* evokes images is an empirical question. Perhaps it does for some people, or maybe only before it becomes a conventional part of the wine vocabulary. If metaphors evoke images and other kinds of associations, that reflects on the vivid prose of the writer. But one can see why wine scientists would ignore this effect since they are presenting scientific information.

SYNONYMY

A controversial proposal with which I will conclude concerns synonymy. There are many wine words that mean *heavy*: *big, robust, fat, solid* in the older literature, and *brawny, muscular, big-boned, fleshy* and *stout* in contemporary writing. Certainly in isolation these words are not synonymous and any dictionary would give them different definitions. This is because each word has a range of senses that differ from one another. If those who use these terms as wine descriptors were to define them, I suspect that they would come up with discrete definitions. A *muscular* wine might have properties *a,b,c,d,* a *brawny* wine *a,b,c,e,* and a *big-boned* wine *a,c,d,f.* My impression is that the differences are in fact neutralised and that most of these words become synonyms in wine discourse. However, even if semantic differences can be expressed by definitions and paraphrases, can wine experts consistently apply these words to wines in a differential way? Can they consistently and consensually distinguish between *brawny, muscular* and *big-boned* wines? This is an interesting empirical question.

The same point can be made with words from other semantic fields, for instance *focused* and *integrated.* As with words associated with body-building, these descriptors could perhaps be differentiated by words—that is, by careful definitions, but it remains open whether a sentence like "Wine X is not focused but it is still integrated" would be labelled as contradictory. Moreover, I would be surprised if a panel of wine experts could consistently distinguish and agree on wines that are *focused* but not *integrated* and vice versa.

SUMMARY AND CONCLUSION

In this chapter I have sketched out how new, trendy, wine descriptors can be linked by intra-linguistic relationships and associations to a basic vocabulary of perception. Through these links a speaker or writer can use old metaphors and associations and create new ones, and hearers and readers can construct interpretations that are close to the speaker's intentions. Many new terms are invented by wine writers who want both to enrich their wine descriptions and entertain readers. After all, there is pleasure in both drinking wine and talking about it. Moreover, linguistic playfulness and creativity is highly valued today in advertising, journalism and other domains.

Utterances that use these colourful and novel words can be true or false, but they must be indexed in ways that are often inexplicit; this may well lead to miscommunication at the level of application, that is, in the way that words are applied to wines, even if there is agreement that *muscular* is the same as or similar to *heavy.* Many words in the wine domain are synonyms, although in other contexts they are not. The consequence is that any theory of meaning has to take into account the fact that most words are polysemous, that is, they have several related meanings. Also a theory requires an understanding of the intra-linguistic relationships among senses of words as well as among the words themselves.

There are intriguing questions that remain to be answered, but they are empirical issues. Does a phrase like *muscular wine* trigger visual images in some people? Do wine experts agree on the intra-linguistic links and metaphorical meanings of new wine descriptors? Will playful new words remain as descriptors or will they, like slang, be quickly replaced by new terms? What other discourses are like wine? I don't know the answer to these questions, but I would love to find out.

Appendix

Lexical Structure

The main lexical relationships found in the wine vocabulary are synonymy, antonymy, class inclusion (hyponymy), and incompatibility. In addition, there is a more general, somewhat vaguer notion of association, which also plays a significant role.

Synonymy is a familiar concept which has been discussed and analysed at length by philosophers, linguists, and lexicographers. Since most words have a range of senses, it is rare to find two words that are complete synonyms, allowing substitutability in all contexts. Therefore, we use the term *synonym* in a looser way for words that can substitute for each other in some salient contexts. For example, *big* and *large* are synonymous in the semantic field of size, but each word has other senses not shared by both. So a *big brother* is not necessarily a *large brother*. In the wine vocabulary, a type of partial synonymy is very common.

Antonymy is also a familiar lexical relationship although philosophers of language have not examined it as much as other structures. There are several types of antonyms, the most interesting of which are gradable opposites, such as *heavy* and *light*. In these structures there is a scale with a middle point or a middle interval, and the antonyms name opposite parts of the scale. Gradable antonyms are closely connected to comparative structures. The operators *more, less, very* and a few others modify terms, most often adjectives, on this scale, as illustrated in Figure 1.

<pre>
            heavy   light
    <— very, more   very, more —>
        less, not as —> <— less, not as
</pre>

Figure 1: Weight Scale

Sometimes a gradable scale will be lexicalised by two antonymous pairs, an inner and an outer pair, as with *hot, warm, cool, cold,* the middle interval occurring between *warm* and *cool*. An interesting feature of the temperature scale is that the middle interval, in limited contests, is also named by *tepid* or *lukewarm*.

Incompatibility refers to contrast sets like *dog, cat, horse, pig, snake* etc. where to assert that *X is a dog* entails that *X is not a cat, horse, pig* or *snake*. Antonyms are a subtype of incompatibility, so to say *Wine X is heavy* entails that *Wine X is not light*.

Class inclusion and incompatibility together give us a taxonomic structure. Consider Fig 2.

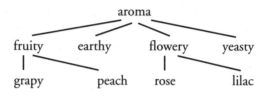

Figure 2

Entailment relationships hold between a word and any words above it in the taxonomy. For example, the sentence *Wine X has a peach aroma* entails *Wine X has a fruity aroma* and *Wine X has an aroma*. A wine can be both *fruity* and *earthy* because it can have both properties.

Association is a general, loose term that is not strictly semantic. It is a term employed by psychologists, but I am using it here for other kinds of semantic relationships, including emotive and connotative (in the linguistic sense) meanings. For example, *heavy* and *big* are not normally synonymous, but they are in wine descriptions. This kind of association arises because in our everyday experience, big things tend to be heavy and vice-versa.

Any truth conditional analysis will have to deal with indexical, contextual, and metaphorical constraints on truth conditions, either in the semantics or pragmatics. Indexicals include pronouns, tense, and deictics of time and place.

Context includes the norms. If A says, "This 1999 BV Cabernet Sauvignon wine is heavy," what is the reference class? Also in the category one might place the audience. An audience of wine writers might be willing to evaluate an utterance like "This wine is brawny," while an audience of oenologists might regard it at meaningless.

Metaphor provides interesting problems with a huge literature. I will only point out that some philosophers, like Goodman and Kittay handle the truth conditions of metaphor in their semantics, while many others, e.g., Davidson and Reimer, place it in the pragmatics. My account leaves that question open.

References

Davidson, Donald. 1979. "What Metaphors Mean". In *On Metaphor*. S. Sacks, ed. Chicago: University of Chicago Press.

Goodman, Nelson. 1968. *Languages of Art*. Indianapolis: Bobs-Merrill.

Kittay, Eva F. 1987. *Metaphor: Its Cognitive Force and Linguistic Structure*. Oxford: Clarendon Press.

Lehrer, Adrienne, 1974. *Semantic Fields and Lexical Structure*. Amsterdam: North Holland.

Lehrer, Adrienne. 1983. *Wine and Conversation*. Bloomington, IN: University of Indiana Press.

Lehrer, Adrienne and Keith Lehrer. 1994. "Networks, fields, and vectors". In *Grammar and Meaning: Essays in honor of Sir John Lyons*, F. Palmer, ed., pp. 26-47. Cambridge: Cambridge University Press.

Lehrer, Keith and Carl Wagner. 1981. *Rational Consensus in Science and Society*. Dordrecht: Reidel.

Lyons, John 1977. *Semantics*. Cambridge: Cambridge University Press.

Noble, Ann C. et al. 1987. *American Journal of Viticulture and Enology* 38.2. 143-146.

Noble, Ann C. 1990. *The Wine Aroma Wheel*. www.winearomawheel.com.

Parker, Robert M. 1998. *Bordeaux: A Comprehensive Guide*. New York: Simon & Schuster.

Putnam, Hilary. 1975. "The Meaning of Meaning". In *Language, Mind and Knowledge. Minnesota Studies in the Philosophy of Science*, vol. 7, Keith Gunderson, ed. Minneapolis: University of Minnesota Press pp.131-193.

Robards, Terry. 1994. *New Book of Wine*, NY: Putman's Sons.

Reimer, Marga, 2001. "Davidson on Metaphor", *Midwest Studies in Philosophy* XXXV: 1422-155.

Stevenson, Tom. 1997. *Sotheby's Wine Encyclopedia*, London & New York, Dorling Kindersley.

Trier, Jost. 1931. *Der Deutsche Worschatz im Sinnbezirk des Verstandes*. Heidelberg: Winter.

chapter seven

WINE AS AN AESTHETIC OBJECT

Tim Crane

Art is one thing, the aesthetic another. Things can be appreciated aesthetically—for instance, in terms of the traditional category of the beautiful—without being works of art. A landscape can be appreciated as beautiful; so can a man or a woman. Appreciation of such natural objects in terms of their beauty certainly counts as aesthetic appreciation, if anything does.[1] This is not simply because landscapes and people are not artefacts; for there are also artefacts which are assessable aesthetically without being works of art (e.g. an elegant car or a mathematical proof).

The category of the aesthetic, then, is a broader one than the category of art. Let's use the term "aesthetic object" for something that is capable of aesthetic appreciation, and "art object" for something which is capable of appreciation as a work of art. Thus: some aesthetic objects are artefacts, and some of those artefacts are art objects.

What makes any artefact an art object—a work of art—is, of course, a fraught and contested question. One of the difficulties is that in some of its uses the concept *art* still has an evaluative, commendatory and honorific connotation. This is not to say that *art* is a purely evaluative concept; "bad art" is not a contradiction in terms. But calling something *art* must have some sort of normative import if we are to understand the reaction many people have to certain kinds of avant-garde art. The reaction I have in mind is that of those who say that the work of John Cage, say, is "just not music" or that Tracey Emin's random objects are "just not art". The evaluation here implies that some mistake has been made by those who present their work as art: they are claiming to achieve a certain standard, but fail to do so.

Wine certainly admits of aesthetic evaluation. Wines are praised as elegant, refined, balanced; they are criticised for being crude, brash or unbalanced. These are plainly aesthetic descriptions: expressions of the aesthetic value of the sensory experiences of those drinking the wine. Anyone who has drunk good and bad wine and has tried to assess their experience knows what such descriptions mean. Those who say they don't—or say that these descriptions can only express snobbish prejudices, rather than genuinely aesthetic attitudes—are either incapable of tasting wine or are not telling the truth.

Wine is a natural product, of course; but wine does not occur naturally, even if fermentation does. Wine-making is the result of centuries of inherited wisdom about grapes, places and seasons, of detailed scientific knowledge, and of trial and error on a huge scale. The wine-maker makes a contribution to the character of a wine at almost every stage, fully deserving the evocative French title *éleveur*. Wine is not discovered but made: it is an artefact that can be appraised aesthetically.

But wines are not works of art, and wine-makers are not artists. And this is not because they are aspiring or confused artists who fail to meet the standard for art. Compare the rejection of wine as an art object with the typical rejection of avant-garde art just mentioned. When someone says that Carl Andre's famous pile of firebricks, *Equivalent 8*, is not a work of art, they normally mean that Andre is trying to do something—create a work of art—and failing miserably. Certainly, they will agree, Andre is an artist; he is just mistaken in thinking he has created art. The artist is aiming to do the usual sort of thing which artists do, including get their works into museums etc.—but he simply fails. "It's just not art: no matter what the critics say." (I'm not endorsing this view, only describing it.)

It seems to me that this is not what people are saying when they deny that wine is a work or art. For a wine could succeed in all the ways the wine-maker intended, but still not count as a work of art. This is because the wine-maker cannot even be *trying* to create a work of art. The wine-maker is doing something else: practising a craft, engaging in high-end agriculture, making a beautiful drink, a fine luxury consumable item etc.—but not making a work of art. Wine-makers have not tried and failed to do something because of some confusion about the nature of their activity—as the critic of the avant-garde would say about Carl Andre—rather, they have not even *tried* to do that kind of thing.

Here I shall explore some of the reasons for and against taking wine to be an art object. Although some of the arguments against taking wine to be an art object are not very persuasive, there do not seem to be any positive reasons for it, either. Our difficulty in answering this question is largely due to the fact that we lack a satisfactory understanding of what it is to be an art object. Despite this, it is clear that wine can appeal to us aesthetically in many of the ways that some art objects do—so long as we have the right conception of aesthetic appeal and aesthetic value. For we should not be misled by a narrowly intellectual conception of the aesthetic. Although the predominant meaning of the word "aesthetic" these days is *pertaining to beauty*, the word derives from the Greek word for sense perception, *aesthesis*. It should be a commonplace that a proper understanding of the aesthetic and aesthetic value must give a proper place to the contributions of sense perception. Once we realize this, we see how wine is indeed a central example of an aesthetic object, whether or not it is an art object.

I am starting with the assumption that wine is not generally regarded as an art object as opposed to an aesthetic object. I want to look first at why this might be so; I will then venture more widely, and tentatively, into the field of aesthetics.

According to the so-called "institutional" theory of art, roughly speaking, anything which is in an art museum (gallery, concert hall etc.) is a work of art, and anything that is a work of art is in an art museum. On a normal understanding of what a museum is, this would immediately disqualify wine, since wine rarely appears *as such* in art museums—anyone offering a vertical tasting of Château Lafite to London's National Gallery *as an exhibition* would be making a joke or a big mistake.

But the institutional theory of art is very implausible, so perhaps it should not dominate our theorising about art. One difficulty with the theory is that it can push the definition of art back onto a further question of what makes something an art museum or institution. The Penfolds winery outside Adelaide consists of displays of old vintages of its classic Grange wines, and tasting rooms where you can sample Penfolds' wines. It is a kind of museum; but what in the institutional theory disqualifies it from being an art museum? No doubt the defenders of the theory have a response; but the general direction does not seem like the right one to take.

A more interesting objection to wine as an art object is based on the status of wine as an object. A wine cannot be properly appreciated aesthetically unless it is drunk, just as a painting is not properly appreciated unless it is seen. Those speculators who buy and sell wine simply to make money are not appreciating wine aesthetically. So we might think that the aesthetic value of a wine requires an experience which itself has an aesthetic value. The value of the wine is partly determined by the value of the experience to which it gives rise. This is not to say that it is *only* the experiences themselves that are of any value. The wine itself has aesthetic value; but what it is for a wine to have aesthetic value cannot be understood without making reference to the experience of tasting it. (Consider the absurdity of someone saying: "I admit that this wine is beautiful/elegant/refined etc.; but I don't see any need for anyone to drink it.") We will return to this point below. For the moment it should be clear that as with painting, there is a distinction between appreciating a wine aesthetically and appreciating it in other ways.

But wine is essentially ephemeral; and here the comparison with painting starts to breaks down. One notable feature of many works of art is that we can return to them repeatedly and learn more about them. Indeed it is often said to be the mark of a great work of art that it repays frequent visits. There is a sense, however, in which a wine cannot be returned to time after time. It is true that in tasting Château Lafite from a certain vintage one is undeniably tasting a representative of a kind of wine—and if the wine-maker has done his job well, then other bottles will taste similar—and expert tasters can confidently talk about how *Lafite 1996* has changed over the years. But, strictly speaking, we are not tasting the same thing—at least in the sense in which the viewer returns to look at the same painting. At the very best, we are appreciating a specimen or a part of a larger sample of wine. Should we call the larger sample—maybe the whole vintage of the *grand vin* from a particular château—the work of art?

There is something to this, for critics tend to say that the 2000 Margaux was a masterpiece, not some particular bottle of the 2000 wine. But given the significance bottling has on the development of a wine, this way of talking neglects an important aspect of what contributes to quality. There is change across time, certainly, in both the experience of the painting and of the wine. But with wine, what changes are the different aspects of the work itself; in the case of the painting, what changes is your understanding of it. The painting remains the same, you return to it and deepen your understanding of it. Wine changes from bottle to bottle, as each develops differently over time.

In addition, if the whole vintage *were* the work of art then the analogy with painting would break down in another fundamental way. For viewers of the painting can see the whole work at one go; they can return to appreciate the *very same thing* which they saw before. And this is true even if the painting itself changes over time, for instance by its colours fading. There is no comparable experience with wine: one cannot return to the whole vintage and experience the *very same thing* time and again. One can only experience a part of it, and each part may have very different features.

Perhaps we have chosen the wrong analogy. If we take the case of music, by contrast, there is a closer analogy available. A great piece of music is something to which one can return again and again. But to what is one returning? In the days before recorded music, many listeners only had performances and their memories of them to go on. They returned to the same piece again and again, but performances differed. But this performative feature did not undermine the status of these works as art. This is analogous to individual occasions of drinking bottles of the same vintage.

However, the relationship between the individual bottles and the vintage is not the same as the relationship between the work and the performance. Using philosophical terminology, we can say that the work itself is the *type* of which the individual performances are *tokens*. The token performances are not *parts* of the type, in the way that the individual bottles of 2000 Margaux are parts of the "work" which is 2000 Margaux itself. 2000 Margaux is scattered throughout the world; the *Goldberg Variations* itself, by contrast, is nowhere in particular. A piece of music is not located where the original autograph score is—if you burn the latter you have not destroyed the piece.

This shows that the vintage is not a type of which individual bottles are tokens. For the vintage is an evolving creation which will one day go out of existence when the last remaining bottle is drunk. Types do not go out of existence in this way: even if no-one were to perform the *Goldberg Variations* ever again, this would not mean that it had gone out of existence. Moreover, a type does not change in the same way as the vintage does over time. Different performances of the *Goldberg Variations* add to our understanding of the work; but as with paintings, what has changed here is our understanding, not the work itself. By contrast, wines themselves change over time in aesthetically relevant ways, not just our understanding of them.

So wine is in some ways analogous to music, and in some ways not. But no analogy is perfect; the relevant feature of the original analogy was that the ephemeral nature of musical performances does not threaten their status as works of art. Analogously, the fact that wines are ephemeral does not show that they are not works of art.

We have examined some arguments for denying that a wine might be a work of art and found them unconvincing. Yet still I do not believe that wines are works of art, and I'm sure you don't either. What is the significance of this?

You might think that it is of little importance. What does it matter, after all, whether wine is an art object? Wine is not traditionally valued as art, but so what? It is still valued. Why should we not introduce a broader category, *art**, which includes everything we now think of as art and also wine, furniture, certain foods etc.? Art* could mean: *aesthetically assessable human artefacts. Art** could then replace *art* in our discussions and the definition of "art" be consigned to the dustbin of pseudo-questions.

This seems to me a superficial manoeuvre. The concept of art is too important in our culture for the question "what is art?" to be dismissed as a pseudo-question. And even if there is no agreed answer to the question, the attempts to answer it have brought insights of their own. But from the perspective of what is most valuable to us as consumers of aesthetic objects, the similarities between aesthetically assessable human artifacts—works of *art**—matter more than the differences between them and works of art. From other points of view, the distinction between *art* and *art** might be very important, but one thing wine teaches us is that where the value of our artefacts is concerned, it is often the aesthetic or sensory which counts for more than the artistic as such. I will introduce this idea by considering one more reason for scepticism about wine as an art object.

An obvious reason that someone might not want to classify wine as art is because art must have a *message*. This is a widespread view, often associated with political or religious conceptions of art; but its influence goes further than (say) didactic Marxist or Christian ideas of art. If works of art have to have a message, then wine would obviously not be a work of art, since wine has no message. A wine may "speak" of its *terroir*, to be sure, but not in any literal sense. Unlike art which contains a message, wine conveys nothing, it has no intellectual or cognitive content.

But to my mind, it is a mistake to think that art must contain a message. Some art does, and when it does, its value might wholly or partly derive from the (moral, political or other) value of the message it conveys. And understanding the message of a work of art can be essential to understanding the work: the message of *Guernica*—the vivid evocation of the horror and senselessness of human slaughter, say—is not something which merely arises accidentally in the minds of people as an effect of seeing the painting. It is central to understanding what the painting is. So we should not deny that the messages conveyed by works of art can be an important source of their value.[2] The question here is whether this is the *only* source.

The answer is obviously no. For many works of art simply *contain no message*. The plainest, most uncontroversial examples here are provided by purely instrumental (and so-called "non-programme") music—what we might call "abstract music". Music like this is often said to convey or express emotion; how it does this is a difficult philosophical question, but *that* music does this is undeniable. However, in no plausible sense is the emotion expressed or conveyed in a *message*. A message says something, it has some propositional or descriptive content. The emotional "content" (if this is the right word) expressed by a piece of abstract music does not say anything in itself.[3] In concentrating on those art objects which do have messages, we have restricted ourselves to an intellectualised conception of art. Yet as the case of music shows, it is not essential to the value of art that it have a message. So it cannot be an objection to wine being a work of art that wine lacks a message.

Similar considerations apply to those views which claim that art makes you a better person, and this is what its value consists in. In a recent book, *What Good Are the Arts?*, the literary critic John Carey argues against these views.[4] Carey argues that art cannot make you a morally better person because many indisputably wicked people (for example, Hitler) have been enthusiastic art lovers. In itself, this is about as good an argument as contending that eating pasta cannot make you fat because many undeniably slim people (for example, athletes) eat it. Surely no-one who thinks that art makes you a better person would agree that reading George Eliot or listening to Mozart *all on its own* can do the trick, or that other deficiencies of character cannot override the otherwise beneficial effects of art.

Nonetheless, even if his argument fails, Carey is surely right in his conclusion: there is no reason why art should even contribute towards making you a morally better person. The puzzling question is why anyone would think that it should in the first place. If we move to the case of music, the absurdity of the idea is even more apparent. It is entirely incredible that listening to Haydn's string quartets can make you a better person. There is no intelligible or causal connection between these two things. There is a parallel here with wine. Some have argued that wine has a civilising influence in a way that other alcoholic drinks do not.[5] But the idea is as implausible as the idea that art is improving. It may be true (with one or two exceptions) that wherever there is civilised life, people drink wine. But the obvious explanation for this is that wine has developed along with civilisation, and so the virtues of civilisation and wine are each effects of this development. They are, as philosophers say, joint effects of a common cause. But there is no causal connection between these two effects.

Where do these implausible ideas come from? I suggest that they come from the intellectualised conception of the value of art and the aesthetic. Those who believe that art must have a message rarely apply their views to abstract music—and those who do, for example, in Stalin's USSR, make the absurdity of their view all the more obvious.[6] The "message" view of art could only be plausible when applied to literature or to some visual art; when we venture beyond these examples we can see how feeble it is.

However, the message view also rests on a deeper error: that the value of art must always reside in being a means to some other further end. It is often claimed that if art has a rationale or a justification, it must be in terms of something outside the work itself. This assumption lies behind the title of Carey's book, *What Good Are the Arts?*—in other words, "what outside art and the experience of art, is art *good for*?" The assumption is that unless there were something outside art which art is good for, then art would not be good for anything, and therefore of no value. But this assumption seems to me to be false.

Among all the things that have value, we can distinguish between those things that have value in themselves ("intrinsic value") and those that are valuable only as means to other ends ("instrumental value"). Friendship has intrinsic value; no-one thinks (or should think) that real friendship is only a means to an end. Money, arguably, is a means to further ends; it would be bizarre to contend that it is intrinsically valuable, independently of what we can do with it. It is a matter of dispute which things are valuable in themselves and which things are only of instrumental value. Is good health something valuable in itself? Or is it only valuable as a means to other intrinsic goods? Opinions differ. But there should be no dispute about whether there really is such a thing as intrinsic value. If nothing were of intrinsic value, then nothing would be worth doing for its own sake. Since few of us believe that nothing is worth doing for its own sake, then clearly something must have intrinsic value.

The distinction can be applied to wine. For some people, wine has merely instrumental value: as an investment or as a way of enhancing their social status or perceived sophistication. Even the value of the *experience* of drinking wine can be seen as instrumental: the experience is a way of drowning sorrows, or a tool for oiling the social wheels. I am not denying that wine and the experience of drinking it can have these values; but does wine have intrinsic value too? And if so, in what does its intrinsic value consist? To answer these questions, we must first return to art.

Many have said that art only has an instrumental value. Marxists took this approach to art, believing that art should serve the purposes of revolutionary socialism. In Marxist states, art which did not do this was condemned as "bourgeois" or "decadent". Moving closer to home, those in government who have defended "the arts" purely on the grounds that they stimulate the economy and produce jobs are thinking along broadly similar lines. And the claims we have just considered—that art must have a message, or that it makes you a better person—are also attempts to explain the value of art instrumentally.

Yet it seems to me that we do not have to think in this way about the role of art in our lives. I am not denying that people—like Marxists, or those committed to some other ideology—think of art as being fundamentally justified by its role in promoting some other value. But surely those of us who are not committed to any such ideology are not obliged to think of the value of art in this way? Someone who spends their resources (time, money, energy) on attending concerts or reading fiction or looking at paintings need not *have* to think of the value of what they are doing in terms of some externally given goal. The idea that art might be something which has intrinsic value is one which we should have no difficulty accepting—once we have accepted the idea of intrinsic value, of course.

It is one thing to say that something has intrinsic value, however, and another to say what that value consists in. Intrinsic value is not supposed to be something ineffable or indescribable. If someone thinks that friendship is intrinsically valuable, then they are not prohibited from describing what friendship is in a way which reveals its value. If good health is something of intrinsic value, then we should be able to say what good health consists in. Similarly, if works of art, like pieces of abstract music, have such value, then we should be able to say something about what their value consists in.

It is clear that the value of abstract music must in some way be related to the sensory experience of listening to it. The intrinsic value of music must reside partly in its aesthetic (in the etymologically original, but now secondary, meaning of sensory or sensual) effects. But these effects—experiences of music—can themselves be something intrinsically valuable. Music is intrinsically valuable precisely because of the intrinsic value of the experiences to which it gives rise. But this is not to say that it is *only* the experience that has value, and the music itself has only instrumental value, as a means to the end of producing the experience. This is a mistake, because the experience can only be characterised as an experience of *this* music: its value cannot be understood except as deriving from this music. The experience with its intrinsic value cannot be obtained in any other way. And the music can have this value even if it does not give rise to experiences of such value—even if it is not heard, or the correct conditions for producing the right experiences do not obtain.

It is not true of all art that its value resides in the value of the sensory experience of the art. It is not true of all literature, nor of "conceptual art" where the sensory component plays little role. In the case of some conceptual art, its value resides entirely in the message it conveys; one doesn't necessarily have to see it in order to get the message, and the work does not demand seeing more than once. Duchamp's *Fountain* seems to me to be a good example of this. I've never seen it; yet I feel I have fully absorbed its message, and its value derives entirely from its message. What is more, even if I had seen it, I don't think my understanding of the work would be enhanced by seeing it many times.

But much art is not like this. Most art, even art that has a message, will have aesthetic qualities too, in the sense of "qualities pertaining to sensuous perception" as well as in the sense of "qualities pertaining to beauty". Excessive concentration on the extra-artistic purposes of art can obscure this crucial element in art's value. In particular, I have claimed, an excessive concentration on the cognitive content—e.g. the "message"—of a work of art can obscure whole areas of art which are valuable to us. This is not supposed to be a controversial or original idea; my purpose in saying it here is to remind you of its importance.

The intrinsic value of music derives from the intrinsic value of the experiences of listening to music. This, I suggest, should be our model for understanding the intrinsic value of wine. A wine cannot be appreciated for its intrinsic value unless it is drunk; the value of the wine is intimately related to the kinds of experience to which it gives rise. Again, this is not to say that it is *only* the experience which has intrinsic value. The value is in the wine, just as the taste is in the wine, there to be apprehended by many perceivers.[7] Nonetheless the only way to apprehend the aesthetic value of a wine is to taste it; just as the only way to apprehend the aesthetic value of a piece of music is to listen to it.

What kinds of sensory experiences have such value? Clearly, value is not an on-or-off phenomenon: some things can be more or less valuable than other things, and the same is true of experiences. In talking about the value of wine here, some of our points apply to the finest wines only. But lesser wines can still have intrinsic value. Our interest here is in the features of experiences which explain why a wine, any wine, has the intrinsic value it does.

Let us return to our earlier point about the ephemerality of wine and the experience of it. Although experiences of tasting wine are essentially ephemeral, they do nonetheless give us a reason to return to the object of the experience. As we saw above, this is not exactly like returning to a painting, it is more like hearing another performance of the same piece of music. We return to the wines we like to grasp more of the kinds of experience they give us, just as we return to music that we like to grasp more of the experience of hearing it. One reason for this is that the experience is often an experience of *complexity*. In the best wines, we experience various elements balancing in harmony. We find them difficult to classify, fascinating, elusive. We want to pin them down, as we might want to isolate the tensions and resolutions points in a piece of music. With wine, unlike with music, the complexity can be the product of more than one sense: the look of the wine, its taste and smell, the texture in your mouth all contribute to this experience of complexity. And although ephemeral, the sense of complexity can linger, as the finish of a wine can stay in your senses, and its memory can provoke you to return to it again.

Returning to a wine in this sense is not just a matter of merely wanting the same physical stimulation again, as one might want another salted peanut. One often returns to a wine to pursue its qualities: to find out more about its tastes and to classify them properly. Returning to a wine is, in a broad sense, a search for understanding: understanding the properties of the wine that make it produce experiences like this. But it isn't like a scientific understanding, since a scientific understanding of the mechanisms of taste and the chemistry of wine could in principle be had by someone who had never tasted wine. The understanding we seek having had the experience is an understanding of *that* subjective experience, from the inside, to so speak. The search for understanding which is consequent upon an experience of a great wine is part of what explains the enormous amount which is written about wine. It is also what distinguishes wine from almost all the other things we eat and drink. The starting point for a proper aesthetics of wine should be a recognition of this particular relationship between the intrinsic value of wine, the intrinsic value of the experience of wine and the need for understanding which arises out of that experience.

I started with the question of whether a wine could be a work of art. I claimed that where most art is concerned, the value of a work of art cannot be exhausted by the value of its message, and also that there is art which has no message at all. Music is an art whose appreciation requires appreciating the sensory experiences to which it gives rise. If wine-making were an art, then this is the kind of art it would be: the creation of art objects whose value had to be understood in terms of the value of the experiences to which they give rise.

Yet, lacking a satisfactory answer to the question "what is art?", I am reluctant to insist that wine is a work of art. Despite the fact that the arguments against the idea that wine is an art object are not very good ones; and notwithstanding the fact that we seem to have a model of aesthetic value of an artefact where its value derives from that of the sensory experience of the artefact (i.e. music); despite all this, it seems like a pointlessly provocative linguistic stipulation to insist that wine is a work of art.

However, what our reflections on art objects and aesthetic objects have shown is that it is not necessary to insist that wine is a work of art in order to claim many of the privileges of works of art. For music provides us with a model of the essentially sensory elements in the appreciation of the aesthetic value of an artefact; but there is no reason why this essentially sensory element should only be common to art objects, as opposed to aesthetic objects more generally. With aesthetic appreciation comes the application of standards, evaluation, and judgments of quality—all things which we can apply to wine as well as music. Wine is an aesthetic object rather than an art object. But the claim of this essay has been that much of what makes certain art objects valuable is something which can be shared with many aesthetic objects. Art objects may matter to us partly because of their aesthetic qualities; but mere aesthetic objects can matter to us for exactly the same kinds of reasons, and wine might be like this. In this sense, perhaps, the aesthetic is a more fundamental category than the category of art.

NOTES:

Thanks to Alex Hunt for very helpful discussions of the aesthetics of wine, and to Roger Scruton, whose fascinating paper at the London Philosophy Programme conference in 2004 provoked me to write some of these thoughts down. Special thanks to Barry Smith for his good editorial advice and many discussions.

1   See Malcolm Budd, *The Aesthetic Appreciation of Nature*, Oxford University Press, 2006.

2   In Malcolm Budd's *Values of Art* (Harmondsworth, Penguin, 2005), he argues that the value of a work of art is greater if the message it conveys is actually true. Nonetheless, this is consistent with saying that the value of the message does not exhaust the value of the work.

3   By using the phrase "in itself" I mean to ignore here the very important phenomenon of works coming to be associated with a certain message. Association with a message is not the same as having a message.

4   John Carey, *What Good Are the Arts?* London, Faber and Faber, 2005.

5   For more in this idea see the chapter by Scruton in this volume.

6   For a fascinating account of Stalin's criticism of Shostakovich, see Leonid Maximenkov, "Stalin and Shostakovich: Letters to a 'Friend'" in Laurel E. Fay, *Shostakovich and his World* Princeton University Press 2004, pp. 43-59.

7   For more on this idea see the chapter by Smith in this volume.

chapter eight

ON THE EVALUATION OF WINE QUALITY

Steve Charters

THE CONTEXT OF THIS STUDY

The nature of wine quality is slippery. The concept of quality is widely used; judges at wine shows talk about the evaluation of wine quality, wine producers market their wine on the basis of its purported excellence and consumers make purchase decisions as a result of the assessment of a wine by themselves or others. Even more, a horde of contemporary wine writers and critics earn money (and occasionally even make a living) from their assessment of wines and the willingness of the wine consumer to accept the validity of their recommendations about what is, or is not, worth drinking; in other words about what is or is not good quality. Nevertheless, while "quality" is widely adopted as a concept applicable to wine it is much less frequently explained. The great American oenologist Maynard Amerine famously claimed that "quality in wines is much easier to recognise than to define" (Amerine & Roessler, 1976, p.2), but part of the problem is that if quality is hard to articulate then how do we know what evaluative mechanisms are operating when we drink wine, and how can we convey our judgments to others?

There are a series of related difficulties around the notion of wine quality. The first focuses on the form which a drinker's perception of wine quality takes; what we might term a psychophysical response. This is particularly concerned with whether our consumption of wine evokes primarily a sensory reflex, or cognitive analysis, or an affective (emotional) reaction. Another issue is to know whether there are any common features in the way that different drinkers evaluate the quality of a wine, and if so, what those features are. Third is the issue of whether or not our judgments of it have an external validity, or if they are merely personal—in other words, is wine assessment an objective or a subjective process? The consideration of these conundrums may help to provide us with a clearer view on how we appreciate wine.

The context for this investigation is the philosophical sub-discipline of aesthetics. It is my belief that wine drinking is an experience which is, at least partially, an aesthetic process (Charters & Pettigrew, 2005). This is a contentious assertion; there is a stream of philosophical thought which denies that wine is capable of providing an aesthetic experience (for instance, Beardsley, 1980; Kant, 1790/1987; Scruton, 1979) although others take a contrary view (Coleman, 1965; Osborne, 1977; Sibley, 2001; Taylor, 1988). However, the assumption that wine is capable of stimulating an aesthetic experience means that the appreciation of wine is perceived to share in common some of the aspects of the pleasure taken from an intense involvement with music, or art, or poetry.[1] Crucially, it is worth noting that aesthetics has also become a concern of psychologists over the last 150 years[2] and the psychological tradition of aesthetic enquiry is less likely to dismiss the experience of wine consumption as entirely non-aesthetic. In parenthesis we can note that often the philosophical and psychological theoreticians of aesthetics pronounce in complete isolation from each other.

Nevertheless, despite the aesthetic context for this inquiry, my chapter differs from others in this volume. My academic interest in wine is in the field of consumer research, a discipline that draws on marketing, sociology, anthropology, psychology and history to understand how consumers engage with products. This engagement involves not merely the use of products for utilitarian ends, but is also crucially concerned with their hedonic purposes—the experience that can be gained from consumption (Holbrook & Hirschman, 1982)—as well as the symbolic function of goods; their ability to convey meaning both to ourselves, about the nature of our existence, and to those around us, sending messages about how we wish to be seen (Richins, 1994), and these touch on philosophical concerns.

As an academic working within the field of consumer behaviour my interest in wine is focused less on pure mental analysis, and more on the results of empirical research. I have not constructed an *a priori*, rational argument to explain how the appreciation of wine occurs. The ideas that follow arise primarily from a substantial piece of qualitative research involving in-depth discussions with 105 wine drinkers ("informants") across Australia. These informants were selected to reflect a wide range of backgrounds, and specifically they had different consumption patterns. Some were very interested in wine, others much less so; some drank daily and others only monthly; some spent a lot on their wine purchases, others very little. Included in the research were a number of wine industry professionals, the intention being to compare their understanding of the quality of wine with that of non-professionals. Some of the interviews took place in focus groups, which included wine tasting, so that observation and analysis of the methods of tasting provided further data for the study.[3]

It is important to remember, consequently, that this study has been based not on a scientific analysis of what happens in the process of wine tasting, but on what consumers perceive to occur when they try to evaluate wine (although where the science tends to support my arguments I have noted it). My conclusions are thus rooted in the everyday experience of wine drinkers, rather than in physiological and psychological measurement.

The three core issues of this chapter (the psychophysical response to wine, the dimensions of wine quality and the nature of the subjective and the objective in the evaluation of wine) will be addressed in order, with a focus on the wine drinker's perspective on those matters. Each section will start with an examination of past theory on the issue, before considering what the informants interviewed in the research project thought about it. However, before doing that, it may be instructive to examine what the wine industry itself thinks about the nature of the evaluation of wine quality.

THE PROFESSIONAL PERSPECTIVE ON WINE QUALITY

The "wine industry" comprises a range of functions and therefore of perspectives. There are those who are involved in production, which includes viticulturists, wine-makers and oenological researchers and consultants, as well as analysts and technicians. There are also those involved in the many aspects of distribution—including wine writers and critics, sommeliers and wine merchants. In wine producing countries the professional perspective tends to be dominated by producers, but in countries which do not make wine distributors and critics may be more important. This range of backgrounds, and the complex, rather abstract nature of quality, is also reflected in a diversity of views on the topic. The aesthetic perspective of Amerine and Roessler has already been noted, although only a few other professionals explicitly concur with their view (Abbott, Combe, & Williams, 1991; Jackson, 2002). Others may take a more subjective or objective perspective.

The influential French oenologist, Emile Peynaud, offers one definition:

> A very simple, obvious and very clear definition is this: "The quality of a wine is the totality of its properties, that is to say the properties which render it acceptable or desirable." In effect it is the totally subjective pleasure provided by drinking the wine which conditions judgment (Peynaud, 1987, p.220).

Peynaud's perspective is thus explicitly subjective. Others follow his line (Groves, 1994; Jackson, 1997), but even some of those who comment on the essentially subjective nature of judging wine still end up wondering if there is not some level of quality that is inherent in the product itself (Noble, 1997).

Whereas Peynaud saw quality as subjective, increasingly other oenologists are attempting to use scientific, analytical processes in order to try to predict wine quality "objectively". Grapes are being analysed by near infrared spectroscopy or by a technique known as GG Assay to determine their composition in an attempt to predict how a wine will turn out (Goldberg, 1997). In one case this has been linked to the final quality of the wine by means of descriptive analysis (Abbott *et al*, 1991). All of these methods make unexpressed assumptions about what wine quality actually is. They are also based on grapes—and the process of moving from grape quality to what is actually sold in the bottle is still multi-stage and subject to many variables.

A number of scientists have also sought to analyse the finished product in chemical terms in an effort to determine its quality. An overview of such a perspective was given by Acree and Cotterell (1985). Unlike many other commentators starting from a scientific perspective, they did offer a definition of wine quality, as "an estimate of its aesthet-

ic worth by a particular group of humans" (1985 p.147). They suggested that faults in wine—which are susceptible to chemical analysis—are
only half of the issue of quality. The other is that the wine must offer aesthetic value to those consuming it.

A more precise, albeit complex, attempt to link organoleptic wine
quality to an analysis of the products chemical make-up has been offered
by Somers (1998; 1999). Somers argues that the quality of red wine can
be predicted using UV spectrometry to analyse the total phenolic make-
up of the wine within the context of its relationship to sulphur dioxide.
His argument is complex and has not so far been widely adopted by the
industry. Other consultants have sought to use other methods of chemical analysis to predict wine quality. Thus in the United States, a
company called Enologix has produced a computer programme to
measure the "quality metrics" of wine, using a database of existing wines
to compare the chemical make-up of a sample and predict its likely
market position (Penn, 2001). They define wine quality as the "colour-
flavour-fragrance intensity of a given wine with respect to all the other
wines in its appellation" (p.59). This, again, is a production-led definition of quality and at present is no more than a guide to likely market
position rather than the consumer's perceived quality of the wine. As we
shall see, it is also arguable whether or not intensity is the core determi-
nant of wine quality. However, even some of those who actively promote
methods of chemical analysis accept that the evaluation of quality is ultimately an organoleptic process (Acree & Cottrell, 1985; Jackson, 1994;
Linskens & Jackson, 1988).

Professionals who argue that tasting wine necessitates a form of evaluation have to create appropriate benchmarks or guidelines to facilitate
that evaluation. Wine critics and judges regularly offer a number of
aspects of wine which, it is claimed, show its quality. These can include:
complexity, intensity of flavour, harmony, finesse, balance, length, personality or distinctiveness, and purity (Amerine & Roessler, 1976; Basset,
2000; Broadbent, 1979; Jackson, 2002; Peynaud, 1987; Thompson,
2000). It should, however, be stressed that this apparent unanimity is not
absolute. An alternative and fairly extreme perspective has been given by
a New Zealand wine judge, Dr G. Watson, who has argued that as long
as a wine is fault-free then the benchmark by which it should be assessed
is how faithfully it reproduces its varietal character (Merritt, 1997).

It is also useful to note that a wide range of vocabulary is adopted by wine professionals in the course of their assessments of wine. Each tends to have his or her preferred terms, which may be precisely graded according to the perceived quality level of the specific wine. Thus, the following words are commonly used: class (Stevenson, 2000); good, fine and great (Broadbent, 1979); sound or special (Schuster, 1992); profound or awesome (Parker, 1997).

In summary it can be noted that the wine industry differs on whether or not the evaluation of wine quality is a subjective or objective process, with a technocratic group arguing for the latter. A series of terms have been adopted both to grade quality and to benchmark it, but even on these there is no common agreement. Gawel (1999), who has researched the process of show judging, notes that each judge's view of quality varies slightly from the rest; some common markers for quality are used, but how the judges weight these will vary from judge to judge according to their background, experience and personal perspective.

THE PSYCHOPHYSICAL RESPONSE TO WINE

There is a debate, within aesthetic theory, about whether or not an aesthetic experience is an affective, cognitive or sensory process; that is, does it primarily entail an emotional, an intellectual or (as it would in the case of wine) an instinctive sensory response of taste, smell and touch? The argument began with the start of modern philosophical aesthetics in the eighteenth century. Voltaire, for example, considered that an aesthetic experience was a felt process; Edmund Burke, on the other hand, claimed that the demonstration of good taste was a mental activity (Schaper, 1983). It has also been noted (Osborne, 1979) that the work of Kant and others at times implies that aesthetic engagement is primarily a matter of sensation (although in practice Kant would not have accepted this, arguing that the experience includes the sensation of pleasure but that such a feeling was not in itself sufficient for aesthetic judgment). In this case aesthetic appreciation is seen to lie not in the area of mental judgment but "within the field of immediate perceptual awareness" (Osborne, 1979, p.137). A similar uncertainty can be observed amongst psychologists who study aesthetics. Some focus on the emotional aspect (Csikszentmihalyi & Robinson, 1990; Funch, 1997). The Gestalt school, on the other hand, considers cognition to be the primary element of aesthetic experience (Arnheim, 1974, 1988), whereas for experimental psychologists the process is essentially about arousal, so that sensation is the key to the encounter (Berlyne, 1971, 1974).

A related concern is the issue of pleasure. In the early eighteenth century pleasure was assumed to be an integral part of any aesthetic response (Hume, 1757/1998). Since Kant, however, pleasure as an end in itself has been discounted as an element of aesthetic appreciation (Osborne, 1979). Instead, within the aesthetic experience pleasure has been seen effectively as a co-incidental "symptom" (1979 p.137, although this is not Kant's view), a point which some contemporary philosophical aestheticians would agree with (Scruton, 1979). On the other hand, psychologists would generally agree with Kant that pleasure is a critical part of any aesthetic event, even if it is not its primary element (Funch, 1997), and the work of Csikszentmihalyi on the "flow experience" (Csikszentmihalyi, 2002; Csikszentmihalyi & Robinson, 1990), which is explicitly paralleled to Beardsley's (1980) philosophical analysis of an aesthetic encounter, focuses very much on the sense of enjoyment one undergoes. It is therefore a matter of some debate whether or not a sense of pleasure should form part of the evaluation of a wine's quality.

This research project indicated that drinkers appear to take different psychophysical approaches to quality. The conclusion must be treated tentatively; it has not been examined experimentally, nor has it been integrated into any psychological framework. Nevertheless the language used by informants ("I think", "I feel", "I taste/smell") tended to imply that varying processes were at work, and observation of the focus group participants suggested that people use different approaches at different times.

Some drinkers placed great emphasis on smell and taste, conveying a strong sense of the sensuousness of a wine. Others would discuss the complexity of flavour or analyse the balance of acid and alcohol in a very cognitive fashion. Almost invariably, however, all drinkers would ultimately record a definite affective response, whether positive or negative. Thus two drinkers give contrasting views on a wine:

Siobhan:[4] I think the bubbles [in that wine] are nice—it's quite fine. And probably just a little bit sweeter, I think, than the first wine. Length a bit longer, a bit more complex.

Neville: [That] is a wine that I really like. It's almost like everything else just floats away it's lovely. It's almost like an intoxicating aroma—it's … You know, any better and your eyes roll back a bit—it makes you really focus on it.

This apparent variety of approaches and of emphasis by informants suggests variation in the way they dealt with quality as an issue; some placing more emphasis on cognitive dimensions and others giving more weight to the sensory or to the affective. This, however, was no more than a tendency; there seems no doubt that elements of the sensory were important to all, and that some cognitive mechanisms were adopted by all or most. This triadic analysis of sensation, thought and emotion has been noted in some consumer research on perceptions of music (Holbrook, 1982). It has also recently gained some support following research into the physiology of tasting. The analysis of brain activity while wine is tasted has revealed differences between the more cognitive responses of wine professionals compared with the less cognitive experience of non-professional drinkers (Styles, 2003). The professionals displayed neural activity in the brain's frontal cortices, where cognitive processes are carried out, whereas the non-professionals showed no such response. (See also Jamie Goode's chapter "Wine and the Brain" in this volume.)

The triadic psychophysical approaches to drinking wine can be shown visually (Fig. 1).

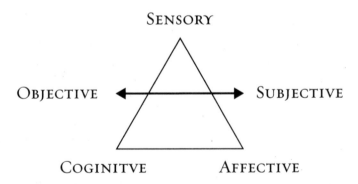

Fig. 1 – The cognitive, sensory, affective approach to drinking

As this figure suggests, the three approaches to wine drinking may be employed on their own but, more usually, in some combination. The figure also suggests that the triadic approach to consumption may function on an objective/subjective axis. Affect reflects the subjective, personal, response of pleasure. Cognition, on the other hand relates to the mental processes that may take place during the assessment of a wine, which may focus more on the evaluation of that wine against benchmarks of some kind. Sensation has aspects of both the objective and the subjective, including both cognitive assessment of a physiological response and a subjective sense of attraction or disgust.

This assertion about the psychophysical approach to wine is a simple, seemingly exact explanation for what is in fact an interactive and complicated process. The sensation of drinking may be fleeting and replaced rapidly with a feeling of pleasure; alternatively with some drinkers the mental analysis of the wine seems to be the initial response, and the cognitive conclusions merely reinforce any passing sensation and are the precursor of an emotional response. Drinkers cannot be classified as only being sensory, affective or cognitive in approach. The varying approaches may have a different level of importance for drinkers and all interact in a very involved fashion.[5]

THE DIMENSIONS OF WINE QUALITY

If the perception of quality requires an evaluative judgment then it is helpful to consider how that evaluation may be formulated for something like wine, which stimulates an aesthetic response. While some modern aesthetic thought is relativist so that it denies any validity for common evaluative criteria (Bayley, 1991), even with a subjective view of perceived quality it may be possible to establish standards by which consumers evaluate "quality" in aesthetic products, and indeed compare and/or grade them. Certainly the continued use by aestheticians of the concept of aesthetic value suggests that most researchers accept the existence of these criteria even if they are hard to pin down (Beardsley, 1980; Sibley, 2001). It is, nevertheless, a matter of dispute as to whether any evaluative criteria relate exclusively to discrete aesthetic product types, or if there are overall criteria that may be applicable across a range of products. To give an example, can wine only be assessed by flavour, aroma, acidity and mouthfeel (which we can term its "local" properties), while music can solely be judged by melody, tempo, and expressiveness or are there common measures that can be applied to both? Again the nature of the appreciation of art objects is subject to vigorous philosophical debate, but one particular approach may be helpful. Beardsley (1980) suggests the existence of three "general canons", "objective", evaluative criteria capable of being used to analyse all aesthetic objects equally. The three suggested general canons consist of unity, complexity and intensity (Beardsley, 1980 pp.462ff.). Does the object display coherence or harmony (which is positive) or is it disparate and are its component parts in conflict? Is it complex (and therefore does it stimulate interest) or is it simple? Does it strike one with its power or stimulate little affective response?

Other researchers, in different disciplines, reflect the use of these canons although without according them that title. Gestalt psychology sees harmony (balance and unity) as fundamental to aesthetic value (Arnheim, 1974, 1988). Intensity—so long as it is in balance—has been posited by psychologists as being significant (Berlyne, 1971; McBride, 1990). Complexity is also perceived by some psychologists to be important to aesthetic value, at least up to a point (Berlyne, 1974).

These general canons can usefully be compared with the criteria used by expert wine tasters. For instance, Basset (2000), who offers a fairly standard framework, suggests five factors for the assessment of wine quality. The first is balance (which, focusing on the interrelationship and harmony of the various dimensions of an aesthetic stimulus can be equated with Beardsley's idea of unity). Second is complexity, which correlates to Beardsley's second "general canon". Next is length (the time one continues to taste the wine having swallowed it)—which has a relationship to the general canon of intensity (Basset, 2000, p.92ff.). Basset's fourth criterion of quality is "definition", which he describes as the wine being "uniquely different". Basset's fifth criterion is the importance of the appearance of the wine. In aesthetic terms this is a local property and therefore cannot be subsumed in any of the general canons. Other wine writers, like Michael Broadbent and Michael Schuster, have adopted a broadly similar approach to that of Basset.

What are the criteria by which general drinkers measure the quality of wine? This may seem an impossible question to answer, and indeed the consumers approached in my study came up with thirty-eight different terms when asked what wine quality is. However, it was also clear that a number of the different terms were in effect synonymous, and with careful analysis it was possible to reduce them substantially to a number of groups—labelled in the study the "dimensions" of wine quality. These dimensions fell into two broad types. The first, smaller, type were extrinsic, that is, they were related to factors extraneous to the wine in the glass. Key among these were the quality of the grapes used, and production processes, particularly those which guaranteed that the wine was fault free and was fit for its purpose. The second type of dimension, a much more substantial group, was termed intrinsic because it related directly to what was drunk. Typically, one informant suggested:

> Morag: [A good wine] should have no obvious faults, so that's number one … It should be true to its type. So it should have some distinctive characteristics, of where it's come from, or what grape variety it's come from. Then it should display character and interest, complexity and length.

There were four significant intrinsic dimensions. The first was pleasure, and it is important to note that this was clearly the most important single dimension to the informants in the study; all of them, when asked what wine quality entailed, used words like pleasure, enjoyment or fun. The other three intrinsic quality dimensions were gustatory, paradigmatic and potential. The gustatory was the largest dimension, and contained a number of sub-dimensions such as taste, smoothness, body and mouth-feel, balance, concentration (a combination of the intensity of flavour of the wine and the length of time its taste remained after it was swallowed) complexity and interest. The paradigmatic dimension was so named because it was based on the notion that good-quality wine should reflect something else—primarily either the place where the grapes were grown and/or true varietal character. To this extent the paradigmatic dimension was similar to Plato's theory of forms (Plato, n.d./1951), whereby the highest quality wine must measure up to an independent and timeless ideal. The fourth intrinsic dimension of wine quality was potential, the idea that a high-quality wine should have the ability to age and improve in the bottle. That this is an element of quality is a contentious point but is held by some in the wine industry (Broadbent, 1979) as well as a few of the informants, and is considered intrinsic as it can only be effectively judged when the wine is tasted.[5]

It should be noted that in their discussion about these intrinsic dimensions, while many drinkers talked about smoothness, length and balance, fewer discussed concepts such as complexity, potential or the paradigmatic dimensions, and very few mentioned interest (although a number used words that suggested that the interest generated by a wine was significant to them—ideas such as memorableness or distinctiveness). Additionally, where those latter dimensions were referred to it tended to be by drinkers who were among the most interested and educated about wine, and it was acknowledged that not all wines—even generally good wines—showed great complexity or interest. There was an implication that these dimensions tend to mark out the highest quality wines, whereas taste, smoothness and balance, for instance, were more generally necessary for any wine to be considered good.

It will be clear to the attentive reader that some of the sub-dimensions of gustatory wine quality (notably concentration and complexity) bear some relation to two of Beardsley's general canons outlined earlier. It will also be evident that the intrinsic quality dimensions are of two categories. Pleasure is a terminal state—the end result of drinking a good wine. The other three dimensions, and their sub-dimensions, can be termed instrumental or catalytic. That is they do not represent pleasure itself but, for instance, the taste, body and ageing potential of the wine act to catalyse that sense of pleasure in the drinker. This has some relevance as we turn to consider the way in which drinkers conceptualise the process of assessing wine.

THE SUBJECTIVE AND OBJECTIVE IN WINE QUALITY

Since the time of Hume there has been a fundamental debate among philosophers about the "objectivity" or otherwise of aesthetic judgments (Hume, 1757/1998; Railton, 1998). Hume (1757/1998) noted the incongruity between the fact that "taste" seemed such a personal faculty, subject to individual biases, and yet overall some works continued to be held in high public esteem over long periods. He uses the example of the first, great Greek poet, Homer, who was revered amongst ancient civilisations and remained admired two thousand years later in the Paris and London of Hume's time. And, we could add, still remains respected today for the beauty and power of what he wrote. Following Hume, Kant (1790/1987) devoted substantial attention to this problem, which he termed the antinomy of taste, attempting to resolve it by focusing not on the nature of the aesthetic object but on the potential universality of the individual's experience. This conflict between the universal validity of aesthetic judgments and the subjective nature of personal taste has a direct relationship to our analyses of the quality of wine.

One contemporary philosopher (Gale, 1975) has used wine specifically as an example of how these types of judgment can be considered objective. Gale's (1975, p.343) argument is that wine evaluation rests on "a fairly well-defined observational base"; that evaluative judgments are based on these "true" observations; and that this relationship between an object and perceptual judgments about it has an empirical validity. However, much modern thought, certainly since the time of Hegel, Schopenhauer and Nietzsche, has been to shift the emphasis more towards the subjective nature of aesthetic judgments and most recently the influence of post-modernism has been to stress the relativism of aesthetic value.[6] This shift from the potentially objective to the more subjective has reflected—and partly results from—a change in focus by theorists away from the intrinsic worth of the aesthetic object itself and onto the subject who is undergoing the experience.

It has also been argued that experiences based on the senses of smell and taste are inherently less "objective" than those based on sight and hearing—because the latter are more cognitive and invoke thought processes (Korsmeyer, 1999). However, that may be based on a false assumption that aesthetic appreciation is almost entirely a cognitive process, which I have already suggested is debatable. It also assumes that wine tasting or the enjoyment of a fine and complexly flavoured meal is unlikely to incite cognitive analysis—a proposition which most keen wine tasters and gourmets would dispute.[7]

This philosophical uncertainty about the subjective or objective nature of wine quality is mirrored by wine drinkers themselves. Some informants considered quality to be subjective, and essentially a matter of personal taste—so that any criteria used for evaluation were merely idiosyncratic. Others claimed that wine quality is objective and thus measurable by extrinsic, impersonal criteria.[8] The following extracts—the first from a wine critic, the second from a consumer, illustrate this dichotomy:

Frederick: I do start getting a bit picky if somebody says "this is the best because I think it's the best wine." I say "well actually it isn't. You absolutely have the right to say 'yes it's my preferred drink' but it may not be the best of its type. And you won't know that unless you do the type of stuff that I do on a regular basis, and you want to learn about that type of thing."

Ellie: I suppose whether you like music, or whether you like poetry, or whether you like wine all comes down to personal taste—which is [what] we've been very much talking about.

This focus on both objective quality criteria and preference led a few to argue that it was therefore possible to assess wine and conclude it was of high quality without actually enjoying it; in one case a wine-maker claimed that he could judge and appreciate the quality of sparkling red wines even though he disliked the style wholeheartedly. If this is correct it may be that the appreciation of wine can be divorced from personal preference (Charters & Pettigrew, 2003a). Some informants, however, took a more paradoxical perspective, and argued that wine quality could be both objective and subjective simultaneously. It was even suggested that quality was seventy to eighty per cent "objective" and capable of external, objective verifiability—but the other twenty or thirty per cent was subjective—a personal response to what was tasted.

It has been suggested occasionally by academics that the quality perception process is more complex than a mere either/or dichotomy (subjective or objective) and involves both concepts jointly—labelled here "interactionist". Sociologists, particularly, use the idea of intersubjectivity to express this, although intersubjectivity is generally perceived to reflect consensus; that is, an idea takes on part-objective characteristics because it is generally accepted. The interactionist perspective rather suggests the coexistence of both personal response and external, impersonal criteria by which it may be judged. Another way to view the idea of quality as an interactionist process is to view it as a tension between a subjective element and an objective element. This can be visualised in graphic form (Fig. 2). This perspective was developed by many informants in the study, including some of those who initially argued for a subjectivist position.

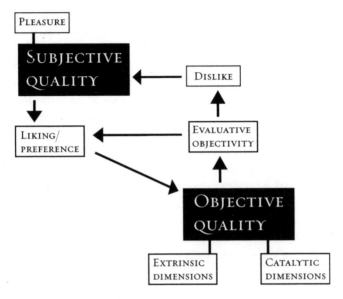

Fig. 2 – Subjective and objective quality

In this model the extrinsic and catalytic quality dimensions of wine have a close relationship with an objective notion of quality (they can, after all, be seen as being quantifiable). Subjective quality is the core of the individual's relationship with the product, and relates closely to the terminal quality dimension of pleasure. It is rooted in the individual's inability to have absolute certainty in the external validity of their evaluation of wine. There are two ways in which the consumer can reconcile this paradox of the subjective and the objective. One, generally for low-involvement consumers, is to accept the existence of objective quality, but claim no ability to discern it, merely to "know what I like". These drinkers start from a subjectivist position but accept that objective quality exists paradoxically alongside that viewpoint. Objective quality as a means of determining preference has no relevance for them, for they cannot engage with it—they do not understand how to analyse wine's objective elements. To that extent they are divorced from objective quality. It can be suggested that the subjective element of the process tends to focus on the activity of engagement with wine, and the objective part tends to focus on the defined dimensions of quality.

The second way of reconciling this paradox outlined in Fig. 2 was adopted by a few of the more interested and experienced informants. They approach wine systematically, with a checklist of points to be considered and/or a benchmark of what the wine should be like against which it can be evaluated. These approaches are consistent with many professional studies of wine tasting (Amerine & Roessler, 1976; Basset, 2000; Broadbent, 1979; Peynaud, 1987; Rankine, 1990). Such systems give these drinkers an "objective" way into engagement with the product. While checklists and benchmarks offer a framework for evaluating the quality of the wine, they do not necessarily guarantee enjoyment. Thus an individual who drinks wine within this framework starts from an objective standpoint, evaluates the wine using objective standards (marked as "evaluative objectivity" in Fig. 2), but may reach the subjective position when he/she gains little pleasure, despite the wine apparently displaying the indicators of quality.

In some ways these two processes (preference and evaluative objectivity) can be seen to be a way by which wine consumers try to resolve the antinomy of taste—the paradox of personally-rooted evaluation with apparently universal judgments of products. If it is accepted that individuals have a personal perspective on an aesthetic product, constrained among other things by personal taste, it is impossible to offer a truly objective aesthetic analysis of a product. Yet, accepting that there may be some external criteria by which the product is judged, and applying those criteria (albeit subjectively and thus imperfectly), one may be able to contribute towards a "universal" and personally recognisable judgment of wine. Alternatively consumers with limited experience may lack the framework to engage with objective quality. They accept the universal judgment about a wine, that it is objectively good or bad, but rely on their own preference for a decision on whether or not they want to drink it, irrespective of that universal judgment.

THE EVALUATION OF WINE QUALITY

What does all this tell us about the evaluation of wine quality? We have examined a series of apparently loosely linked issues related to the evaluation of wine quality; do they allow us to reach any conclusions about what actually happens when the drinker drinks? The paradoxical subjective and objective facets of wine quality have been noted. I have suggested that the psychophysical approach consumers take to wine has an impact on how they evaluate it—the complex interaction of sensation, cognition and affective response. I have also proposed that drinkers consider that wine quality has a number of dimensions which together define what it is. The integration of these disparate ideas must begin with a more detailed analysis of how the wine quality dimensions might operate.

As suggested, the dimensions of wine quality include the extrinsic (centred primarily on the production of the product) and the intrinsic, which are discerned in the wine as it is drunk. The intrinsic dimensions may also be catalytic ("creating" the awareness of quality) or terminal (the pleasure that is taken in the act of drinking a particular wine). It can also be suggested (and some informants in the research tended to agree with this) that there is a fundamental distinction in the apprehension of the extrinsic and intrinsic dimensions. The extrinsic—faultlessness and fitness for purpose—tend to be a *sine qua non* for quality. Rather than a direct contributor to pleasure it is their absence that would actually impact on quality. This idea has also been mooted by Emile Peynaud (1987) who suggests that

> A distinction is made between the negative aspect which is the absence of faults and corresponds to a minimal quality threshold, and the positive aspect which concerns real qualities: pleasure, appeal, complexity, personality, purity (1987, p.223).

The catalytic wine quality dimensions are local or specific to wine; we may or may not claim to make any comprehensible judgment about a wine based on its smoothness or taste, but those factors only relate to wine. Is it possible to make any more substantial, any more "objective" judgment about wine? I have already noted the similarity between some of the intrinsic, gustatory sub-dimensions and Beardsley's general canons—specifically concentration. It will be interesting to consider whether or not these general canons have any applicability to wine, although it is only fair to Beardsley to add that he would not have accepted any such link, being of the opinion that wine is not capable of aesthetic appreciation.

Before developing this theme, however, it is also useful to consider whether or not Beardsley's three general canons of unity, complexity and intensity are sufficient for this process. Again, Beardsley himself argued cogently that these three are the only canons applicable across a range of aesthetic situations, and that no others existed which were not specific to the particular type of aesthetic object, such as poetry, or sculpture or drama (Beardsley, 1980). However, other philosophers of aesthetics (including those who are generally considered to be sympathetic to Beardsley) have disputed this and claimed that there may be other general canons (Dickie, 1997; Sibley, 2001). It is possible, on examining the work of psychologists who research aesthetics, to suggest a further general canon, which could provisionally be named distinctiveness. Distinctiveness, it may be argued, includes a number of similar ideas: novelty (Csikszentmihalyi & Rochberg-Halton, 1981), character (McBride, 1990) and the surprising (Child, 1969). While philosophers have not necessarily recognised distinctiveness as an evaluative component of aesthetic value some have suggested novelty (e.g., Cothey, 1990). It has also been suggested that Kant considered uniqueness to be a "formal element in aesthetic interest" (Scruton, 1974, p.23). The concept of distinctiveness may be similar to what the wine writer Gerard Basset (2000) termed definition, when listing his five components of quality or to what Amerine and Roessler (1976) termed memorableness.

There may also be another addition to Beardsley's three general canons, based not so much on the academic perspective on aesthetic value but rather stemming from the research carried out for this study. On the basis of what informants said it seems clear that appropriate methods of production are fundamental to the overall nature of wine quality; as noted above, however, this dimension tends to be a prerequisite of quality, rather than a catalyst for quality. Clearly, if a wine suffers from brettanomyces or is oxidised it is precluded from being high quality, so that by extension it can be argued that a level of technical competence is essential if a wine is to be good. This is not to argue that a wine should be technically spotless; there are those who would argue that the limited brettanomyces to be found in some red Rhône wines or the controlled oxidative handling of certain white Burgundies add to, rather than detract from, their quality. Informants complained about wines "made to recipes" which were boring, and noted that slight technical imperfections could result in a more interesting wine.

Consequently I suggest that although technical perfection is not essential as a dimension of wine quality, technical acceptability, providing a minimum level of flavour without any substantial faults is necessary to underpin wine quality. It can be noted that pre-modern aesthetic philosophers, like Plato and Aquinas, would not have agreed with this, instead arguing that perfection was fundamental to the aesthetic object (Dickie, 1971; Plato, n.d./1951), yet it could be argued that a minor "flaw" makes a product less technically perfect but more aesthetically interesting. Modern theorists have generally given less attention to the criterion of superior aesthetic technique.

The process of evaluating wine quality, which attempts to integrate all the issues discussed, can thus be shown in graphic form (see Fig. 3). The consumer engages with wine through a series of local quality dimensions, which in turn produce general criteria for aesthetic quality. One of these latter relates to the technical acceptability demonstrated by those who create the drink, which operates as a precursor to wine quality necessary but not sufficient for excellence. The other local quality dimensions result in the four proposed catalytic general canons: intensity, unity (which includes ideas such as balance, harmony and finesse), complexity, and interest (which may include concepts such as novelty, distinctiveness and memorableness). These general canons—like the local quality dimensions—tend to range from the more sensory (intensity and balance) to the more cognitive (complexity and, especially, interest—both of which require a great deal of intellectual effort and concentration to disentangle when drinking). The more sensory canons may be used by all wine drinkers but the more cognitive tend to be adopted more by the most interested and experienced. The more cognitive canons, it is posited, also tend to be used to make distinctions at the highest level of quality, whereas the former are more significant for good-but-not-very-good quality wines.

The catalytic general canons in turn produce a greater or lesser amount of pleasure—terminal quality—depending on the precise balance of each of the four components. At this point the affective takes over from the sensory and cognitive as the key element in the drinker's response to the

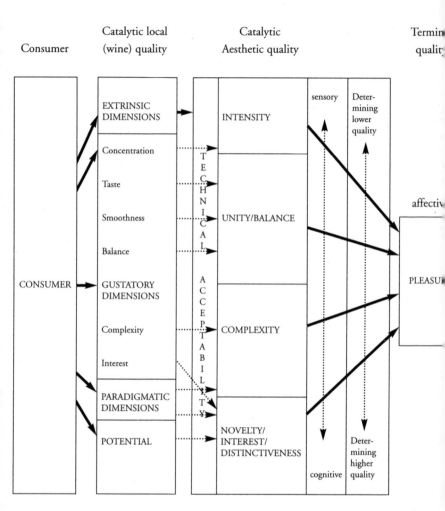

Fig. 3: The quality engagement process for aesthetic products

wine. In principle the highest quality wines will produce the greatest pleasure, although with the caveat that there may be experienced wine tasters who can evaluate the intensity, unity, complexity and interest of a wine, consider that they are all profound, yet—for other, idiosyncratic, reasons—decide that they personally dislike the wine.

It is also possible to see how the subjective and objective paradox fits in. A novice wine drinker may respond unconsciously to the intensity and balance of a wine; if there is a great deal of fruit, if their palate senses instinctively that the acid, alcohol and sugar are in harmony, it is "pleasant", and thus subjectively liked. The same wine can be evaluated by another drinker against external criteria, such as the length of flavour on the finish, the wine's ageing potential, its ability to reflect the region of vineyard from which it originates and the interrelationship of its component parts, and gain a great deal of pleasure from it; in the case of the very best wines that pleasure may be profound, resulting in a deep "flow" experience. This is typical of the aesthetic concept of psychical distance (Cupchik, 2002), with attention focused on the aesthetic event, a loss of awareness of the past and the future and of self-consciousness, as well as an intrinsically satisfying sense of personal integration (Csikszentmihalyi & Robinson, 1990).

REFERENCES

Abbott, N.A., Combe, B.G. and Williams, P.J. (1991), "The contribution of hydrolyzed flavor precursors to quality differences in shiraz juice and wines: An investigation by sensory descriptive analysis", *American Journal of Enology and Viticulture*, 42, pp.167-74

Acree, T.E. and Cottrell, T.H.E. (1985), "Chemical indices of wine quality", in G. Birch and M. Lindley (eds), *Alcoholic Beverages*. London: Elsevier Science, pp.145-59

Amerine, M.A. and Roessler, E.B. (1976), *Wines: Their Sensory Evaluation*. New York: W. H. Freeman and Company.

Arnheim, R. (1974), *Art and Visual Perception: A Psychology of the Creative Eye*. Berkeley, CA: University of California Press

Arnheim, R. (1988), *The Power of the Center: A Study of Composition in the Visual Arts*. Berkeley, University of California Press

Basset, G. (2000), *The Wine Experience*. London, Kyle Cathie

Bayley, S. (1991), *The Secret Meaning of Things*. New York, Random House

Beardsley, M.C. (1980), *Aesthetics: Problems in the philosophy of criticism* (2nd edn). Indianapolis: Harcourt, Brace

Berlyne, D.E. (1971), *Aesthetics and Psychobiology*. New York: Meredith Corporation.

Berlyne, D.E. (ed.) (1974), *Studies in the New Experimental Aesthetics*. Washington: Hemisphere

Broadbent, M. (1979), *Pocket Guide to Winetasting* (sixth edn), London: Mitchell Beazley

Charters, S. & Pettigrew, S. (2003a), "I like it but how do I know if it's any good?" Quality and preference in wine consumption, *Journal of Research for Consumers*, 5

Charters, S. & Pettigrew, S. (2003b), "The Intrinsic Dimensions of Wine Quality: An Exploratory Investigation", Paper presented at the 3rd Annual Wine Marketing Colloquium, Adelaide

Charters, S. & Pettigrew, S. (2005). "Is wine consumption an aesthetic experience?" *Journal of Wine Research*, 16(2), 37-52

Child, I.L. (1969), "Esthetics". In G. Lindzey & E. Aronson (eds.), *The Handbook of Social Psychology* (Vol. 3, pp.853-916). Reading: Addison-Wesley Publishing

Coleman, F.J. (1965), "Can a smell or a taste or a touch be beautiful?",

American Philosophical Quarterly, 2(4), pp.319-24

Cothey, A.L. (1990), *The Nature of Art.* London: Routledge

Csikszentmihalyi, M. (2002), *Flow: The Classic Work on How to Achieve Happiness.* London, Rider

Csikszentmihalyi, M. and Robinson, R.E. (1990), *The Art of Seeing.* Malibu: J. Paul Getty Trust Publications

Csikszentmihalyi, M. and Rochberg-Halton, E. (1981), *The Meaning of Things.* Cambridge: Cambridge University Press

Cupchik, G.C. (2002), "The evolution of psychical distance as an aesthetic concept", *Culture and Psychology,* 8 (2), pp.155-87

Dickie, G.L. (1971), *Aesthetics: An Introduction.* New York, Pegasus

Dickie, G.L. (1997), *Introduction to Aesthetics: An Analytic Approach.* Oxford: Oxford University Press

Ferry, L. (1993), *Homo Aestheticus* (R. de Loaiza, trans.). Chicago: University of Chicago Press

Funch, B.S. (1997), *The Psychology of Art Appreciation.* Copenhagen: Museum Tusculanum Press

Gale, G. (1975), "Are some aesthetic judgments empirically true?", *American Philosophical Quarterly,* 12(4), pp.341-8

Gawel, R. (1999), "Quality Ratings—Why they Vary", *Winestate,* 24

Goldberg, D. (1997), "Fine wine takes glycosides", *Search,* 28, Nov /Dec, p.302

Groves, S. (1994), "Wine quality versus personal taste", *Australian and New Zealand Wine Industry Journal,* 9(4), pp.323ff

Holbrook, M.B. (1982), "Mapping the retail market for esthetic products: The case of jazz records", *Journal of Retailing,* 58 (1), pp.114-31

Holbrook, M.B., and Hirschman, E.C. (1982), "The Experiential Aspects of Consumption: Consumer Fantasies, Feelings and Fun", *Journal of Consumer Research,* 9 (Sept.), pp.32-40.

Hume, D. (1757/1998), *Selected Essays.* Sydney: Oxford University Press

Jackson, R.S. (1994), *Wine Science.* London: Academic Press

——— (1997), *Conserve Water, Drink Wine.* Binghampton, NY: Food Products Press

——— (2002), *Wine Tasting: A Professional Handbook.* London, Academic Press

Kant, I. (1790/1987), *Critique of Judgment* (W.S. Pular, trans.). Indianapolis: Hackett

Korsmeyer, C. (1999), *Making Sense of Taste.* Ithaca: Cornell University Press

Linskens, H.F. and Jackson, J. (1988), "Wine Analysis", in H. Linskens and R. Atkin (eds.), *Modern Methods of Plant Analysis no. 6: Wine analysis* (vol. 6, pp.1-9), New York: Springer-Verlag

McBride, R. (1990), *The Bliss Point Factor*. Melbourne: Sun Books

Merritt, F. (1997), "Problems of Judging Wine Quality", *Australian and New Zealand Wine Industry Journal*, 12(1), pp.79-82

Noble, A.C. (1977), "The Catch-22 of Scoring Wine Quality", *Slow*, 6, pp.14-17

Osborne, H. (1977), "Odours and Appreciation", *British Journal of Aesthetics*, 17, pp.37-48

—— (1979), "Some Theories of Aesthetic Judgment", *The Journal of Aesthetics and Art Criticism*, 38, pp.135-44

Parker, R. (1997), "What Makes a Wine Great", *Food and Wine: the Guide to Good Taste*, 20, Oct., pp.138-41

Penn, C. (2001), "What is Quality? An American Perspective", *Australian and New Zealand Wine Industry Journal*, 16(3), pp.58-9

Peynaud, E. (1987), *The Taste of Wine* (M. Schuster, trans.). San Francisco: The Wine Appreciation Guild

Plato (n.d.), *Symposium* (W. Hamilton, trans.). London: Penguin, 1951

Railton, P. (1988), "Aesthetic Value, Moral Value and the Ambitions of Naturalism", in J. Levinson (ed.), *Aesthetics and Ethics: Essays at the Intersection*. Cambridge: Cambridge University Press, pp.59-105

Rankine, B. (1990), *Tasting and Enjoying Wine*. Adelaide, Winetitles

Richins, M.L. (1994), "Valuing things: The public and private meanings of possessions", *Journal of Consumer Research*, 21(Dec.), pp.504-21

Schaper, E. (1983), "The Pleasures of Taste", in E. Schaper (ed.), *Pleasure, Preference and Value*. Cambridge: Cambridge University Press

Schuster, M. (1992), *Understanding Wine*. London: Mitchell Beazley

Scruton, R. (1974), *Art and Imagination*. London: Methuen

Scruton, R. (1979), *The Aesthetics of Architecture*. Princeton NJ: Princeton University Press

Sibley, F. (2001), *Approach to Aesthetics: Collected Papers on Philosophical Aesthetics*. Oxford: Oxford University Press

Somers, C. (1998), *The Wine Spectrum: an Approach Towards Objective Definition of Wine Quality*. Adelaide, Winetitles

Somers, C. (1999), "The Wine Spectrum: Problems and Solutions for the Wine Industry", *Australian and New Zealand Wine Industry Journal*,

14(3), pp.52-4.

Stevenson, T. (2000), "Will Cava Ever Have Class?", *Decanter*, 56, Aug.

Styles, O. (2003), *Official: Wine Tasters Use Intellect*, retrieved 6 August from http://www.decanter.com/news/newsdefault.asp?newsstoryid=1135&List Start=11

Taylor, C.S. (1988), "Prolegomena to an Aesthetics of Wine", *The Journal of Speculative Philosophy*, 2 (2), pp.120-39

Thompson, B. (2000), "20 top cask wines", *The Sunday Times Food and Wine Supplement*, p. 8f., Aug. 13

NOTES:

1   For discussion of whether wine can be considered a work of art see Crane's chapter: this volume.

2   For different approaches within psychology see Arnheim, 1974; Berlyne, 1974; Csikszentmihalyi & Robinson, 1990; Cupchik, 2002; Funch, 1997)

3   Details are available elsewhere about the process used to collect, analyse and interpret the data and as a defence of the appropriateness of the research methods used (Charters & Pettigrew, 2003a).

4   All quotations are taken from my research. Each speaker has been given a pseudonym.

5   For further information on the dimensions of wine quality see Charters and Pettigrew (2003b).

6   For discussion of these ideas see Bayley, 1991, Dickie, 1997 and Ferry 1993.

7   For related issues see Bach's chapter: this volume.

8   For further discussion of the various things meants by the subjectivity of taste see chapter by Smith: this volume.

chapter nine

WINE EPISTEMOLOGY: THE ROLE OF REPUTATIONAL AND RANKING SYSTEMS IN THE WORLD OF WINE

Gloria Origgi

Ever since Pliny the Elder, talk about wine and its aesthetic appraisal has oscillated between giving allegiance to the subjectivity of taste and appealing to systems of ranking and reputation. Book XIV of his *Historia Naturalis* is dedicated to wine, its cultivation and its benefits. In chapter 8 of the book, Pliny acknowledges the subjective dimension of wine tasting: *quam ob rem de principatu se quisque iudicem statuet* (*His. Nat*, xiv, 8), while presenting, a few lines above, a long and structured ranking list of the best wines, based on the reputation they had for emperors and other distinguished people. Famous proverbs such as *de gustibus non est disputandum* or *chacun à son goût* are often mentioned alongside remarks on the need for some "standards" or rules of taste to help our sense of discrimination.

Even Robert Parker, the internationally acclaimed "taste-pundit" in the world of wine, whose 100 points-based system of wine rating has revolutionised the wine market, entitles subjective taste as the ultimate judge. He writes in his subscribers-only website of wine rating *www.erobertparker.com*: "There can never be any substitute for your own palate nor any better education than tasting the wine yourself." Or take this declaration in one of the most authoritative books on wine ever published, Hugh Johnson's *World Atlas of Wine*: "The best judge of the right styles of wine for your palate is you. There are no absolutes of right and wrong in wine appreciation" (p.49, 5th edn). Yet, the book is a monument to the reputation and the rating systems of the various regions in which wine is produced all over the world.

Wine taste is the paradigmatic case of subjective experience: it is highly variable, not only from one person to another, but also within the same individual from one particular occasion to another; it is highly incommunicable and depends upon a unique combination of external and internal conditions. Yet, the world of wine is a domain in which experts have a major role in defining the very experience of taste. This is of course no surprise: Wine is an aesthetic experience, and as such, needs evaluative criteria.

Hume's famous essay *Of the Standard of Taste* is an attempt to argue for the need of a principle, a rule that allows us to discriminate between good and bad taste, and which he finds in the "joint verdict of true judges":

> Strong sense, united to delicate sentiment, improved by practice, perfected by comparison, and cleared of all prejudice, can alone entitle critics to this valuable character; and the joint verdict of such, wherever they are to be found, is the true standard of taste and beauty.

For Hume, a true judge is thus a *connoisseur,* that is, a person well acquainted with an aesthetic domain, and competent to transmit his or her judgment on the matter.

Connoisseurship is an elusive concept which vaguely refers to a special kind of expertise. If most of us are able to recognise a connoisseur in an aesthetic domain, like fine arts or interior decoration, it would be hard to precisely say what defines him or her as such. Is a connoisseur just someone who has *good* taste or does she or he have an objective expertise in a domain? The tension between subjective experience and objective expertise is especially vivid in the world of wine because, on the one hand, taste, like smell, is considered a lower sense, whose relation to aesthetic judgment is less clear-cut than that of sight and hearing (see Scruton, this volume), and, on the other hand, knowledge of wine is not a well defined epistemic field, so connoisseurs in the world of wine are often considered as no more than snobs who bluff their way by pretending an expertise that doesn't have any serious objective grounds.

What is wine connoisseurship about? In trying to define it, the Italian gastronomist Carlo Petrini,[1] founder of the *Slow Food* movement, plays with the common etymology of the two Italian words *sapore* (taste) and *sapere* (knowledge), both coming from the Latin word *sàpere* which means at the same time "having taste" and "knowing". Taste requires knowledge to become good taste, that is, to belong to the licit sensory pleasures that a particular society considers as legitimate. Yet, the word *gastronomy* entered the European lexicon quite recently, through the 1801 poem by Joseph Berchoux, *La gastronomie ou l'homme des champs à table*, nearly as a joke, an oxymoron in which two markedly contradictory terms are put together to convey the idea of an impossible "science of the stomach" alluding hilariously to the word *astronomy*.

Sensory pleasures such as food and wine have been quite recently admitted among the proper pleasures in our society. Alcohol consumption is still forbidden by some religions and in many countries, and food restrictions and proscriptions are found in every culture. The way in which talking about wine and food has become so cultivated may perhaps depend on the need to detach it from the lower origins of the pleasures of palate. But I don't want here to provide a sociological account of wine talk and its place in the mechanisms of social recognition and social distinction. This is an interesting topic that has been explored at length in sociology, especially in Pierre Bourdieu's seminal work on the social critique of taste.[2]

Rather, I would like to approach the question from the point of view of social epistemology, trying to understand how sets of knowledge structures, such as classifications, ranking systems, reputational systems, guide us in acquiring a capacity for discrimination in a particular *epistemic domain*.[3] Taste, as Kant says, is an acquired disposition to discriminate and appraise.[4] I shall consider wine taste in this sense as an interesting example of a more general epistemic process of appraisal that underlies our acquisition of expertise in so many different fields of knowledge and practice.

Wine seems of a special epistemological interest because it is an epistemic domain that we enter as adults and sometimes with relatively little cultural background to influence our taste and our judgment. (We don't undergo any obligatory institutional education in wine tasting even in those places, like Southern Europe, where one is very likely to be exposed to wine talk and appraisal from childhood on.) We deliberatively decide to learn about wine, defer to experts and acquire their manners and expertise. Thus, trying to elucidate what sorts of epistemic strategies are at stake in the case of acquiring wine taste seems at a first glance easier than in the case of other domains whose acquisition can be affected by age, school education and coercive teaching.

My general point will be that acquiring a wine expertise is not so radically different as it may seem at a first glance from acquiring epistemic competence in any domain of knowledge. Acquiring taste as a discriminative ability, a "sense of quality" that allows us to sort items of cultural knowledge, is a process that is not very well investigated in epistemology and cognitive science, but that plays a crucial role in knowledge acquisition. We need experts, tags, labels and rating systems in order to acquire a capacity for discrimination, to understand the style[5] of thought that is proper to a particular body of knowledge. Without the mastery of some credible procedures for sorting information and enabling us to navigate through bodies of knowledge[6] we would face the impossible task of *Bouvard et Pécuchet*, the two heroes of Flaubert who decided to retire and to go through every known discipline without, in the end, being able to learn anything.

Let me state my point in this way: coming to know a body of knowledge involves, at least at the beginning, the ability to identify those whom other people trust for that knowledge. Assessing an expert's or a label's reputation is a way of orientating our trust in a new domain of knowledge so as to appropriately defer to the expertise (the expert or the labelling institution) of others in the early learning phase when a totally autonomous judgment is not possible. This is a controversial epistemological point and I would like to explain it better. The classical view, a crucial requirement of any epistemology—whose aim is to tell us how we ought to arrive at our beliefs—is to ensure the autonomy of our process of knowledge acquisition. Various criteria, rules and principles on how to use our mind have been put forward throughout the history of philosophy as a guarantee to preserve the autonomy and freedom of thought necessary for the acquisition of knowledge. Recent approaches in epistemology have challenged this view and tried to account for the epistemic reliability of the inevitable trust and deference that permeate our cognitive life. Following this latter line, in my work I try to understand the place of deference, trust and reputation in our acquisition of knowledge.[7] I defend the idea that deferring to indirect criteria to evaluate information—like reputation or trustworthiness of our interlocutors—is a fundamental epistemic strategy that has to be taken into account in any serious investigation of the processes of knowledge acquisition. To put it another way, we do not acquire information in order to assess other people's reputation: rather, we assess their reputation in order to acquire information.

By adopting this approach, a number of epistemological questions arise:

- What are the processes of construction of systems of reputations and ranking in a given domain of knowledge?
- How are different processes used to obtain information about that domain?
- How do people use these systems to orient their discrimination?
- What is the role of experts' trustworthiness in maintaining or challenging these systems?

In order to elucidate these questions I will analyse three examples that illustrate the complex relations between the institutional systems of classifications, the trustworthiness of experts and the acquisition of wine taste: the French appellation systems, the Californian systems, and the rise of the credibility of the taste-pundit Robert Parker and his influence on the wine market.

CLASSIFICATION AND REPUTATION. THE FRENCH- VS. THE CALIFORNIAN APPELLATION SYSTEM

In her book, *How Institutions Think*, the famous anthropologist Mary Douglas compared two systems of wine classification, the famous 1855 classification of Bordeaux wines in France and the more recent classification system of Californian wines, as an example of the institutional/public pressure on our ways of acquiring categories in a domain of knowledge. After a detailed description of the two different labelling systems—the Bordeaux regional-based system vs. the Californian grape-based—she concluded that the Californian labelling system marked a transition in our thinking about wine from the old and complex French regional-based system, whose way of condensing information "can only be unpacked by a connoisseur", to the new, more pragmatic and market-oriented grape-based system. In her words: "This is how the names get changed and how the people and the things are rejigged to fit the new categories [...] They make new kinds of institutions, and the institutions make new labels, and the new labels make new kinds of people" (p.108). According to Douglas, this difference between the two classificatory styles expresses a conceptual shift in our way of thinking about wine. Yet, her prediction of a transition from the French classification system to the Californian one has not been fulfilled: Hugh Johnson's *World's Atlas of Wine*, which she mentions as irrelevant to understanding the contemporary wine market, has attained its sixth edition and is still the number one best-selling book in the world of wine. It is true that the two systems are very different, and it is worth exploring in more detail how these differences have an impact on our discernment. But the resilience of the regional-based French classifications systems suggests that the distinct role of these labelling systems exists not just to provide us with the categories that enable us to classify reality: these labelling systems are resilient as long as they are also reputational systems; that is, as long as the label informs us how to appraise the value of the items in question. In this perspective, the Californian appellation system is not a rationalisation of the French system towards a more pragmatic or market-oriented wine categorisation. It just establishes a different network of deferential relations that consumers use in order to orient their choices. But let us have a closer look at these systems of classification.

QUALITY AND REPUTATION: THE FRENCH BOURGOGNE AND BORDEAUX CLASSIFICATION SYSTEMS

French appellation systems are very idiosyncratic and vary from one region to another. The two most famous areas of wine production, Bourgogne and Bordeaux, have completely separate classification systems:[8] the Bourgogne is based on a complex system of quality classification of land whereas the Bordeaux is based on the *châteaux* system. The Bourgogne classification system was systematised and unified in 1906 by the *Institut National des Appellations d'Origine* (INAO), by appealing to previous local classification systems. It divides, according to their position and their soil composition, the lands into small vineyards that form the various *appellations*: Chablis, Meursault, Beaune, Côtes de

Nuits, Vosne Romanée, etc. It further sorts the vineyards into four quality classes: *Grands Crus* (a rank that is deserved only by thirty-two small vineyards or *climats*, whose name represents the best wines in Bourgogne: Musigny, Chambertin, Montrachet, Chambertin Clos de Bèse, Romanée-Conti, etc.), *Premiers Crus* (about 600 vineyards which are usually indicated on the wine by the name of the village plus the name of the vineyards (like Gevrey-Chambertin Clos St. Jacques or Chambolles-Musigny Les Amoureuses),[9] the *appellation communale,* which allows a wine to be called by the name of the village in which the vineyard is situated (like Meursault or Pommard, but also Gevrey-Chambertin, Chambolle-Musigny, Puligny-Montrachet—all village wines unless from a specific *climat*), and finally, a generic appellation *Bourgogne blanc et rouge* reserved to less well situated vineyards, or to grapes taken from many, sometimes quite good, vineyards, in the case of good producers. This classification is a reputational system that establishes in a fairly robust way quality standards on a double level: first, by fragmenting the whole region into small portions of land and attributing appellations to them; second, by imposing on this fragmentation a four-level ranking system of vineyard quality. A connoisseur's eye will thus read in a bottle's label detailed information about the wine's reputation according to the quality of the vineyard in which it is produced.[10]

Bordeaux wines are classified according to a variety of local ranking systems, whose best known is that of the *châteaux* in the Médoc region (with the exception of Château Haut-Brion in Graves) that was established in 1855, in response to Napoleon's III request to rank Médoc wines for the Parisian *Exposition Universelle,* a very selective showcase of French *élite* culture. The ranking was established by wine industry brokers according to the *château* reputation and its trading prices over the previous 100 years. The *Grand Crus* were already produced differently from ordinary Bordeaux wines, typically from older wine stocks that often reached more than fifty years of age,[11] thus raising the reputation of those *château* proprietors who could afford to keep large stocks for so long. The *château* reputation, calculated in terms of prices, was the key ingredient in establishing the 1855 ranking system, a very different criterion than that of the land quality used in the Bourgogne system. A *château* is a controlled vineyard which has wine-making and storage facilities on the property. Its reputation depends thus not only on the vineyard's position and soil quality, but also on the *savoir-faire* and past performances of the proprietors. As Hugh Johnson explains in his *World's Atlas*, a *maître de chai* is a central figure of the *château*, one whose craft is supposed to be inherited from father and grand-father (cf. 5th edition, p.82). The 1855 classification included sixty *châteaux* from Médoc and one from Graves, ranked as first, second, third, fourth and fifth growths (*crus*). Only four *châteaux* were ranked among the *Premiers Crus*: Lafite, Margaux, Latour and Haut-Brion (a fifth *Premier Cru*, Mouton-Rothschild, was added almost 100 years later).

By giving a primary role to the *châteaux* reputation, the Bordeaux reputational system provides different cues to the consumers. Wine-makers' mastery and their credibility over the years are the relevant cues for assessing whom to trust among producers in this highly fragmented market. An experimental study in economics on quality expectations, reputation and prices in the Bordeaux wine market shows that the price premium associated with a better reputation exceeds twenty times the price associated with current quality.[12] In a highly fragmented market, where information gathering about individual producers is very costly, the epistemic role of a château's reputation is crucial to orient one's taste.

DEFERENCE RELATIONS. THE CALIFORNIAN 1978 APPELLATION SYSTEM

The Californian appellation system was established in 1978 by the Bureau of Alcohol, Tobacco and Firearms (ATF), with the aim of improving the reputation of American wines (California produces more than ninety per cent of the wine made in United States), by allowing a wine to be named after a "politically designated" region. In 1980 "American viticultural areas" (AVA) were created, that is, delimited wine-growing regions that have distinctive geographical features, such as Napa Valley, Sonoma Valley or Anderson Valley. A wine-maker who uses one of these legal appellations doesn't need to produce wine inside the designated areas: it suffices that at least eighty-five per cent of the grapes present in the wine should come from it. The AVA system doesn't fix which variety of grape or yield should grow in a particular area and in which percentage. A wine produced with eighty-five per cent Napa Valley Chardonnay grape will deserve to be a Chardonnay with the Napa Valley appellation. A Californian winery has much more freedom than a

French one in choosing its appellations. Many producers still ignore the AVA classifications, and prefer to stick to the simpler labelling used before 1980, that is, naming the winery plus the grape variant. Others are not only committed to the AVA systems, but have also started to put on their labels the name of locally renowned vineyards now associated to a grape variety, such as Zinfandel in Dry-Creek Valley and Pinot Noir in the cooler hills of Carneros. Differentiation of areas and vineyards is still ongoing, producing a very different picture from that drawn by Mary Douglas, who predicted an inevitable simplification of the classification systems towards a grape-based labelling. In fact, the more the reputation of Californian wines grows, the more fine-grained and stratified the classification system becomes, thus incorporating information that can be unpacked only by the expert's eye.

The relative freedom of labelling of Californian wine-makers doesn't simplify the classification system. It leads rather to the establishment of a complex network of deferential relations among appellations and wineries, as has been shown by the economist J. M. Podolny.[13] If a winery in one region puts the name of another region on its labels in order to indicate a better quality of grapes coming from that region, this is interpreted as an act of deference towards that region, and will contribute to its overall reputation and to the impact of the appellation on the price of wines. As Podolny shows, half of the bottles which bear the name "Napa Valley" on their labels are not produced within Napa Valley, as a clear act of deference and acknowledgment of the superiority of the grapes coming from this particular AVA. An example of a strategy used to influence status perception through affiliation to an appellation is the recent association of the Gallo winery, the largest producer of wine in the US whose reputation is associated with cheap and mediocre wines, with the appellation Sonoma Valley, as an attempt to change its reputation and improve the perception of its wine (cf. Podolny p.113). The use of the label "Gallo of Sonoma" is an act of deference of the Gallo vineyards towards the Sonoma region, thus signalling a more careful selection of the provenance of the grapes. This act of deference has a double effect: on the one hand, it makes transparent to the consumers the relationship between the two entities, that is, the fact that Gallo buys grapes from Sonoma Valley. One the other hand, it contributes to stabilising a distinct identity of the label "Gallo of Sonoma", which will orient consumers' choice.

Podolny's case study of the reputational network created by Californian wineries' affiliations shows that this network has an influence on past evaluations of quality, an important parameter for fixing prices in a market. That is, the reputation that a particular winery gains through affiliations not only isn't determined by its past, but influences how its past is evaluated.

So, here we have a third kind of reputational system, in which people rely on "who is associated with whom" in order to get information about a particular wine, given that it would be too costly and cumbersome to obtain this information from direct inspection of the quality.

These three examples show how different reputational systems provide consumers' evaluation heuristics with different cues: the Bourgogne system provides cues about the quality of the vineyards, the Bordeaux about the mastery of the *châteaux*, and the Californian about the social network of status relations. These different types of cues incorporate evaluations that are used by the consumers to get information that would be very costly to obtain otherwise. The "normative landscape" encoded in this ranking systems orients the novice in his or her first steps within the new domain of knowledge of wine.

CREDIBILITY, TRUST AND MORAL QUALITIES: THE RISE OF ROBERT PARKER'S TRUSTWORTHINESS

As Steven Shapin pointed out in a recent article,[14] it is remarkable that the most famous taste pundit over the last decades, Robert Parker, comes from the United States. A former lawyer, born in Baltimore in 1947, Parker began writing wine reports around 1975 and has since become the most respected critic throughout the world. His publication, *The Wine Advocate*, has more than 40,000 subscribers. His rise coincides with the rise of American wine and its now worldwide reputation. Parker's best known revolution is his rating system based on a 100 point scale, a much more flexible system than the usual twenty point scales: 96-100 points correspond to an *extraordinary* wine, 90-95 to an *outstanding* wine, 80-89 to a *barely above average to very good* wine, 70-79 an *average* wine, etc. Almost every wine shop in the United States displays the Parker points below the prices of wines to orient the customers.

How did Robert Parker succeed in imposing himself as the most authoritative *connoisseur* in the domain of wine expertise? Why do people all over the world trust his judgments? His fame is related to his judgment on the 1982 vintage of Bordeaux, which "British experts" judged as overripe and not worth buying for the long term. His positive evaluation was eventually endorsed by the rest of the world. Yet his rise was not without controversy. In 2004, so the story goes, he was heavily criticised by one of Britain's leading wine critics, Jancis Robinson, for having rated a 2003 vintage Château Pavie 95-100, a "ridiculous wine" according to Robinson, and one whose appreciators deserved a "brain and palate transplant". Still, despite a few attempts to discredit the reputation of his palate, Robert Parker is internationally considered a man of exquisite and precise taste, a "true judge", in Hume's words, whose infallible taste buds dictate the laws of oenological excellence. Wine experts in the wine industry play a key role in balancing the effects of reputation that we have seen in the previous section of this chapter: blind-tasting is a way of ensuring a criterion of quality independent of the classifications described above. When different blind evaluations converge, one may consider that one possesses an objective measure of the "perceived" quality of a wine (as opposed to its "expected quality", that is, its reputation). Professional blind evaluations are performed under controlled conditions by panels of experts. But Parker has never accepted to be part of these panels. He presents himself as an independent critic and has not been formally trained in wine. He started his bimonthly publication as a vocation, abandoning his legal career against the advice of friends and relatives. So, again, why is Parker trusted? Given that he doesn't appeal to any professional expertise or rigorous standard of evaluation, should we admit the thesis of the superiority of his taste apparatus: exceptional palate, taste buds and memory that are never mistaken? Against this superhuman view of a "million dollar nose", which can be used as a litmus test to determine the quality of a wine, I would rather explore an alternative view: Parker is identified as a modern version of a gentleman, a man of honour, and for this reason he is considered trustworthy, a friend of the ordinary consumer, not siding with the experts and the elite. The socio-epistemological role of the moral qualities of gentleman status and honour in evaluation truthfulness has

been superbly addressed by Steven Shapin in his work on truth and credibility in the emergence of modern science.[15] He explores "the
connections between the identity of individuals making claims and the
credibility of what they claim" (p.126) and the way in which judgments
of the truth or falsity of knowledge-claims incorporated assessments of
the knowledge source during the emergence of experimental science in
the seventeenth century. A similar connection between the acceptance of
normative standards and the display of moral qualities, such as integrity
and freedom of action, can be traced also in the case of the assessment of
the credibility of a taste expert such as Robert Parker. Parker is suppos-
edly incorruptible: *The Wine Advocate*'s subtitle is: "The Independent
Consumer's Bimonthly Guide to Fine Wine". He sees himself as a self
appointed consumer's advocate, a crusader whose mission is to free the
world of wine from hypocrisy and bad faith. His publication does not
accept advertising; he does not accept gifts from wine producers or invi-
tations to vineyards; does not speculate on the wine market, and prefers
to taste alone at home, without the pressure of social occasions. His
detachment is a guarantee of trustworthiness. He also shows a total dis-
regard of the lore of hierarchies of wine. He is not a snob as he claims are
his British competitors, too sensitive to the lineage of wine. As his admir-
ers claim, he brings a democratic breeze into the wine industry by
detaching the evaluation of wines from the reputation of their location
and history. His simple and synthetic reports lack the verbosity of those
by other critics and are easy to understand. Integrity, democracy, intelli-
gibility are constituents of Parker's self-professed identity and it is
through the appraisal of his identity that consumers decide to trust him.
While usually convergence of content and other indirect epistemic criteria play a role in assessing the credibility of reports, the case of Parker is
somewhat different: it is the display of his moral qualities that reinforces
his authority.

The relation between experts' trustworthiness and historically determined reputational systems is thus quite complex: experts are not simply
tools or instruments, as Smith claims (see Smith, this volume) that allow
the consumer to assess the real quality of the wine by proxy, or to unpack
unintelligible information out of a wine label. Experts participate in the
maintenance and the transformations of the reputational systems by coun-
terbalancing their role, challenging their hierarchies or reinforcing them.

A novice who approaches a complex and traditional corpus of knowledge such as wine expertise is confronted with a normative landscape, rich in cues that he uses to orient his sense of discrimination. The lore of tradition is structured by the classifications, ranks and reputational systems that teach us what is canonical for that corpus of knowledge, that is, what defines the threshold of identity below which that corpus ceases to exist. We learn these maps fast, by using heuristics that allow us rapidly to associate values to items. But we are not blindly deferential to this lore. To the extent that we acquire an autonomous capacity of discrimination, we challenge and revise it, by relying on our own experience and on those experts whom we consider trustworthy in that domain. A socio-epistemological investigation of the different heuristics we construct and use to structure a body of knowledge is a worthy project, even in those cultural domains where facts of the matter are difficult to pinpoint. I don't think that there exists a "science of wine". But nor does this imply that our acquisition of discrimination is deprived of any objective value.[16] Although a science of wine is still beyond our reach, the sketch of an epistemology of wine that I have outlined is an attempt to describe how people structure their knowledge, which heuristics they employ and which experts they trust in navigating an historically embedded and epistemologically entangled corpus of knowledge such as wine expertise.

Gaston Bachelard used to say that science has not had the philosophy it deserves. In the case of wine, it would be perhaps more appropriate to say that philosophy has not the science it deserves.[17]

REFERENCES

Albert, J.P., "La nouvelle culture du vin", *Terrain*, 1989, no. 13 (Oct.), *Boire*.
    See also: http://terrain.revues.org/document2961.html

Bourdieu, P., *La distinction*. Paris: Editions Minuit, 1979; translated as
    Distinction: A Social Critique of the Judgement of Taste. London,
    Routledge, 1986

Douglas, M. *How Institutions Think*, London, Routledge and Kegan Paul,
    1987

Foucault, M., *Les mots et les choses*. Paris: Gallimard, 1966; translated as *The
    Order of Things*. London: Tavistock, 1970

Hughson, A.L. and R.A. Boakes "The knowing nose: the role of knowledge in
    wine expertise", *Food Quality and Preference,* 13, 7-8, 2002, pp.463-72

Origgi, G., "Is Trust an Epistemological Notion?', *Episteme,* vol. 1, no. 1,
    2004, pp.61-72

Origgi, G., "What Does it Mean to Trust in Epistemic Authority?" in P.
    Pasquino (ed.) *The Concept of Authority*. Rome: Quaderni della
    Fondazione Olivetti, 2005

Podolny, J.M., *Status Signals*. Princeton, NJ: Princeton University Press, 2005

Solomon, G., "Psychology of novice and expert wine talk", *American Journal of
    Psychology* 105, pp. 495-517

Solomon, G., "Conceptual change and wine expertise", *The Journal of the
    Learning Sciences* 6, pp. 41-60

Shapin, S., *The Social History of Truth*. Chicago: Chicago University Press,
    1994

NOTES:

1   Cf. C. Petrini , *Buono, giusto, pulito. Principi di nuova gastronomia,* Einaudi, Torino, 2005, p. 97.

2   Here I refer to Pierre Bourdieu's work on social distinction. Marcel Proust is another great explorer of social distinction, as he defined it in the *Recherche*: "L'art infiniment varié de marquer les distances" Cf. P. Bourdieu, *Distinction. A social critique of the Judgement of Taste,* London, Routledge, 1979.

3   I use the expression "epistemic domain" in a very intuitive way, that is, referring toany structured field of knowledge in which some principled discriminative criteria for what counts as knowledge within it exist and can be learned.

4   Cf. I. Kant (1798), *Anthropology from a Pragmatic Point of View,* translated by R. B. Louden, Cambridge University Press, 2000.

5   For an epistemological interpretation of the notion of "style" see ch. 12, "'Style' for historians and philosophers", I. Hacking, *Historical Ontology,* Cambridge, MA: Harvard University Press, 2002. He refers to A.C. Crombie's notion of "style" in scientific thinking. I use the word here in a more relaxed way that also involves traditional corpuses of knowledge that don't belong to science.

6   The expression "body of knowledge" in the sense I'm employing here is due to Michel Foucault (cf. *The order of things*). It refers to any structured domain of cultural knowledge that distinguishes itself by its systematic criteria of classification and its internal procedures of representing and sorting information. In this sense, Western music, astronomy and gastronomy are all bodies of knowledge.

7   Cf. G. Origgi (2004; 2005).

8   Even the right bank Bordeaux wines of St. Emilion and Pomerol have a different classification from the 1855 in which none of them featured.

9   Some of the villages annexed to their names the nearest famous vineyard, like Puligny-Montrachet or Chassagne-Montrachet. A *Premier Cru* is often indicated by this village name and the name of the *climat or vineyard.*

10   Of course, given the fragmentation of Burgundy, the reputation of the producer counts a lot: Clos de Vougeot is 125 acres and is divided among eighty growers. You'd better know which ones are the good ones when you buy a bottle. But I don't want to insist on growers' reputation in Burgundy because I want to contrast its land-marked reputational system with the Bordeaux's system of *châteaux.*

11   Cf. R .C. Ulin (1995) "Invention and Representation as Cultural Capital", *American Anthropologist,* 97,

12   Cf. S. Landon, C.E. Smith (1998) « Quality Expectations, Reputation and Price », *Southern Economic Journal,* 64(3), pp. 628-647.

13   Cf. J.M. Podolny (2005) *Status Signals,* Princeton UP, ch. 5, p. 109: "The California Wine Industry".

14   Cf. S. Shapin (2005) « "Hedonistic Fruit Bombs", » *London Review of Books,* vol. 27, n. 3.

15   Cf. Stephen Shapin, *A Social History of Truth,* Chicago University Press, 1994.

16.   Cf. on this point Hughson (2001)

17.   I wish to thank Noga Arikha, Roberto Casati, John Fehrjohn, Pasquale Pasquino, Barry Smith and, especially, Dan Sperber, for having shared with me their expertise about wine, philosophy and good taste.

chapter ten

THE ART AND CRAFT OF WINE

Andrew Jefford
and
Paul Draper, Ridge Vineyards

Paul Draper was born in 1936 and spent his childhood on a farm in what was then rural country west of Barrington, Illinois. When the Depression came, his father walked away from business life and turned to his family roots as a farmer. He grew vegetables and corn, kept bees and cattle and ploughed with horses. Paul's earliest memories are of the striking natural beauty of this environment: the green rolling hills, the oak woodlands and the streams. After school—with the nearest neighbour a mile away, and his best friend five miles away—he rode alone through the open meadows and woodlands of the surrounding countryside. His imagination was given free rein, and he credits those hours on horseback with his becoming a romantic. While studying at the Choate School in Connecticut from 1948-54, he got to know wine at the family home of a Swiss room-mate. He went on to University at Stanford, drawn to California in part by the idea of living where wine was grown. With an interest in mythology, world religions and the big questions, he chose to study philosophy. Though the department was becoming known for its focus on logic, Paul pursued value theory, studying ethics and aesthetics, graduating in 1958 with a degree in philosophy.

With compulsory military service still in effect after the Korean War, he volunteered to attend the US Army language school and study Italian, even though it meant a longer commitment to the military. He was assigned to Northern Italy for two and a half years in a civilian role to work in liaison. He followed this with a year's study at the Sorbonne. These years in Europe deepened his knowledge and love of wine. He considered making it a career but was dissuaded, on the incorrect assumption that it required technical training. Instead, he began a career as a development consultant in South America, working initially on nutrition and family planning in Chile. His stay in the country convinced him of its potential as a wine producer, and he tried to encourage Chile's wine producers to increase exports by improving the quality of their wines. Frustrated by their lack of interest, he and his partner and friend from university, Fritz Maytag, leased a bodega, contracted for Cabernet grapes and began making Chilean wine themselves. The idea was to show how exports, especially to the US market, could be increased. After two vintages, the economic situation in Chile began to deteriorate and they decided to return to California.

Paul, why did wine appeal to you? Why does wine matter?
Certainly it appealed for the pleasure it can bring to each day. And it matters because when wine is present as we break bread with family and friends, it brings a sense of ritual and of community, of caring about one another. Enjoyed in this way, in moderation, it opens our hearts and civilises us. I felt that to be a winegrower would be to do something I loved doing. It would be what I would do everyday. I would eat well if simply, and enjoy each day. Perhaps my time in Italy affected me most deeply here—the Italians taught me the joy of living in the present.

Now you were finally making wine, did you discover that it was simpler than you had anticipated?
Yes, I remember being very struck with the idea that something so sophisticated, so complex as fine wine, comes from nature, the sun, the rain, the earth. The separation from nature we impose on ourselves with concrete, glass and air-conditioned environments is continually drawing us away. This chance to work with wine, not just as agriculture but as something weighty with cultural and symbolic meaning was—what can I say?—irresistible. It feels to me as if my life has simply flowed in these directions because they were right for me. The Buddhists say that whatever happens is what should happen. I was never consciously striving to change my life or become a winegrower; it just happened.

I became more and more intrigued, however, by the process. Chile was where it all really started: when you're alone in the cellar with fermenting wines, punching down the cap, and the natural yeasts are transforming sugar into alcohol and it's all taking place in front of you day by day, it's intoxicating, even if you haven't ingested any alcohol. Magical, too: a spontaneous metamorphosis, an alchemy. You haven't added anything; you've just broken the skin of the grape, yet this thing is bubbling away and changing. Then of course the process continues: it finishes its malolactic without your having added a starter, and then clarifies itself by settling, and on and on, and you grow more and more amazed. Chile was where I first experienced that. Being alone, or there with a couple of workers: that's when personal intoxication touches you. That was when I realised how wonderful this thing I had become involved with is.

We are of course dealing in a drug, a mind-altering substance, yet it is nourishing as well. You have to take in the cultural antecedents of how it was used. For the Mediterraneans, wine is used with food, as a food, as part of a meal. It's more intimately integrated both into the culture, and literally into your body, than if it's drunk (as distilled spirits might be) alone. There's an historic and cultural symbolism behind wine which can tend to mitigate its negative aspects.

So wine is a wholesome drug?
Yes, but I'm absolutely aware of the seriousness of what it is, what it contains, and that we have to recognise that there are people within every culture who cannot deal with it.

You loved the naturalness of wine and relished the opportunity it gave you to work intimately with nature, but why do those things matter? Isn't making a nice drink all that matters?
For me, it's a bond of trust with the soil, the place, the land itself. What is fine wine all about? Let's start from the point that making wine is a natural process. In Chile, I wasn't adding anything or taking anything out. We sourced Cabernet grapes from four hillside vineyards miles apart. We kept them separate, and once they were fermented, you could taste clear differences. And we had preferences. One was rather ordinary; the others were more individual and more interesting, but different. So not only did the wine with our guidance and care make itself, but you could find distinctive character in the wines that you hadn't created by blending or adding or subtracting, but that actually came from a piece

of ground. So it struck me that if you were really talking about wine as a natural product, as something authentic, then you should be seeking out those parcels, those pieces of land, where there was individuality of character and real quality in the grapes themselves. You would tend the vineyard and guide the transformation in the cellar, but the wine would reflect nature and the natural process, more than your winemaking.

This all came through experience. I was already philosophically and culturally attuned to this idea, but it was the practicalities of wine-making which proved conclusive. To this day, I have only one response to a wine-maker who dismisses the idea of *terroir*. "How many Cabernet vineyards do you work with?" I ask. "Three," he says. "Are the wines that come off those three vineyards identical?" "Oh no," he says; "this one is such-and-such and that one is so-and-so…" "Are some of them consis-tently better than the others?" "Yeah, sure." "So why don't you keep them separate, instead of blending them?"

That was always the philosophy at Ridge?
Well, I think we can assume it was even in the earliest years because the grapes came from the vineyards surrounding the Monte Bello winery. The winery had been built in the 1880s, and the first vintage was made in 1892. But all those nineteenth-century vineyards had been abandoned during Prohibition. In the 1940s, a theologian and conscientious objec-tor had bought part of the place and had replanted Cabernet Sauvignon and a small amount of Chardonnay, so there were mature vines when the Ridge partners arrived in '59. They made wine in the first years just from Monte Bello grapes, then in '64 added a Zinfandel, this time from nine-teenth-century vines. They added Geyserville vineyard in Sonoma in '66. But all the vineyards were kept separate in our search for the best *terroir*.

The Ridge partners got in touch with me when I got back to the States from Chile, asking if I'd be interested in taking over from Dave Bennion as wine-maker. I went up to Ridge in 1968 and tasted the 1962 and 1964 Monte Bellos. I was astonished: they seemed to have the depth and complexity of a very good Bordeaux; I'd never tasted that in California before. So I accepted the job. My first vintage was 1969.

Dave and I worked together on the '69 vintage, including the Geyserville, and for the first time I really saw that Zinfandel from old vines grown in the right soil and climate could produce something of real interest. It was very different from the Bordeaux varietals, but had great sensuous potential. So once I was there, I started looking around myself, and brought in more old Zinfandel vineyards, most notably Lytton Springs, in '72.

We were so fortunate with Monte Bello. When the partners bought the land, the replanted vines were already twelve to fifteen years old, mature enough to show their true quality, and that quality convinced them to reopen the winery. In fact that was never the point anyway; they bought the land to divide up when they retired and build houses for themselves up there in the hills, but in the meantime came up at weekends with their kids and camped out. However once they had made wine from the land, their wine-knowledgeable friends saw the quality, and said "My God, you've got to reopen this place, you've got to do this." So with the Monte Bello, we lucked out. We also tried Cabernets from elsewhere—from York Creek on Spring Mountain in Napa most successfully, but also from Mendocino, from down south of us on the Central Coast, and from other places in the Santa Cruz Mountains. Indeed we made the Eisele Vineyard Cabernet (now Araujo) in '71, the first time it was ever made commercially. We saw that, good as all those wines were, they didn't *make themselves* to the extent that Monte Bello did. We had to work with them in the winery to be as good as we needed them to be. Whereas the Monte Bello, it was what it was and didn't need tarting up. We didn't have to do anything to the wines; we didn't have to be "wine-makers", we could be wine growers. We've thought a lot about what in the site makes Monte Bello distinctive. Geological studies show that the ridge was formed near the equator as part of the major die-off of the tiny sea life that forms limestone. The ridge moved north on the Pacific plate over millions of years and was jammed against the edge of North America as the Pacific plate moved on below. Because Monte Bello Ridge was formed far distant from the land around it, geologists refer to this as an "exotic terrain".

With Zinfandel, I wouldn't even look at a young vineyard. If the vines weren't seventy or eighty years old, I wouldn't consider it. With Lytton Springs, in mid-winter of '71, I happened to meet the man who had recently bought the vineyard. I was standing in the simple tasting room at the old nineteenth-century Nervo winery, and this guy from LA and his wife were standing next to me and there was this big, white

Cadillac out front. We got talking, and he said "Oh, you make wine. I just bought a vineyard two miles away from here. I sold the fruit to Mondavi last year; it was my first year. Would you be interested in coming over to see it?" So we drove over in the rain, and stood out there in the mud, and the vines, you know, they were much as they are today, with these big trunks, seventy-year-old vines at that time. "Would you be interested?" he said, and I said, "Yes". That was the test. They had survived the thirteen years of Prohibition because they were so good the owners couldn't bring themselves to pull them out, though they lost money each year.

So the potential of a special place given articulacy by deep-rooted, mature vines is, for you, the point of departure for fine wine?
Yes, and in that respect I'm amazed to see how new vineyards are established in California and much of the New World. People hire a consultant, and he tells them that this is a good place to grow grapes and they buy the piece of land as an investment. They spend hundreds of thousands of dollars, maybe millions, on the land and plant vines; they put up their winery at even greater cost. They've planted Cabernet Sauvignon or Chardonnay or whatever has the greatest cachet, wait four years for the vines to produce a crop and start to make the wine. And that's the very first time they have any idea of the quality of what they've invested in! They have to wait another six to eight years for the vines to fully mature and for the wine to show its true quality and consistency of character. Often it's ok, but not particularly distinctive, yet they've committed a fortune.

In my thirty-eight years, we've purchased grapes from more than fifty different Zinfandel vineyards, but most of them couldn't live up to Lytton Springs or Geyserville. Even though they were from Dry Creek and eighty years old. Everything looked right, and yields were low, but we couldn't get the same quality and consistency from them. We had to step in and be wine-makers too often. Once we realised that, we'd drop them. So my advice to anyone in the New World would be—don't start by building a winery. Put some equipment in a custom crush facility, so that you've got control over when things happen; then go out and look at all the vineyards and the fruit available on the open market and start making wines from several of the most promising parcels. When you find something that has distinctive quality, that makes itself, then offer a price that cannot be refused. But to go out and plant a piece of land, and spend all that money, and put up a winery, and then find out that the site doesn't produce anything truly distinctive or interesting; that's heart-breaking.

Of course you have to give your land a chance to show what it can really do by keeping yields low. I'm constantly on that soapbox. I disagree with my French friends who say that great *terroir* is less than one per cent of what's planted world wide; I tend to think that it's at least ten per cent or more. But so many vineyards have never been given a chance. They've been blended from the start, or the yields in those vineyards have been kept too high. My feeling is that there are many, many places where you could find character and quality, but it's just never been sought out.

What's so special about Monte Bello? What does it give to the vines?
It's quite different from Napa, first of all, because the climate's cooler. Yes, it's got limestone soil, so of course my French friends say that's a big part of it. OK, maybe; there's no limestone in Sonoma or Napa; but I think it's chiefly the cooler climate and the higher acid from the colder nights. We get full flavour at more moderate alcohol levels. It's not better, but stylistically different from other good wines like Pride Mountain on Spring Mountain, and Shafer in Stag's Leap. I've seen wines come from those two producers that, to me, are some of the most interesting Bordeaux blends in California. I've never looked at their soils; they're very probably quite different. I certainly don't covet either piece of land but I admire the wines coming off them.

You stress the primacy of nature. Nonetheless wine is still a made object and fine wine requires a particularly solicitous approach. Do you ever view wine as a created object with an artistic dimension, or is winemaking at best a craft?
I avoid the word "create". I regret the word "wine-maker"; I vastly prefer "winegrower". But of course the majority of New World wine producers and indeed many in Europe are wine-makers, not winegrowers. They process their wines; they take this out and put that in; they have in fact created the wine.

So for you great wines are grown and not made, whereas ordinary wines are made and not grown?

Yes, but most good wines as well are made not grown. Remember that includes more than ninety per cent of the world's wine. That's the speciality of the larger companies and some of the small producers as well. It's impossible to produce major amounts of consistently decent branded wine except by making it, rather than growing it. What they're doing is absolutely essential in providing the market with reasonable quality, reasonably priced, everyday drinking wine.

Is there no conflict between that kind of wine and what you're trying to do? In the old days, after all, even cheap wine would have been grown rather than made. It might not have had a lot of ambition or complexity, but it would have been of a place. Most branded wines today are not of a place at all. Isn't the comprehension of wine with a sense of place therefore disappearing?

That is our role: to tell consumers that there is a choice. Part of my problem with the University of California at Davis is that they don't tell the student of wine-making that he or she has a choice in how they make wine; they tell them that there is only one way to make wine, and that way is industrial, and that there's no such thing as wines of place, and natural process.

I'm not arguing against commerce, by the way, but I am opposed to the abusive commercialisation of wine. Unless you make a profit, you're not improving your vineyard or your winery, or looking after your staff. However, beyond that level of being able to pay your people well, give them proper benefits, improve your vineyards and your winery and make a reasonable profit yourself, if you consider what you are doing an artistic endeavour, there's no justification for charging exorbitant prices. You're in steady state. Once you make the bottom line the centre, and push that as hard as you can, by charging prices which don't reflect quality, but rather what the market will bear, then you've veered off the straight and narrow of fine wine growing.

All we can do is keep our drinkers alive to the fact that there is a choice, and that the heart of the matter, what wine is all about, is place and natural process. I would claim that the majority of wine drinkers see wine consciously or unconsciously as a connection to the earth, a connection to the seasons. They don't see beer or spirits that way. But they do see wine in that way; and that's why they're interested in it, that's one reason they love it. And if that is lost, we will be left with nothing but industrial wine.

Of course, the Big Guys exploit that connection. Gallo's advertising in the old days was brilliant: all that folksy little old wine-maker stuff… But Gallo's PR department knew better than the wine-makers how important that culture of wine is, how important it is to feel that wine is connected to the earth. The wine-makers in those days probably didn't think about it, but the PR guys did and knew that if they didn't make that connection, they were not going to build their market.

But maybe what bothers me more—whether it's Grange or a California cult wine put together from several vineyards—is charging an exorbitant price for something which is made and not grown. That does bother me. And I'm not arguing that all wines of place are good, either. Everything depends on what's in the glass. A wine's first duty is to be good. Beyond that, *terroir* is bullshit.

So you disagree with Nicolas Joly's statement that "Before being good, a wine should be true?"
I would say that a wine has to be both good and true. If it is simply true (meaning authentic) and mediocre, I'm sorry: that's not enough.

So how do you transcend the mediocre? What do you know about your vines? What do you feel to be your responsibility towards them? What are they asking you for?
That goes to the heart of what a wine grower's role is, which is one of tending, of husbandry, of learning from the land the best approach. One example is pruning, where you are focusing the energies of the vine. The vine's like a dilettante, who will never do anything of superb quality in any field because her interests are too broad. So you're taking that vine and focusing it, getting it to do the very best it can. But every site is different; you can't say "This is what we do at Monte Bello so this is what you should be doing at Shafer"—absolutely not. As you walk the vineyard each year, you have to look at the individual vine and see what it needs, rather than its neighbour which may be much stronger and so can carry more crop. Understanding not just crop level but the shaping of a

vine is at the heart of the relationship between the grower and the plant.

So is there any progress in fine-wine viticulture? The rise of biodynamics, after all, suggests that the past was wiser than the present. Is Ridge's future biodynamic?
I know the Leflaive domain, and I think since Anne-Claude Leflaive switched to biodynamics, those wines have acquired another dimension because of what she's doing in the vineyard. We have a marvellous vineyard manager who's been with us fifteen years. We've moved slowly, initially, to an approach called sustainable agriculture, which is very broad, but at least it's on track. But from this year we've decided to set biodynamic certification as the goal. We may never achieve it, but without that focus, we are never going to move as far or as swiftly as we will if we have that aim.

Do you think the chief advantage of biodynamics is that it helps foster a vital, living soil medium—or that it opens the vineyard to the upper world of the moon and the planets with their influences and their rhythms?
Soil is much more easily measurable than the moon and the planets. But that upper world counts too. I always remember an incident with a winery assistant who was a UC Davis graduate. We had been tasting on a Friday and we agreed "OK, on Monday, let's start racking the Monte Bello. It's time to get it off its lees." The weekend went by, but on Sunday evening it started to rain. On Monday I came in and it was still pouring with rain; a big low-pressure system had moved in. I said to my assistant "You cancelled the racking of the Monte Bello, of course." And he gave me this strange look and said "No, we've just started."

"Have you looked at the wine?"

"No," he said.

"It'll be cloudy." And we went down in the cellar, and took a glass. Cloudy. He just stood there. "Low pressure system," I said. "The pressure changed; it stirred the sediment back into suspension."

We haven't timed the work in the vineyard biodynamically, but the idea that the moon has an effect on vines makes sense to me. The planets may have an effect. I have to think about that a little more. But the whole point is that all of this is connected. Every part of the natural world clearly affects the totality in one way or another.

Are there some interventions that you will never contemplate?

Yes, though in some cases only after we have put them to the test. I'll tell you a story about York Creek Zinfandel. Fritz Maytag owns York Creek and we are old friends from university days and from Chile, therefore I have less ability to influence him than I do our other growers. We were unable to control the ripeness at which he picked for several years in a row. One year the grapes came in and we fermented them. The older vines made a wine which was riper than ideal, but had the body to carry the higher level of alcohol. So though it wasn't the style that we prefer, it was interesting wine, good wine, and we labelled it and sold it. The wine from the young vines did not have the body to carry what turned out to be an even higher level of alcohol, so we were going to sell that portion of the wine in bulk. At that point I realised that for years I have been criticising reverse osmosis, but I had never tried it. So I decided to send out a portion of the wine to the guys who do reverse osmosis. They reduced its alcohol dramatically and we blended that portion with the rest, bringing the final wine down from 16.5 per cent to 14.8 per cent or something like that. Its balance was vastly improved, but we could no longer identify it as York Creek. The wine that hadn't gone through that process was indeed York Creek: the pepper, all the elements were there, we could instantly recognise it.

Anyway, we decided to bottle the wine which had gone through reverse osmosis as well, but we declassified it and called it Spring Mountain instead of York Creek, and I took care to describe everything that had happened on the back label. I even sent a bottle to Robert Parker with some further description in a letter. The specialists offering spinning cone and reverse osmosis technology have over 1,000 clients in California. Who are they? No one ever talks about it, let alone mention it on the label.

The thing we learned was that with that intervention the wine loses its sense of place. Needless to say, beyond this one trial we will never do it again.

You have to be careful whatever you do. I can see the point in minor acidification or de-acidification, to taste. Not enzymes. Not the "death star" that kills everything in the wine. Certainly not concentrates. Concentrates can add tremendous body and colour to otherwise weak wines, yet they are 2,000 to 1 concentrations of junk grapes from all over. And those concentrates are even going into some expensive wines as well as cheap ones. I don't see the point in centrifuging when you can settle wines naturally and more gently. We have done tests over the years with no filtration, very open filtration, tighter filtration and membrane sterile filtration, and we see a small but noticeable change in overall complexity as the wine ages, depending on how far you have gone with filtration. Our white wines are rarely filtered at all, and single vineyard reds are filtered but never membrane sterile filtered.

Are your greatest wines those you have had to do least to?
Absolutely.

So we can be clear: greatness in wine comes primarily from its place of origin, but requires the will and the experience of the wine grower to be able to express its greatness. Wine is not, therefore, an artistic creation like a piece of music or sculpture.
Wine is not a created work. What we do is more akin to what a performer does with a piece of music. My wife is a musician and she and I have a friend, a classical pianist, Paul Hersh. "I do a live performance," he said to me once, "and when that performance is over, it's finished, it's gone. CDs? I'm sorry, those are copies; they're not the live performance. But you have cases upon cases of the live performance, to be experienced again and again each time a bottle is opened. They're not copies; they're originals. You are so lucky!" Of course the score—a Bach partita or whatever—will go on through time far beyond the greatest wine. Perhaps the *terroir* and the natural transformation of the grapes into wine are the score brought to life again with each performance. Is the fine wine grower more like the musician bringing the score to life in the performance?

Yet a bottle of wine is destroyed by time, which a piece of music isn't.
Wine's link with time connects it to the human. It has its birth, youth, its maturity, its old age and its death, whereas the work of art is immortal.

Is this mimicry of the human part of the reason why wine has a compelling fascination for us?
It may be. That idea can be reinforced when you move back another step

in the cycle to the vineyard. In spring, with flowering and fruitset, the grape is born; it develops through summer; changes colour at mid-life and becomes something quite different; matures to full ripeness in autumn; is crushed, dies, and then in winter is reborn as wine. In most cases, remember, we outlive wines. I was born in 1936; I still have some Yquem and Latour from that less-than-stellar year, so every tenth birthday I open a bottle of each. The Latour is interesting for about a half an hour. The Yquem for somewhat longer. Then again, I should be careful. The same might be said of me.

You make a strong case for the primacy of nature in the creation of great wine, but as you've pointed out, nature doesn't always make great wine. On certain key issues—let's take ripeness, for example—there is little agreement, either among wine growers or critics. Nature delivers a spectrum; humans make a choice. Where do you stand on this question? What statement do you allow nature to make in this instance?

Depending on the region it is true that nature delivers a spectrum, but also dictates its own point of ideal ripeness. In any year, weather permitting, there is a point of full flavour in the fruit and mature tannin in the seeds. You could say that just as a note on the violin is in or out of tune, the experienced wine grower will choose that moment to harvest—the wine grower's equivalent of perfect pitch. Nature can push the sugar ahead of flavour in a warm year or warm region and force the grower to wait, ending up with higher alcohol than ideal. However, that is not typical with mature vines and balanced yields, and if the grower goes beyond full flavour consistently, it is his or her choice, not nature's. If the fruit is overripe, those overripe flavours will dominate the wine and mask the sense of where the grapes were grown, the sense of place. Just as the excessive use of new oak produces nothing more than an over-oaked wine, so excessively ripe fruit produces nothing more than an overripe wine.

This is a particularly sensitive issue with the Bordeaux varieties. Grown in the right place, they have potential in a good year to develop incredible depth and complexity with age. In today's "now" culture, we are told that consumers seek instant gratification. The response of a growing number of producers is to make overripe and therefore lower acid wines in which the richness of body and sweetness of fruit mask the

tannins. The wines are much more approachable young and, complemented by new oak, can be appealing, but they have lost any sense of
place and the chance with age to become something greater.

In our case, besides the Monte Bello and Santa Cruz Mountains
which are from Bordeaux varieties grown on the estate vineyard, we also
work with a number of Zinfandel vineyards. Nature makes it more difficult to pick at ideal ripeness with this varietal. First you need a slightly
warmer climate to burn off acidity and fully ripen flavours. Napa,
Sonoma and Paso Robles are ideal. If there's warm weather at vintage,
Zinfandel ripens incredibly quickly. If you're not on top of it, and you
have a few days of really warm weather, by the time you've finished the
first blocks, you'll find that the last ones are already overripe. And that
we simply cannot have. In vineyards we don't farm ourselves, it is even
more difficult to control ripeness, so for some of the small-production
wines which we release only at the winery, we have had a number of late-
picked wines over the years. Luckily some of our customers think those
are the best, though I wouldn't agree. But with the vineyards which we
farm ourselves, like Lytton Springs and Geyserville, let alone Monte
Bello, that is just not an option for us. In some years with Zinfandel
there is nothing you can do, so some blocks will have to be kept out of
the single vineyard wine because you couldn't pick them in time.

As harvest approaches, the whole staff, bolstered by interns, are sam-
pling every day. As we get close, we are tasting the juice from the samples
and saying "Ok—that could be in the next day or two," or "Boy! Get in
there tomorrow morning," or "That's probably a week off …" Everyone
has their opinion, so we discuss it. We want to see the green tones gone.
And with Monte Bello and its cool climate, we see that happening at reasonable sugar levels. In the case of Zinfandel, with young to middle-aged
vines, you don't see that until you reach 14 per cent. We think you see it
between 14 per cent and 14.9 per cent. You should never have to wait
beyond 14.9 per cent to have full fruit flavour in Zinfandel. If you're
making 15.5 per cent, 16.5per cent or 17.5 per cent, the chances are you
are making an intentional choice though occasionally you might have been
caught by the weather in that particular year.

Those wines would for you be overripe?
Yes. And when I make them myself, they're still overripe! Flavour matu-

rity in Cabernet at Monte Bello comes typically at around 12.5 per cent, 12.9 per cent, 13.3 per cent, averaging somewhere around 12.9 per cent to 13.1 per cent over our last forty-four vintages. The 2001, which was a warm vintage for California, went to just over 14 per cent for the first time in all our years. We were horrified. You can see its clear family resemblance in a line-up of Monte Bellos, but we're not sure it will be as classic or typical as, say, the 1996. It's not what we aim for each year, but it was the nature of that vintage.

Even in Napa Valley, I don't think you have to go over 14 per cent in most years to get flavour maturity in Cabernet. Maybe if you're over-producing or have very young vines, but otherwise it's an intentional choice.

Flavour maturity (or phenolic maturity) is what counts, yet how much subjectivity is there involved in assessing flavour maturity?
I had a conversation with our vineyard manager, David Gates, a few years ago. "David, you can't be the only one to determine what day we pick. It's not intentional on your part, but you are so concerned about underripe flavour in those grapes that, unconsciously, the safe thing for you is to go slightly overripe. So the Production team, John Olney, Eric Baugher and myself are going to work with you on determining what day to pick." But I'm afraid that's not generally the approach in California. Producers are not as concerned about over-ripeness as they should be because of the critical praise they receive for wines that are more than ripe.

The Australian wine producer Brian Croser uses the term "dead fruit" about such wines.
I've never used that term, and of course there are some super-ripe wines which are in balance with their acidity and their tannins and so on. They are, quote, "balanced wines"—except that they are in a whole different category. I would hesitate to say that the balanced wines are dead wines. It's just that you have a wine that is so rich and so high in alcohol that it is no longer a complement to food. It's the whole meal itself. It's hard to have it share a place at table with food.

I remember being in New York once showing Monte Bello at the Wine Experience, and being next to Latour and Las Cases. I'd got round to tasting some of my favourite wines, and right across the room was Screaming Eagle. Someone carried a glass over, and it was syrup compared to the Bordeaux I had been tasting. I would have called that a dead wine. It would not be enjoyable with a normal meal, and yet it's getting, I don't know, ninety-eight points and selling for $400 a bottle; it was absurd. That kind of excess I don't agree with, even if it is from a single vineyard.

What is the role of the critic? Are they simply surrogate drinkers hunting down exquisite sensory experiences, or is their job to help provide a conceptual and verbal framework for the beauty of nature as expressed in wine?
The last thing wine needs is to be seen as elitist. Wine is food. It brings us together. It can have a most civilising effect. An article describing a dinner where wines from the 1860s to the present were tasted has no place in the daily press. Wine is meant to be drunk not tasted. The critic's role depends on his audience. If he is writing to interest a more general public in wine or for those just beginning he could make it clear that virtually everyone can pick a favourite between two different equally priced wines; that the best wine for you is the wine that tastes best to you; that the glass does need to be a wine glass, not a tumbler or made of plastic. And for this audience, as for the most knowledgeable, to provide what you so elegantly stated: "a conceptual and verbal framework for the beauty of nature as expressed in wine."

As a wine grower, I would like to see the critics distinguish between wines that are actually fermented and aged by the maker, not just bought on the bulk market, blended and bottled. Perhaps for the beginner to find wines that represent place is too much to ask, but at least they could represent the person who made them. The role some critics have taken on themselves is to taste through the many wines lining the merchants' shelves and distinguish between the poor, the good and the very good for their readers. Robert Parker is the most influential of these and because his opinions on the wines he tastes are his alone, he is quite consistent. His readers can learn the characteristics of a wine from his words and choose the one they think they would prefer. They have the choice of buying his preferences based on his scores or their own, if it differs, based on his descriptions. My hope is that more and more of his public focus on his words rather than the points.

Do critics taste too much and not drink enough?
Absolutely. Bob Parker's a good taster…

Is he a good drinker?
Yes, he is also a good drinker. At table with friends he doesn't sit there
and spit. One of the great things about Parker is that he loves wine. His
love of wine came first. The power his readers and the producers gave
him followed. There are other critics where the power has come first and
love of wine has never come or seems secondary. What I require of any
critic is that he or she love the art or the craft that they are criticising.

Does Parker drink Screaming Eagle with pleasure?
I would speculate that if you were to have dinner with Parker, and you
were to have a great vintage of Latour or Margaux, and a very fine
Californian Cabernet, and Screaming Eagle too, blind, all in decanters,
you could watch which decanters would get emptied first. And I don't
think the Screaming Eagle would be one of them.

*Would you like to see more critics base their assessments on drinking rather
than tasting?*
Yes. I did a tasting in London for some top sommeliers; the wines were
undecanted, just opened. Later we all sat down at table and had them
decanted, with a nice meal. For me, the quality and enjoyment of those
wines took a huge step the moment we had them with food. The '92
Monte Bello was somewhat closed by itself, but with food and having
been decanted it was just glorious, and that was true of the other wines
as well.

I belong to something called the Vintners' Club in San Francisco,
and we recently tasted six Bordeaux and six top California Cabernets
from the '96 vintage, blind, then rated them. I liked the Lafite '96 a lot,
whereas most of the California group, even if they consistently buy the
first growths, tended to prefer the California wines when tasting blind.
But I felt the tasting was such a terrible waste. Any one of those wines
would make a glorious evening with friends, and there we were just dis-
secting them. Personally an event of that kind is not my favourite
approach.

Has criticism done the wine world a disservice?
We have a huge materials company in California. It sells concrete, and the slogan on the sides of their trucks reads "Find a need and fill it". Parker found a need and filled it. In this world of ten thousand different labels there is a need to give the consumer some help. But I would like to see it done much more generally—much less specifically.

Do you feel your wines are critically understood?
Does the critic have a broad experience of the world's wines, and does he or she taste relatively objectively? If those two are true, I think we will always get a fair hearing.

Do you resent having your wines scored?
We don't see any choice. But if you read Parker's descriptions, you get a very clear idea about the wine, and if it's not your style you don't have to buy it; you don't really need the points.

So Parker would be better without the points?
He would be better without the points. But he'd have half the number of subscribers.

You meet your drinkers regularly. Have you noticed an evolution in taste over the last thirty years?
There's been growing experience with the years. The comments that I got in the mid-1970s were less specific than they are today. People are also learning to trust their own taste more. Plenty of people still buy the label or the Parker points, but plenty of others are working out their preferences for themselves. That's the beginning of everything. And I have to say that in the States, that trend has progressed faster with Zinfandel than with any other variety. Internet chat rooms and bulletin boards have had an astonishing effect, too; every enthusiast can now post his impressions and opinions of a wine worldwide, within seconds. I think today, at least for many interested in learning more about wine, that's an important check on the power of the wine press.

Is critical tasting assessment too far removed from most people's experience of drinking wine—with a meal, with friends, in a situation where pleasure and significance can readily accrue?

For me, meeting and talking with our customers is one of the most satisfying aspects of the craft. I tutored a dinner at Berry Bros in Britain for about forty guests.[1] At the end of this dinner, a group of six or eight gathered round, all very passionate about Ridge, and one woman said "I have to thank you for all the pleasure you have brought to our family table down the years. We can always count on a bottle of Ridge—it's such a joy to us." At that point, you sense that what you are doing nourishes the soul as well as the body. That's what wine is all about for me. I'm part of a big tasting in the States each year and hundreds of people come by in an evening to get a taste of a ten, twenty or thirty-year-old Monte Bello, and typically thirty or forty people a night say something close to what that woman said. It reminds me of Alice Waters of Chez Panisse saying she opened her restaurant to feed her friends. That's what we try to do.

NOTES:

1   The Ridge dinner took place at Berry Bros. and Rudd in December 2005.

INDEX